MOTHERS & MURDERERS

A True Story of Love, Lies, Obsession
... and Second Chances

KATHERINE ELLISON

WILDBLUE
PRESS

WildBluePress.com

MOTHERS & MURDERERS published by:
WILDBLUE PRESS
P.O. Box 102440
Denver, Colorado 80250

WILDBLUE PRESS is registered at the U.S. Patent and Trademark Offices

ISBN 978-1-948239-40-0 Trade Paperback
ISBN 978-1-948239-39-4 eBook

Cover photo of Judith Singer and her son, Daniel Witkin, is courtesy of The Mercury News.

Interior Formatting by Elijah Toten
www.totencreative.com

MOTHERS &
MURDERERS

For John, who knows Y

What allows some people to hurt others without conscience or remorse?

As a journalist, I've interviewed many textbook villains, from a death squad leader in El Salvador to Filipino officials who stole billions in government funds to a Chilean secret police chief who oversaw the torture and mass killings of thousands of dissidents. What all of them shared was a combination of entitlement and self-absorption that is often labeled narcissism. Narcissists think they're special—more important than others and entitled to do what they want, no matter whom they hurt. Some are convinced they serve a higher purpose. Some feel free to harm others out of a belief that *they've* been victims. The worst of them are easy to hate.

What's harder is to face the less barbaric self-absorption we so often see in our families, in our workplaces and, if we're being honest, in the mirror. The kind that doesn't murder or maim but may still leave scars.

Narcissism, like heat or light or autism, fits on a spectrum. Most of us are at least a little self-centered now and then. Move along the line and you'll find such annoying behaviors as taking credit for other people's ideas, boasting about the size of one's body parts, and tweeting one's every thought. It's here you'll also start to meet the sort of wounded people who unintentionally wound others, trapped in a cycle that can last for generations.

Only at the farthest end of this spectrum do we find the certifiable illness known as narcissistic personality disorder. More than sixteen million Americans reportedly meet the criteria for this diagnosis. Among them are those iconic rogues who manipulate, exploit, and destroy others without shame.

Everybody loathes a narcissist—at least theoretically. The Ancient Greeks warned about the risks of too much self-love in the story of Narcissus, the handsome youth who fell in love with his own reflection in a pond and by varying accounts pined away or drowned. The Bible is full of tirades against vanity and praise for humility. Today there's even a Wikipedia page devoted to the annual worldwide injuries and deaths related to the use of selfie sticks. Hundreds of internet sites, blogs, and books dole out advice on coping with hopelessly self-centered bosses, lovers, and spouses. But somehow we keep getting hurt by them.

My interest in this subject began early on in my career, after I was assigned to report on one of the most bizarre and high-profile murder cases in the history of California's Silicon Valley. My involvement in the case changed me, not least by pushing me into psychotherapy, where I was obliged, at first unwillingly, to confront my own unique variety of self-absorption.

Among other things, I realized how tempting it can be to find someone or something else to blame for your own bad behavior. Look closely enough, after all, and almost everyone deserves a little sympathy. Each of us is at least partly the product of all sorts of influences beyond our control, from genes to parenting to peer pressure. Still, in the midst of covering the murder case, I kept wondering about the line between explanation and justification. When, if ever, should we stop trying to understand and even sympathize with someone else's hurtful behavior, and simply condemn it or punish it—or if it's ours, own up to it and do whatever it takes to change?

The murder story, which began in 1981 and is still having repercussions today, featured several extraordinary characters, including two hapless hitmen, a flamboyant Beverly Hills attorney, a rodeo-riding prosecutor, and a woman who initially seemed to be as far as anyone could be from a narcissist. This was Judi Singer: a thirty-two-year-old, stay-at-home mother of three and former religious studies major who volunteered at her synagogue in her spare time. Judi was the ex-wife of the murder victim. She was also the wife of the man on trial for killing him.

Her story would haunt me for more than three decades.

1

San Jose, July 1981

In the summer of 1981, Santa Clara County looked nothing like its future as the hub of the soon-to-be-famous Silicon Valley. No Google. No Facebook. No traffic jams or Zagat-rated restaurants. The coming tech explosion was still a slow burn, and the fertile basin bounded by the Diablo and Santa Cruz Mountains, fifty miles south of San Francisco, was little more than a stretch of urban and rural sprawl, dotted with plum and apricot orchards. Tourist brochures called it "The Valley of Heart's Delight." No one had a cell phone. Coffee was served black or with cream. Homes were affordable and newspapers were profitable.

Title IX, banning gender-based discrimination in schools, was less than a decade old. The Equal Rights Amendment still had a fighting chance. At twenty-three years old, in my shag haircut and shoulder-padded jacket, I must have looked like a billboard for that era's female ambition. I felt like one, too, until the hot summer morning when I first heard the news that changed everything for me.

I was sipping a Tab and frowning at the dim green screen of the monitor of my Coyote word processer when Bill Melcher burst through the glass double doors of the Santa Clara County pressroom.

All four of us reporters in the room turned our heads. The Beverly Hills defense attorney was a spicy departure from our normally bland diet of blue-blazered, reticent county bureaucrats. Bill wore tailored European suits, chomped on a pipe, and seemed to love nothing more than telling us about his client, Robert "Bob" Singer, the owner of a Michigan franchise restaurant. Bob Singer was on trial and facing the death penalty, charged with murder-for-hire in a case that was pure reader catnip. The victim—an heir to a prominent and wealthy local family—had only recently been married to Singer's wife, Judi.

All that would have sufficed to land my stories on the front page of the *San Jose Mercury,* where I'd been working for less than a year in my first fulltime job. But Bill had been telling us throughout the pre-trial hearings that there was more to be revealed. The case, he assured us, was no mere tawdry family drama, but an epic saga involving shadowy, vengeful drug mobs who had framed his innocent client. "It's the trial of the century!" Bill declared. "Right here in San Jose!"

I longed to believe him, callously hoping all those front-page stories would speed my promotion to a job as a foreign correspondent, a career I'd dreamed of since the age of thirteen. Covering the news from distant lands was the most romantic and meaningful work I could imagine, even though very few women were doing it. Those were years when most female reporters were stuck covering society or education. Miraculously, however, the foreign assignment I'd coveted for so long finally seemed within my reach.

Newly ambitious and flush with cash after a merger with a national newspaper chain, the *Mercury* had recently opened a new bureau in Mexico City. I spoke Spanish, sort of, and had built up my resume since high school, when I edited the school newspaper, after which I interned at *Los Angeles Times, Foreign Policy Magazine, Washington Post,* and *Newsweek.* My editors prized my energy, imagination, and reliable willingness to work night after night of overtime without ever trying to charge for it. They'd even seemed willing to overlook a few clumsy recent mistakes: a name misspelled here; the wrong date there. To my delight, one editor had recently told me that I was a top candidate for the Mexico job. At my age, as he acknowledged, that would be a meteoric rise—*as long as I didn't blow it*. The Singer story was sure to help, which made me doubly glad to see Bill Melcher heading toward my cubicle.

I stood up to greet him but he didn't return my smile as he looked down to rummage in his briefcase. He pulled out a stapled set of papers. Perhaps it was another of his outlandish press releases. Maybe this time he'd come to give me a scoop.

I smiled more broadly.

Bill still didn't smile back.

"I'm sorry, Kathy," he said, as he handed me the papers.

It took me a moment to recognize that he was giving me a summons to a civil suit, for libel. Bob Singer's wife, Judi, was suing the *Mercury* and me for eleven million dollars.

The suit was a shock, but the reason for it wasn't. Two weeks earlier, the city editor had called me at home to point out a mistake I'd made in a story published that morning, July 16, on the prosecutor's closing argument.

His call caught me just as I was leaving for work. Cradling the phone on my neck in the kitchen of my tiny studio apartment, I gazed at the brightening sky through the window over the sink.

"This is a big deal," he began.

The error was way down in the tenth paragraph of the story and might well have gone unnoticed had Judi Singer not called to complain. I suppose she had good reason. I'd misquoted the prosecutor, Deputy District Attorney Jack Marshall, as having said that "*Judi and* Robert Singer" had plotted to kill Judi's former spouse. If true, that would have meant that Judi, together with her husband, was guilty of criminal conspiracy to murder. But Judi had not been charged with any crime.

My first thought was to suspect someone else had messed up. Maybe Jack Marshall *had* said it! Or if he hadn't, he'd certainly suggested it! His whole closing argument had focused on Judi and some dispute she'd been having with her ex. And what about the copyeditor? Shouldn't he have caught my error?

The editor was still talking. Throughout my life, I've had an unfortunate habit of letting my own nervous soundtrack drown out the rest of the world, but I tuned back in again in time to hear him say: "Make sure to check your notes." Alas, I knew that wasn't going to help. Jack Marshall would never have been so careless to have spoken the words I'd written.

The *Mercury* published a correction the next day, and I burned from seeing my screwup so publicly exposed. Still, I figured that was the end of it, and I'd be able to move on, just as I had after all my previous—albeit smaller—mistakes.

Judi's suit told me just how wrong that was. I read her list of charges as I stood frozen under the fluorescent lights of the pressroom, breathing its scent of tobacco and sweat.

She claimed my error had exposed her to "hatred, contempt, ridicule, and obloquy"—making her "unemployable in any field whatsoever, possibly forever." She accused me and the newspaper of "malice," an essential ingredient of a successful libel suit, saying we'd published the mistake either with "knowledge of its falsity or with a reckless disregard as to whether it was true."

It would take me some time to appreciate how someone else in my situation—someone more mature and less self-absorbed—might have paused then, even for an instant, to consider how her carelessness had harmed an innocent woman's reputation. But that didn't cross my mind. I was too busy worrying about my career.

Adios to the Mexico job, just for starters, I figured. But maybe worse. Maybe I'd be fired and never find another job in journalism.

Malice!

My face felt hot. What a groundless accusation!

Or was it?

I couldn't deny the strange mix of emotions I'd come to feel toward Judi Singer. In some striking if superficial ways she resembled my mother, another upper-middle-class Jewish native Midwesterner who, like Judi, had married at nineteen, stayed home to make her children her life's work, and even volunteered for the same good cause: Hadassah, the national Jewish women's fundraising group. I adored my mother, so at first all of this made me feel friendly toward Judi, and she'd been friendly right back. She'd always been happy to talk when I'd asked her to comment on the case, praising me, at one point, in her flat Michigan accent, for a writing style she said was "so clear and concise!"

But at the same time, I resented her. She embodied a way of life that I hoped was finally vanishing—and which I desperately wanted to escape. With her high heels, bleached blond hair, and flirty smiles at every man in the room, she seemed ripped from the pages of *The Total Woman*, the 1970s blockbuster anti-feminist bestseller that famously implied that wives should greet their husbands at the front door, nude and swathed in Saran Wrap.

Women like Judi, as I believed, all too willingly appeased powerful men, even men who were violent and abusive. My own mother had never stood up to my father when he drank and beat up my brothers, and Judi's behavior was significantly worse. Evidence strongly suggested that Bob Singer, her second husband, had killed her first husband, *the father of her children*. And yet there she was, blowing kisses to Bob in the courtroom!

But now here comes the crazy part. I also envied her.

Despite her sordid circumstances, with one husband murdered and the other on trial for his life, Judi radiated pampered self-confidence. A big diamond flashed on her finger; her thin-knit summer dress clung to her Barbie-doll hips, and her tote bag, marked LV for Louis Vuitton, screamed status that year, long before the cheap Chinese knockoffs flooded the market. My own purse was a five-year-old black LeSportsac; I was chronically ten pounds overweight, and while I'd never have said it aloud, I wouldn't have minded owning a nice, big diamond ring, to prove to the world how much some man cared for me ....

Bill Melcher must have wondered why I'd stood there silent for so long. Now he was turning toward the door.
Should I grab his legs? Beg him to reconsider?
Instead I glanced behind me to meet the cool stares of the three or four other reporters in the pressroom. They weren't close enough to hear our conversation and probably thought I'd gotten that scoop.

Only after Judi Singer sued me did I realize I had to figure out the reasons for my growing string of errors or lose my career. That's how I ended up in therapy, where, as hard as I initially fought against it, I had to face other issues I hadn't even suspected were problems—such as why, after libeling Judi, my first thought was to think I was the victim.

For decades to come, Judi and her lawsuit would inspire me to wonder about this and other aspects of unhealthy self-absorption.

In the short term, they made me want to know a lot more about her ex-husband's murder.

2

Santa Clara, California, March 1980

On the afternoon of Friday, March 21 of 1980—the last day of Howard Witkin's short life—he sat in his private office at the Havlin-Witkin Picture and Mirror Corporation, composing a brief letter to his three kids. Danny, ten; Marie, thirteen; and two-year-old Nathan were living with his ex-wife, Judi Singer, in Michigan.

"Dear Dan The Man
Marie the Ski
Nate the Skate," Howard typed on office stationery.
"I've missed you a lot but I've been very busy .... Your Grandpa Barnett came into [sic] see your Zadi and me today. He looks pretty good so does your Aunt Millie. I'm going to Carmel for the weekend with Bob and Kathy, Gary & Lynn and Stephanie. So I have to run cause they are all waiting for me in the car."

The detectives who later read this letter knew that Howard was telling his kids a white lie. No one was waiting for him in a car, and there was no planned trip to Carmel. Instead of going off to have fun, Howard dropped his letter in the mail and headed alone straight to his townhouse on a quiet cul-de-sac a few miles away in Santa Clara, where he ordered a pizza to be delivered for dinner and changed into a torn blue terrycloth bathrobe.

Howard's letter was a small part of his ongoing effort to paint a cheery portrait of his disappointing life in the two years since his divorce. So was his brand-new red Corvette with the vanity license plate ANHOW. He had recently boasted to one friend that he was "finally starting to live." On most weekday evenings, you could find him at the Garden City Casino, a cavernous, dark hall on South Saratoga Avenue in San Jose, where he liked to drink and flirt with waitresses.

Still, Howard's friends worried, as they'd later tell the police. It wasn't hard for them to spot the loneliness beneath the bluster. Howard was thirty-two, but his receding hairline and expanding belly made him look considerably older. He drank too much, ate too much, smoked weed, they said, and snorted cocaine. Shortly after purchasing the new Corvette, he'd crashed it into his garage door after yet another night carousing at the casino.

All this was such a contrast to the role he'd so diligently played when he lived with Judi and their kids in an airy, three-story house in Los Gatos, a woodsy suburb of San Jose. The home was a wedding gift from Howard's father, Harold, a cofounder of the family glass and mirror business. Harold and Howard's mother, Geraldyne, lived just a few blocks away.

Howard and Judi had married in 1968, when both were just nineteen years old, and for nearly a decade, Judi had seemed like a model wife and mother from an all-but bygone time. She doted on her children, cooked casseroles, kept a spotless home, did her volunteer work for Hadassah, and cultivated a close group of women friends. But the family's idyll ended in 1978, about a year after Judi met Bob Singer at a fundraising meeting at San Jose's Temple Emanu-El.

When I first saw Bob in the courtroom, I couldn't imagine why Judi had been drawn to him. He was fourteen years older, with washed-out, pale blue eyes, and pockmarked skin. Nor was he particularly bright. He had dropped out of Wilmington College in Ohio after one semester, got drafted into the army, serving stateside during the Korean War, then moved to San Jose to join his father as a partner in a small family business maintaining vending machines.

Still, Bob in those years had a fatherly, take-charge air that Judi must have found appealing during a time when, as she'd testify, she felt Howard was slipping away from the family. A year or so before Bob and Judi first met, Howard was already spending weeknights playing cards, while she was busy at the temple. She'd also caught him smoking weed, she'd later claim, even though he'd tried to hide that from her, knowing how much she hated drugs. Compare that to Bob, with his sober work ethic and solidly upper-middle-class accoutrements: the wife and three sons, the midnight-blue Mercedes sedan, and the large house in the wealthy San Jose neighborhood of Willow Glen. He even had the same first name as Judi's beloved father, Bob Barnett, a men's clothing salesman in Detroit.

By the fall of 1978, Judi and Bob had divorced their respective spouses, married each other, and moved to Grand Blanc, a wealthy suburb of Flint, Michigan, Judi's home state, where Bob bought a stately home in a high-priced subdivision called "Kirkridge in the Hills." Bob briefly worked with Judi's father, selling suits on commission, before making another large investment—buying a franchise restaurant called The Onion Crock in the Genesee Valley Center mall in Flint. Howard stayed in Santa Clara, with a custody agreement that allowed him to see his children on prearranged holidays and school vacations. He missed his children terribly, as his friends would later tell police. He called them in Michigan almost every day and wrote to them at least once a week.

The TV was still on when police found Howard's body. Based on their estimate of his time of death, they surmised that he'd been watching a talk show featuring Hugh Hefner and five of his Playmates when the doorbell rang.

As far as anyone knows, Howard's assassin—Andy Granger, a twenty-year-old former department stock clerk from Flint, Michigan—was the only witness to Howard's last moments.

Andy would later claim to have clear memories of that night, down to the scent of pear blossoms on the warm breeze as he walked past the redwood chips lining the concrete path to Howard's front door. Still, by the time he reached Howard's townhouse, he had to have been more than a little cognitively handicapped. He'd spent the last three days driving cross-country from Flint with his accomplice and childhood friend, Gary Oliver. As they'd waited out the hours before nightfall, when they planned to drive to Howard's townhouse, they smoked joints and drank beer, after which, as Andy would confide to police, he'd attempted to further calm his nerves by taking five "microdots" of LSD—a hefty dose by anyone's standards. The drugs were just starting to kick in as he approached Howard's door, cradling his .22-caliber Marlin-Glenfield semiautomatic rifle.

Howard took a long time to answer his doorbell—long enough for Andy to suspect he wasn't home. Andy would later testify that he felt a wave of relief, as he lowered his rifle and turned to leave. But then he heard the doorknob click. He wheeled around, recognizing Howard from a Polaroid photograph he'd tucked in his shirt pocket.

For Howard, standing under the porchlight's yellow glare, Andy must have been a terrifying sight. The gun-wielding stranger was six-foot-four, with stringy, shoulder-length hair and size thirteen feet. Yet as homicide detectives will tell you, there's little truth in the Hollywood portrayal of the suave, skilled hitman. Most hired killers sign up for lack of a better option. Andy was no exception.

Before he agreed to murder Howard Witkin, Andy had been looking for work after being laid off from a job as a department-store stock boy. He had never shot anyone or anything other than pheasants, while hunting in Michigan with his Uncle Stu. His only criminal experience had been some shoplifting as a kid, and one night spent destroying mailboxes with a steel pipe while joyriding with friends. After his arrest in 1981, Andy's hometown newspaper quoted neighbors who said they'd seen the tall teenager playing with G.I. Joes in a sandbox in his mother's front yard.

Still, what Andy lacked in experience he made up in determination. At his first sight of Howard, he fell into a crouch, a posture he remembered seeing on TV crime shows. Raising his rifle, he squeezed his eyes shut and fired the first three shots.

"What the hell!?" Andy would remember Howard shouting, as he lunged back behind his front door, slamming it shut and fumbling frantically with the lock.

Andy kept his finger on the trigger as several more bullets crashed through the wooden door and lodged in Howard's chest, arms, and abdomen. Two of them deflated his left lung. Three ripped into his stomach and gut. Two bullets slammed into the signed Picasso print on the wall of his foyer. The coroner would find more metal fragments in the bones of Howard's left arm, elbow, and middle finger, suggesting he had raised his arm to try to protect himself.

Andy crept to Howard's door and leaned down to listen for signs of life, which is when, as he later told police, he heard his victim's last words—a moaned complaint: "Why me?" And then such complete silence that Andy felt free to turn away to rejoin Gary, who was waiting for him in a car parked just around the corner from Howard's cul-de-sac.

"Did you do it?" Gary asked.

"I *think* so," Andy replied.

Andy was right to be uncertain. By the blood stains that led from the door to the kitchen, police assumed that Howard had stumbled around for a while after Andy left, perhaps trying to call for help, although he never managed to do so. Whether Andy heard Howard's last words correctly was also a matter of doubt, as much so as any of his other memories from that drug-addled encounter. But assuming he did, it was a reasonable question.

Understanding the motive for Howard Witkin's murder would preoccupy Santa Clara County police and prosecutors—and me—for many years to come.

3

Hillsborough, California, 1968

The TV was on in the dining room—Walter Cronkite delivering more awful news from Vietnam. But all five of us had stopped watching.

My father thought my older brother Jimmy had disrespected him by not answering a question he'd asked, which maybe Jimmy hadn't even heard. Jumping up from the dining room table, toppling over his chair, he dragged him into the kitchen by his neck, choking him.

Jimmy, sixteen, was my best friend and the smartest person I knew. I was eleven, pressing my back against the kitchen wall near the door that led to the street.

My brother's glasses clattered to the floor. Maybe this time my father would kill him.

My sister was in college, on the other side of the country. I can't remember where my other brother was.

"You little bastard!" my father yelled.

This is the scene that keeps coming to mind whenever I think about my family's dark side, even though there were many other scenes like it. My father's rages lasted throughout my adolescence, and while my two brothers were most often his targets, my sister and I also got hit and screamed at.

Today I know my family's violence didn't make us unique. In the 1960s, U.S. states were just beginning to pass mandatory reporting laws for child abuse. Child Protective Services agencies hadn't yet been established. Many of my parents' contemporaries hit their children, and, just like our family, never talked about it afterward. Even so, from an early age I believed my father was committing a crime and that my mother was covering it up.

Scientists tend to agree about what constitutes narcissistic behavior, some key components being a sense of entitlement, a lack of empathy, and manipulativeness. But when it comes to how narcissists are *created*, the picture gets cloudier, with anecdotal evidence and speculation outweighing rigorous studies. Many authorities agree that this extreme form of self-absorption stems from a combination of nature (genes) and nurture (parenting)—with nurture, or the lack of it, playing the stronger role. But then the consensus splinters. Some say parents create narcissists by treating them as if they're special. Others say narcissists are produced mainly by abuse or neglect or conditional love. One small Canadian study suggests that the most potent recipe is a whiplash combination of extravagant praise and mistreatment. Yet another, larger research project found narcissistic traits in children as early as three and four years old, suggesting that genes may be a strong factor.

Wherever it came from, I'm grateful that my own large helping of belief in my own importance helped me rebuild my career after Judi Singer's lawsuit. But I'm just as glad that I got the chance to understand and modulate it, since that same trait also caused a lot of confusion and pain to me and others along the way.

My dad's explosions made no sense. The furious drunk in our kitchen was by day a respected ear, nose, and throat doctor, and the same loyal family man who for years had made me feel safe as I lay in bed at night listening to him patrol our house, locking all the doors. I was his baby, the youngest of four. He'd whisper that I was his favorite, his *shayna punim*, Yiddish for "beautiful face." I rode on his chest when he swam backstroke in a neighbor's pool. "Put your nose in this machine!" he'd coax, holding his knuckles open close to my face. I always would. He'd then make a loud buzzing noise and squeeze my nostrils, and I would always act surprised.

On weekdays, except for Wednesdays, when he played golf, he cleaned sinuses and took out tonsils to pay for our privileged lives in the super-rich suburb of Hillsborough, seventeen miles south of San Francisco. There are no businesses in Hillsborough, only exceptional elementary schools and mansions sprouting behind tall hedges and fences, shaded by redwoods and pines. Bing Crosby, Jenny Craig, and William Randolph Hearst were just a few of our notable neighbors.

On many nights, my father would labor on our family albums, gluing in photographs, report cards, and other records of our achievements. Both of my brothers and my sister followed my father into medicine, although it did say something that the two oldest became psychiatrists.

When my dad wasn't drinking, he was such a charming Jekyll that it never failed to shock me when he turned into Hyde. He'd scream and swear, lash out with fists and feet, and then jump into his car and speed off into the night. My mother and siblings and I were like a meteorologist in a hurricane—no matter how skilled our predictions, we couldn't prevent the wreckage.

What did my father have against Jimmy, who got straight A's and played the Kol Nidre on his violin at our synagogue every Yom Kippur? My brother and I used to lie on the scratchy blue carpet in his room, memorizing stanzas from Shakespeare, Dylan Thomas, T.S. Eliot, and Andrew

Marvell. He taught me to read deeply and to love words. But that night in our kitchen the only words I could think of were: *Why isn't Mom stopping this?*

My dad's arm was still squeezing Jimmy's neck, and he'd started to kick at his back. My brother's face was red and his eyes seemed to bulge. I desperately wanted to save him, to scream or ram myself into my father. Instead, I turned and ran out the door.

Across the street was a mansion, secluded behind hedges, that had been vacant for as long as I could remember. At times like these, I'd often hide out in the garden, where I'd sit at the edge of an empty concrete fountain. Earlier that afternoon, I'd left my journal and pen there, tucked under a bush. I grabbed them now and started writing.

His face was red. His eyes were bulging....

Eventually I understood some of my mother's reasons for never challenging my father: her fear of poverty, the stigma of divorce, and the stiff-upper-lip tradition handed down by her Eastern European ancestors. "My baba used to tell me: "Tell your troubles to a stone," she'd say. But she did more than keep mum about my father's violence. She also worked constantly to show our family's best face to the world, like the little smiley faces she drew on the cards she'd send to family and friends for birthdays, anniversaries, and graduations. A former college beauty queen, with long legs, blue-green eyes and jet-black hair, she was naturally suited for the role of our ambassador.

She braided my hair before I'd trudge to school, where I often ate lunch alone, a chubby kid who stood too close and lost track of conversations. But each day after I trudged back home, my mother would ask me to tell her about my day. "Start at the beginning!" she'd coax, and would reward me with such rapt attention that I trained myself to look and listen more closely and tell better stories.

She taught me the difference between rose and yellow gold and the importance of having your hair cut every six weeks. Her walk-in closet was a wonderland of designer shoes and boots: buttery-soft leather Ferragamos, Bruno Maglis, and Oleg Cassinis. I loved to breathe in the scent of Joy (the "costliest perfume in the world") from the warm silk lining of her ebony mink jacket when she and my father were preparing to leave for another night at the symphony, opera, or theater.

My father worshipped my mother and paid her tribute with expensive gifts—the mink, a silver Rolex, designer clothes, two facelifts—as he struggled to keep up with their richer friends: the department store president, the plastic surgeon, and the orthopedist. To the rest of the world, we were part of the one percent, yet he was paying for everything—including their new BMWs and overseas trips and all four of our elite educations—by siphoning equity out of the Hillsborough house. The bills kept piling up, and sometimes I'd hear him sighing as he read them at his desk. I wondered if his financial worries were what caused his tantrums. I wondered how my mother could get him to do almost anything except to stop hurting his kids.

Eventually my mother made an exception to her grandmother's advice and began to tell her troubles to me. She needed someone in whom to confide her fear, disappointment, and increasing resentment of my father, and I eagerly filled that role. Sometimes she called me her "Little Savior." The crazy-making catch was that the next day she'd almost always deny what she'd confided. "I could never live with a man who beat his children," she once told my brother, who then told me. Yet when I asked her about it, she swore he'd heard her wrong.

As I grew older, I often tried to break through my mother's denial and pleaded with her to leave my father, for her own safety, and ours, even for just one night. She'd never consider it. I began to have a recurring dream, in which she was locked in a tower, waiting for me to come free her.

Within two years of the night my father dragged Jimmy across the kitchen floor, I knew what I wanted to do with my life. At thirteen, I set my heart on becoming a foreign correspondent. As the years passed, I'd have all sorts of reasons for this choice. Journalists were the good guys, the truth-tellers, like the ones at the *Washington Post* who would later chase a corrupt president out of office. There was also the promise of adventure and glory, the chance to travel the world on someone else's dime, with your name in boldface on the front page. And then there were reasons I'd never discuss with my future college professors. One was that I needed some physical distance from my parents. Another was that writing had become a comfort, helping me cope with upsetting events. It felt like taking chaos in my hands and shrinking it into words that made sense. Still another was that I'd gotten hooked at an early age on peering at the messes behind people's carefully constructed facades.

Perhaps most importantly, my love of writing was going to be my ticket to freedom, guaranteeing I'd never again be dependent on an unreliable man. I already knew I could monetize it. When I was just twelve years old, Archie Comics paid me ten dollars for a brief essay I wrote about our pet schnauzer.

On my seventeenth birthday, in 1974, my sister gave me a book of interviews by Oriana Fallaci, the Italian journalist famed for skewering pompous male leaders like Henry Kissinger and Yasser Arafat. I wanted to be just like Fallaci—beautiful, glamorous, and fearlessly exposing the sins of "these bastards who control our lives." This was the start of my mission to expose hypocrisy, corporate corruption, political malfeasance, racism, and all other forms of abuse of the weak.

Still, I never lost my ability to spot a Louis Vuitton bag—or even, for that matter, a Givenchy.

4

Santa Clara, California, March 1980

A full day and a half passed between the time Andy Granger killed Howard Witkin and police discovered Howard's body. This gave Andy and Gary Oliver the chance to flee Santa Clara unhindered. On Sunday morning, a couple of Howard's friends, who'd grown worried after failing to reach him by phone, dropped by the townhouse, saw the blood on the porch and the bullet holes in the door, and called police.

Two Santa Clara detectives, Captain Wayne Britt and Sergeant Steve Derossett, were assigned to the case. Within hours they began canvassing Howard's neighbors. Yet after more than a dozen interviews, they had yet to locate a witness. Three or four residents in the tidy, look-alike townhouses along Howard's cul-de-sac recalled hearing a strange noise, but they told the cops they'd assumed it was a car backfiring. Which of course was odd, considering the seventeen rounds Andy had fired.

In that first week, the closest the police had to a witness' perspective, which at the time didn't seem close at all, was a report called in by one of Howard's neighbors, a house painter who had contacted the station after reading the news report of his death. The notes from the duty officer said that late on the previous Thursday, one day before the murder, the house painter had watched an unfamiliar car with two men inside driving slowly around the cul-de-sac. The painter had been on his way home in his truck but was sufficiently concerned to follow the 1970s gold Chevrolet for a few blocks until he could write down the license plate. It was VNM530.

Britt called the painter several times that week but failed to get an answer. He ran a search of the license plate in California, but after nothing came up he tucked the note into a file. The detective had more urgent priorities. A police search of Howard's townhouse had yielded a surprising discovery: an old sock in a floor safe stuffed with packets containing sixty thousand dollars worth of high-grade cocaine. Subsequently, a few of Howard's friends confirmed that Howard had not only been using but was also selling the drug, mostly but not exclusively to people he knew well. Some described it as his way of making friends, like the baseball tickets he'd also share with buddies.

The detectives made the reasonable assumption that Howard's risky business had helped lead to his death, which is why the first *Mercury* story on the murder, written by the night-shift police-beat reporter and published on Tuesday, March 25, 1980, ran under the headline: "Drug Link Suspected in Exec's Slaying."

Howard's cocaine stash was obviously on Wayne Britt's mind when he called Judi Singer at the Le Baron hotel in San Jose that evening. He'd been trying to reach her for two days and only recently found out that she and Bob Singer were in town with her kids for Howard's funeral.

"Hi, sergeant, how are ya?" Judi greeted him on the recorded call. "I've been kinda waitin' to hear from you."

Judi had gotten word of Howard's death within hours after his body was found that Sunday morning. She'd been having lunch with her husband and children in their favorite booth at The Onion Crock, as was their custom after picking up the older kids from Hebrew school, when the restaurant manager called Bob Singer to the phone. On the line was

Judi's father, Bob Barnett, who'd just heard the news from Howard's parents, the first to be informed by police. When Judi realized who it was, she grabbed the phone out of Bob's hand. After another minute, her daughter Marie, who was watching from the booth, heard Judi shriek, "Oh my God!" and then heard her begin to sob.

Now, on the phone from the Santa Clara station, Britt expressed his sympathy for Judi's loss before asking what she knew about Howard's drug sales.

"Yeah, he used drugs," Judi said. "I really don't know, you know, too much. I'm an anti-drug user—" she laughed quietly—"so he tried to hide it from me, I'm sure. I mean, he certainly used mari*jua*na ..."

Britt pressed her, gently. What was the deal with all that cocaine? Did Judi think Howard had any enemies? Judi had nothing for him there. She didn't know anything about the cocaine, she said.

The detective's halting questions betrayed his frustration. Britt believed that if you don't get a major break on a homicide within the first twenty-four hours, you're likely out of luck. And now, after three days, the Santa Clara detectives knew little more than they did on the morning Howard's body was found. As if as an afterthought, Britt mentioned that Howard's friends had told the detectives that he'd seemed upset recently—something to do with Judi and the children.

"Yes he was," she said quickly. "We have this two-and-a-half year old *child*. And he was scheduled to come for a visit this summer, for nine days, and possibly thirty days ...."

Suddenly Judi's voice rose with what seemed like fresh anger. She told Britt that her ex-husband had even planned to take the three kids on a houseboat in a lake near Yosemite National Park, a prospect that terrified her. "The baby is just a *baby*," she said. "He sleeps in a crib and he is not toilet-trained, and he—he's a baby! And I didn't feel he was ready to be separated from me for that length of time. Nor did his doctor. So Howard and I did not have a really terrific"—she laughed again, although this time it sounded harsh—"relationship, consequently. We were *divorced* after all. And so I was taking some type of legal action to change that situation."

She hadn't been trying to prevent Howard from visiting, she said. "What I was attempting to do was have the baby come at a later time. The baby does not know Howard. Did not know Howard. I mean, we have been divorced since he was an infant ... and I think sometimes"—Judi laughed again—"thirty-two-year-old men who are having, living a good life, don't always be as careful with little babies as the mommy. I'm a little *overprotective* ...."

"Hmmm," Britt said. "Ok ...."

His voice sounded distracted, as if he were ready to get off the phone, but he paused for some small talk, asking Judi if she had a job in Michigan.

"No," she said, laughing once again. "I drive carpools. It's what I do for a living."

This time Britt laughed with her. "Okay, sounds just like my wife."

Toward the end of the conversation, Judi invited Britt to call her at any time if he had more questions. Then she turned the talk to her kids once more. "I hope the end of this will not be something that's difficult for my children," she said. "I was *very* unhappy with the newspaper this morning. I mean I've got *babies*. I just think that was in terrible taste."

"Ah, unfortunately, we have no control of sensationalism by the press—"

"I know, I know—"

"I agree with you, though," Britt broke in. "Unfortunately, they wanna sensationalize these things ..."

A moment later, the detective and the victim's ex-wife said a friendly goodbye. Britt and his partner, Steve Derossett, spent the next seven days continuing to pursue the "drug-link theory." Then Derossett got a phone call that entirely changed their course.

A San Jose police sergeant who was friends with a cop in Flint, Michigan, was on the line. The Flint cop had been talking with Bob Singer's manager at The Onion Crock restaurant, who'd revealed that Bob had recently tried to recruit him to help arrange a "hit" on his wife Judi's ex-husband.

"Hey, this is wonderful. Absolutely wonderful!" Derossett yelped. He turned on his tape recorder and asked the San Jose sergeant to start over.

The Onion Crock manager would later serve as the prosecution's key witness. During the 1981 trial, he would sheepishly admit that he'd initially considered accepting Bob's offer. He'd even accompanied him one night to a seedy Flint night club, The Aladdin, where Bob thought they might find an assassin.

Bob had been behaving out of character, the manager would testify. Normally he was a pretty calm guy, but that night at The Aladdin he seemed highly agitated, using language out of 1930s gangster movies. "Don't say 'murder,'" he coached the manager. "Tell him you need someone to take a long walk off a short pier!"

The manager's conscience kicked in the next day, after which he told Bob he'd better find someone else. Apparently Bob did just that. About one week later, the manager heard that one of the busboys, a twenty-one-year-old kid named Gary Oliver, had left for California. When Gary returned to pick up his paycheck, three days after Howard's murder, the manager said he watched him open his wallet and saw that it was full of hundred-dollar bills. Gary, a ninth-grade dropout, had been earning three-dollars-and-twenty-five cents an hour as a busboy.

"The kid sounds to me like he is not what you call your professional kind of killer," the San Jose cop told Derossett, on the taped call. "That fits," Derossett marveled. "It sounds good," he added. "Damn, it sounds good."

Through most of the week after the call from the San Jose cop, Britt and Derossett sought more evidence to back up their new theory, that Howard had been killed by an inexperienced hitman who had been hired by his ex-wife's new husband in Flint and then traveled to California. They called eight motels near Howard's home to see if anyone from Michigan had checked in during the week of his murder. (No one had.) They looked to see if Bob Singer had a criminal record in Michigan or California. (He didn't). But after half a dozen of these dead ends, Detective Britt got a second lucky break. On a hunch, he tried the house painter again, and this time he reached him. He asked him to check his notes, and the painter confirmed that the license plate number he'd seen was VNM530. But it must have been one of the older California plates, the painter now said—the ones with yellow letters and numbers on a black background.

Michigan plates were black with white lettering, but Britt now remembered the yellowish light above Howard's front porch and wondered if maybe the painter had seen the letters and numbers under a similar glow. Maybe they'd only *seemed* to be yellow. He checked the plate again, this time in Michigan, and it came back registered to a two-door gold 1970 Chevy. The car had last been registered to a man who lived around the corner from Gary Oliver's grandmother.

As the detectives learned more about Gary Oliver— and soon after that about Gary's childhood friend, Andy Granger—they marveled at how the two of them had organized themselves to drive all the way to California, much less to have nearly gotten away with a murder.

5

In the week that Howard Witkin was murdered, I was twenty-two and traveling in the Himalayan mountains of northern Pakistan, trailing after a man I thought I loved. I felt like Ingrid Bergman in Casablanca as Richard and I hopped aboard small planes and checked into five-star hotels. After all those years of studying and work, the life I'd dreamed of—or at least a close facsimile—was finally beginning.

This wasn't what I'd planned when I'd landed in London two months earlier. Back then I thought *I'd* have the leading role. *Newsweek* had just hired me for an elite internship, with my expenses and salary paid by a grant from the Overseas Press Club.

But that was before I met Richard, whom I'd idolized for years. Just seven years older than I was, he already was a legendary foreign correspondent, covering the Middle East and Africa for the *Philadelphia Inquirer*. I'd first read his dispatches as a college senior in 1979, after he won a Pulitzer Prize for his Middle East coverage, with stories that skillfully portrayed ordinary people in the midst of unfolding history. I remember one of his features from Cairo, just after Egypt's president, Anwar Sadat, dared to try to make peace with Israel. It began by describing how proud Egyptian workers were singing their national anthem one morning as they walked on unpaved streets to their jobs. Reading along, I felt like I was right beside him, hearing the music and tasting the dust. Anyone who could write like that had to have a huge heart—not to mention a lot to teach me. So when the *Newsweek* editor who hired me in New York remarked that Richard was his friend, I asked for an introduction.

"Maybe Richard needs someone to house-sit when he's traveling," I suggested. "That would help me save on rent, so I could make the grant last longer ...."

The editor agreed, and called Richard in London, after which Richard called me. In my first week in the city, we met at a bar near his flat in Earl's Court, where skinny, dreadlocked Rastafarians leaned against brick walls, drinking from cans in paper bags, and men in turbans played Arabic music on boom boxes. Richard sat grinning and smoking a cigar; he was an incorrigible chain-smoker, just like my father. Also like my father, he was tall and charismatic, and loved spending money. According to legend, he'd once rented a camel and a goat to bring into the *Inquirer* newsroom. He joked that walking past certain shops in London gave him a "palsy of the wants."

Within the first five minutes, I'd blurted out how much I admired him and proposed my house-sitting idea.

"That could work," Richard said. For a shadow of an instant, his eyes dropped toward my breasts, presented that day in a tight purple cashmere sweater. My mother had given me that sweater, together with the seeds of my ridiculous confusion. In that moment I couldn't have said if I wanted Richard to mentor or to marry me, which maybe wasn't surprising after all those years of her mixed messages:

You're smart enough to be free and independent!
Don't be too smart or no one will protect you!
Mothers are virtuous; career women are selfish.

For God's sake, use my bitter sacrifice to make something more of your life!

At that very first meeting, Richard gave me an extra set of keys to his flat. Within a few weeks I was not only house-sitting when he was away but hanging around on his return, sleeping in his spare room, cooking meals, and running errands. All the while, I flirted like the clumsy amateur I was, growing increasingly frustrated as he failed to reveal anything beyond that first flicker of interest in the bar. The more remote he seemed, the more I longed to get closer.

I had a spy at *Newsweek*'s office back in New York, where Richard occasionally dropped by on his U.S. visits to see his friend, my editor. Sarah was the editor's secretary, with whom I'd struck up a conspiratorial friendship. When I called her from the London office to tell her about my crush on Richard, she warned me to be careful. "He's got a *lot* of girlfriends," she said. We groused together about how unfair that was. Richard was paunchy and reeked of tobacco, with thinning hair he never combed. None of it diminished his attractiveness. That, on top of his contagious enthusiasm—for adventure, food, romance, and journalism—made women like me want to take care of him.

I thought I had my chance one night after Richard arrived home late from Rhodesia and we stayed up talking until dawn, lounging on his overstuffed, tasseled couches in the pre-furnished flat he joked was "done in neo-Iranian." He told me all about his adventures on the road, including how he'd covered the Israeli invasion of south Lebanon by walking across the no man's land between Palestinian guerrillas and the Israeli army, and I asked his advice about stories I was working on at *Newsweek*. But although I smiled and smiled at him, he didn't make a move.

This is hopeless, I thought, as I stumbled into Richard's spare room, closing the curtains against the morning light. I'd yet to learn the secret of how to catch a man.

I woke just after nine in the morning to find the flat empty. A scribbled note on the kitchen table informed me he'd gone off to cover some breaking news in Tel Aviv. I dressed in a rush, took the Underground to the bureau, and within an hour was sitting at my little corner desk, reading a newspaper and silently still berating myself, when I heard the bureau chief's secretary gasp.

"Look what someone got for *you!*" she trilled, looking over at me. I glanced up to see a deliveryman heading out the door, and, on her desk, a giant, flamboyant bouquet of pink lilies.

A few days later, on Richard's next stop home, I was waiting for him at the apartment, having splurged on a couple of steaks to go with a bottle from his stash of Bordeaux. I put a vase of roses on the table, and wore a tight, low-cut burgundy dress. No Saran Wrap, but the same naked offer. This time it did the trick.

After that, Richard readily took on the role of teacher to a worshipful student. I admired his ability to ignore a ringing phone when he didn't feel like answering it. He showed me how to make strong coffee with a French press, his ritual before sitting down to write, and which became my ritual as well.

The French novelist Honore de Balzac once wrote that coffee was a "great power in my life," sending sparks shooting into his brain. "Ideas quick-march into motion like battalions of a grand army to its legendary fighting ground," he wrote. "Memories charge in, bright flags on high; the cavalry of metaphor deploys with a magnificent gallop ...." Balzac drank stronger and stronger cups until he died at fifty-one, his stomach destroyed by his addiction. From my perspective at twenty-two, it didn't seem like such a bad trade.

Making love with Richard was another kind of trade. It didn't send sparks shooting into my brain, but I hadn't expected it to. I'd lost my virginity in the summer of my eighteenth year to the head peach-picker on an Israeli kibbutz, and his wham/bam/shalom approach had set a low bar. And as for me, I wasn't only amateur at flirting. What I loved most about being with Richard was the afterward, lying in bed as I listened to his stories. I pestered him for details about his years of paying dues while covering local politics in Baltimore and Philadelphia. His bottom line was always the same: To follow his path, I'd have to return to the United States and pay my dues on a local beat at a small paper.

I didn't want to think about that then. With Richard I was at least living my dream vicariously, and maybe that was as close as I'd come. The *Newsweek* internship hadn't started off well. The New York editor who'd hired me had failed to get buy-in from my future boss, the London bureau chief. So not only was the bureau chief not waiting for me with a welcome sign at Heathrow, as I'd half-expected, but on my first day in the office, he informed me that he wasn't about to add intern-supervising duties to his crowded schedule. If I came up with a good idea, he'd consider it, but I should limit my demands on his time.

This was a blow, but I stayed hopeful. Each morning I dressed up for work, reported to the office, and was all but ignored for the rest of the day. Occasionally the bureau chief would throw me a small story, but I felt like I was wasting my time. After three weeks of this, I called the editor in New York and queried him directly. What about a story on how leading British feminists loathed their first female prime minister, Margaret Thatcher? He loved the idea and told me to go ahead. But the bureau chief was furious with my end-run.

"You are the most *forward* intern I've ever met!" he sputtered. "You're *not staff*, you know!"

I nodded silently as he chewed me out, then slunk out early to shop for Richard's dinner. *Newsweek* published my Thatcher story, but I'd obviously blown whatever chance I'd had of winning the bureau chief over, so I didn't feel I had much to lose on the night that Richard called me to suggest I accompany him—the next day—on a two-week trip to Pakistan, where he planned to report on the U.S.-backed mujahideen rebels fighting against the occupying Soviet army in neighboring Afghanistan. I left a giddy message on the bureau chief's phone to let him know I'd be gone for a while.

In Islamabad, at the Intercontinental Hotel, Richard and I spent late afternoons sitting by the pool and evenings chatting with diplomats or sipping whiskey together in the hotel's "permit room" for infidel guests. Traveling west, we strolled through the souk in Peshawar, dodging water buffalos and honking Vespas. Shepherding me through the stalls with his hand against my back, he bought me kohl eyeliner in a little silver case, soft Egyptian striped cotton pajamas, a leather purse, and a large lapis pendant. I took notes for him and snapped a photo that got me a byline credit in *The Inquirer*. After all that dissing from the bureau chief, Richard made me feel appreciated, needed, almost like *staff*. He invited me to sit in on his interviews, introducing me as his assistant, taught me how to use a teletype machine, and charged all my meals to his expense account. I listened closely, studying his technique: the friendly, open way he got his sources to trust him.

I was Richard's perpetually awestruck audience, with just a couple of exceptions. The first came one week into the trip, after an emaciated cab driver had taken us from Rawalpindi to Islamabad. I watched in horror as Richard squabbled over the price, negotiating mercilessly over a mere two dollars. After he finally turned away, victorious, I slipped the driver a wad of rupees.

Then one night, during a special candlelight dinner he'd arranged on our hotel rooftop, given as he was to grand gestures at his newspaper's expense, Richard caught me by surprise, telling me that meeting me had led him to "an orgy of bridge-burnings." I assumed this was a reference to all those other girlfriends. "I can see us maybe getting married someday, maybe having some babies," he added.

Babies!? I stifled a gasp. Being with Richard felt like being at the center of the universe: the only place where interesting things were happening, the only place I wanted to be. But I didn't want to think about babies. Having babies would kill my career, condemning me to live my mother's life.

So I didn't answer his indirect question. Instead, I fluttered my kohl-enhanced eyelashes as I suddenly remembered what I'd been meaning to tell him all day. That morning, while still in Peshawar, I'd had a long and promising conversation with the United Nations head of refugee affairs, who I'd originally thought might help us find an Afghan translator. He was lonely, stuck in that isolated post, and had asked me to lunch, where he'd told me how a thousand-member tribe of fiercely anti-Communist nomads from Kyrgyzstan had traveled all the way to Gilgit, in the Himalayas, in hopes of immigrating to Alaska. "Wouldn't that be an amazing story?" I asked Richard in the candlelight.

The Czech novelist Milan Kundera once said he couldn't stand to think about himself in his twenties, when he was "an absolute jerk from every point of view." I'm sure many parents of twenty-something children would confirm that it's an extraordinarily self-involved time. And perhaps all that ego is necessary to meet the profound challenge of finding one's place in the world. Even so, I still wince to think of my behavior that night on the roof.

Richard switched gears easily, agreeing that my story idea sounded promising, the nomads being such picturesque and touchingly deluded characters. He could do the story for his newspaper, he said, while I could try to freelance it.

The next morning, I booked a flight on a small plane for Richard and his growing entourage: a photographer who'd flown in from Italy, our new Pakistani translator, and me, his mistress/apprentice. In Gilgit, we interviewed Rahman Qul, the Kyrgyz tribe's imperious leader, who solemnly asked if we thought he could take his hundreds of goats on the plane to the United States. I wandered through the village, full of blossoming apricot trees and wide-eyed smiling children, and wanted to stay longer. But after just two days, we flew back to Peshawar, where Richard told me I'd have to return alone to London. He planned to slip into Afghanistan, disguising himself in robes and a turban to blend in with a group of mujahideen to continue his reporting on the real news of the rebellion.

When I hinted that I'd like to come along, he looked at me with what seemed like sadness and shook his head no.

"I wouldn't be able to protect you," he said.

I nodded, returning his sad look, even as I knew we were both fibbing. He didn't want to be encumbered, while despite all my talk about aspiring to cover wars, when it came to down to it, at least just then, I was more than half-relieved by the excuse to skip the goat meat dinners and Soviet air strikes.

Back at Richard's flat, I realized I couldn't bear to face the *Newsweek* bureau chief again. I hung out in limbo, sleeping in Richard's bed, writing in my journal, taking long walks, and typing up notes for what I hoped would be that magazine story on the nomads.

All this was just fine until Richard's planned week with the mujahideen turned into two. Then he called from Peshawar with a vague update. He'd need a few days to file his story, and then might have to go to Rome .... He'd let me know, he said. But he didn't.

After the third week, I invited a young British journalist I knew to Richard's flat for dinner. We made a fire in the fireplace and nibbled at a piece of the big bar of hashish Richard had not that wisely smuggled back from a previous trip to Afghanistan. When after an hour nothing happened, we nibbled some more.

What an idiot! I scolded myself the next morning, after my friend kissed me goodbye, and, still reeling from the hash, I shoved Richard's sheets into the washing machine. I wasn't in love with the British guy like I thought I might be with Richard. But I was lonely, which of course I believed was Richard's fault.

I had no idea if Richard had been serious in Islamabad, with his talk about babies. But I'd been thinking more pragmatically about my own prospects: my apparent lack of stick-to-itiveness and how much work it would take to go back home and cover news with no guarantee it would lead me back overseas. As much as I loved journalism and believed I was getting good at it, I was sure I'd never be as talented as Richard. Yet as his wife, I'd be able to keep doing it, under pretty optimal circumstances. I wouldn't have to put up with hostile bosses like the *Newsweek* bureau chief, and I'd be free to be creative, as long as I avoided having those kids.

Alone in Richard's flat, I fantasized about our future together, even as a small, still-functioning part of my brain registered that another week had gone by and I had no idea when he planned to return. My anxiety finally drove me to rummage through his desk, where in no time I found confirmation of my fears: a letter mailed some weeks earlier from a woman in Baltimore. She'd enclosed a photograph— she looked young, like me, and cute, in a homespun kind of way, with blue eyes and red hair peeking out from a straw hat. On the back, she'd written: "I'd be happy just to tend your garden!"

Two more days passed. It rained constantly. I barely left the flat, eating cheese and crackers for dinner and staying close to the phone. No call.

On the third afternoon, a letter addressed to Richard dropped through the mail slot. The return address was the *Newsweek* office in New York, so I figured, correctly, that it was from Richard's friend, my editor. By this point I was so outraged that I didn't hesitate to slide my fingernail under the seal.

What I read made me wish I hadn't.

The editor began by scolding Richard for having asked him to assign me to a story in Ireland so that he could host one of his girlfriends in London in my absence. He went on to rail about how I'd abandoned the internship, warning his friend against getting more involved with such an "opportunistic groupie."

I blinked hard and read the phrase again. *It was impossible that he meant me!*

Breathing shallowly, I found a glue stick to reseal the envelope. I checked the clock, calculating that Sarah should just be coming to work in New York City. Lying with a cup of coffee in a patch of sunlight on the Pakistani rug in Richard's living room, I called her, at Richard's expense, to tell her about the photograph of the redhead and the letter from the editor.

"You poor thing," Sarah said immediately. But then she said something that immediately made sense: "I don't think you really wanted to marry him, did you? It sounds more to me like you wanted to *be* him."

I studied the dust motes rising from the carpet. I recognized that what she'd said was just a slightly more diplomatic version of "opportunistic groupie." Still, Sarah helped me see what I had to do next.

Three days later, Richard finally returned. I met him at Heathrow with a long embrace. But in the cab ride back to the flat I told him I was planning to leave London the next week.

"I'm going to take your advice and start over at a small paper," I said.

If Richard was surprised, he didn't show it. He said I was doing the right thing, career-wise, saying nothing about what it meant for our supposed relationship. When the day came, he chivalrously accompanied me in the cab to the airport and insisted on waiting with me through my flight's four-hour delay. For most of that time, he kept his arm around me as I snuffled into his shirt, overwhelmed by feelings of failure, loss—and rage. Everyone had been against me: the bureau chief, Richard, my *Newsweek* boss, even the red-haired girl. What had I done to deserve that?

This is how I was thinking then, if you can call it that. More like *not*-thinking, in my conviction that I had no share of the blame for the ruin of that internship and quasi-love affair. Not until many years later could I see my part in tearing it all down.

Like the way I hadn't bothered to tell the New York editor who'd hired me—my former champion—that I'd be going AWOL to Pakistan. And the look on Richard's face, during that candlelight dinner, after I switched the topic from babies to Kyrgyz nomads. And how I'm pretty sure he saw me slip those rupees to the cabbie. And his brooding silence in London, after I told him I thought mice had gotten into his hashish.

No wonder the *Newsweek* editor had been so mad. No wonder Richard had lost interest in me as a candidate to tend his garden. And no matter that we wouldn't have lasted a month had we gone ahead and gotten married. Once I was able to see things more clearly, it distressed me to realize how blindly I'd been moving through the world.

6

Flint, Michigan, April 1980

While I was still in London, and still fantasizing about a future with Richard, the two Santa Clara cops were making quick progress in Flint. The weather in the riverside, Rust Belt town was dark and rainy, with the arrival of spring doing nothing to lift the gloom of the oncoming national recession that would soon leave tens of thousands out of work. Wayne Britt and Steve Derossett arrested Gary Oliver at his grandmother's house, where Gary wasted no time in confessing that Bob Singer had hired him to kill Howard Witkin, and that he had then recruited Andy Granger. With Gary's assistance, the cops tracked down Andy and arrested him in front of the Paramount Potato Chip Company, where he had recently been hired as a deliveryman. Shortly thereafter, they also arrested Bob Singer. A prosecutor looking at the case some years later would call the three bumbling suspects "the Three Stooges."

Andy was even more of a willing witness than his pal Gary had been. He brought the two detectives to his mother's house and led them to his bedroom, where he showed them all his mementos from his trip to California, including a map of Santa Clara with Howard's address circled. He'd also kept a Western Union money-gram that Bob Singer had sent the two young men to pay for their journey home. In what seemed a tiny effort to cover their tracks, Bob had addressed it to "Stuart Granger."

The detectives would later tell me how delighted they were by Andy's eager cooperation, sans any legal counsel. He seemed even to enjoy telling them all about his adventure out West—a drama of outrageous bumbling and weirdly serendipitous success that Andy would go on to tell, with some tweaks here and there, several times more over the next few years, in depositions, courtroom testimony, and eventually in a long interview with me. The most important change Andy would make in his story was the identity of the triggerman. In that first conversation in his bedroom, he said Gary, not he, had done the shooting. Only a few days later would he adjust his narrative to fit with the rest of the evidence.

Andy said he'd never met the man who'd ordered the killing and still didn't know his name. Gary had always referred to Bob Singer as "Mr. Big." According to Andy, Gary said Mr. Big planned to pay ten thousand dollars for the hit but had never given a reason why he wanted Howard dead other than saying that he was a "dope dealer" who'd sold drugs to kids.

Here's how the story subsequently unfolded, according to what the cops could piece together. Having gotten part of the payment in advance, Gary spent five hundred dollars to buy the ten-year-old Chevy from his neighbor. Then he paid another couple hundred dollars for a new shotgun: a Remington Bushmaster Deluxe Deerslayer. The two young men packed up the Chevy as if they were headed out for a camping trip, with bags of Doritos, weed, and Gary's guitar. They set out before dawn on Tuesday, March 18, 1980 with sleet pounding on their windshield.

The plan was that Gary would be the shooter. Gary, after all, had the serious criminal experience—he was still on parole for having burglarized a gas station. But after two days on the road, there were several signs that Gary wasn't up to the job. Andy first became concerned in Wyoming, where they'd stopped on a lonely road at night to take target practice at a stop sign. It was there that Gary told Andy that he'd forgotten to buy ammunition for the shotgun. Andy assured him that needn't be a problem, since he'd thought to bring along his pheasant-hunting rifle, with bullets, as a backup. But soon after that, Gary dropped and shattered his one pair of glasses, after which he could no longer see well enough even to do his share of the driving.

Andy could see that Gary was having a crisis of confidence even before they reached Nevada, where Gary asked Andy straight out whether they shouldn't call it quits. They could go back home, return the rest of the money to Mr. Big, and go on with their lives. By then, however, Andy was determined to see the thing through. He had a special loathing for adults who took advantage of children, and the idea that Howard had sold drugs to kids rankled him.

"We have to stick with the plan," Andy told Gary, as he would later testify, adding with no apparent sense of irony: "We have to do the right thing."

So Andy powered through, driving without a break until they came within a mile of the California border. By then he was so exhausted, however, that he fell asleep at the wheel and drove the Chevy into a ditch. He managed to get the car moving again, but there was obviously something wrong, as he could tell by a new and constant loud clicking noise. Distracted by worry about whether the Chevy would last, he then took a wrong turn that brought them all the way to Oakland as they got lost for more than an hour before finding their way to Howard's townhouse to check out the address. This was just before midnight on Thursday, March 20, which is when Howard's neighbor, the housepainter, caught sight of them.

The two men drove around until they found a deserted roadside to sleep for a few hours, and in the morning headed to downtown Santa Clara for breakfast and some sightseeing, killing time as they waited for nightfall. Andy parked in front of a Kmart, where he wanted to buy a comb. As he turned off the ignition, he heard the car make one last, weak grinding noise. He tried to turn it on again, but it had died.

What were they supposed to do now? Take a cab, with the rifle, to Howard's house? The two of them briefly debated calling Mr. Big before agreeing he wouldn't appreciate it. Then Andy told Gary he was going to get his comb and headed off to the Kmart. Gary opened the Chevy's hood and stared inside. He knew almost nothing about cars.

The two were in luck, however—if you can call it that. Several years later, when I interviewed Derossett and Britt, the Santa Clara detectives were still marveling over the way fate intervened at that moment. Just as the murder plot seemed to be irrevocably doomed, an eighteen-year-old stranger and part-time mechanic named Tom Maciolek noticed Gary standing aside the Chevy and walked over to offer his help. Tom couldn't fix the car, but after Gary invited him to share a joint, Tom and his girlfriend drove Andy and Gary to their apartment in his 1969, sky-blue Cadillac. Three hours, a few more joints, and several beers later, Gary offered Tom a deal: one thousand dollars and the brand-new, never-been-used shotgun would be his for simply driving them to Howard's townhouse. Tom agreed.

Thanks mostly to Andy Granger's extensive confession, the Santa Clara County District Attorney's office finally gathered enough evidence to file charges against all four suspects in the crime: the "Three Stooges" and the getaway driver. The plan was for Andy and Bob Singer to stand trial together first, followed by Gary Oliver and Tom Maciolek. All four were accused of first-degree murder.

7

Hillsborough, California, August 1980

Around nine in the morning I was sitting at my parents' kitchen table in my Lanz of Salzburg flannel nightgown, and midway through my second bowl of Life cereal, when my mother pulled up a chair next to me. Fresh and perky in her tennis whites, she had already read the newspaper, taken her morning bike ride, prepared two poached eggs and a cantaloupe slice for my father, emptied the dishwasher, and checked in with a couple of her friends by phone. I knew what she had on her mind.

Two and a half weeks had passed since my return from London, but even though I knew exactly what I had to do next to move forward with my plan to get a newspaper job, I hadn't yet taken the first step. Instead, I was sleeping late and spending afternoons lying slathered with baby oil by a pool at the home of a friend from high school.

It was still summer, and I'd been working hard for months, or so I told myself. I deserved a little downtime, and my parents, at least initially, seemed glad to have me back home.

With my three older siblings all out of the house and no more rebellious adolescent energy or tuition bills to vex him, my dad was no longer routinely getting drunk and exploding. He and I were close again, as we'd been intermittently throughout my life, during the times he wasn't completely off the rails and I wasn't actively hating him. When I was in college, he'd drive down almost every week to take me to lunch, where he'd talk for most of the hour and then, laughing at himself, ask me: "What about you? Tell me your dreams, hopes, and ambitions!"

Occasionally, at times like these when we were comfortable together, I'd gingerly challenge him about his drinking. He always denied that he was an alcoholic, and never directly acknowledged his violence. Even so, he often spoke obliquely about his yearning to be a better man – one of his many poignant traits that kept me from entirely giving up on him. Over and over he told me and my siblings about how impressed he was in medical school when he studied the writings of Sir William Osler, a legendary Canadian physician in the early 1900s. In his essay, "Aequanimitas," Osler wrote that for a physician, "no quality takes rank with imperturbability." My father often referred to that essay, pronouncing its title as slowly and sadly as if it were the name of a lost love.

On my visits home, like this one, we played backgammon together on the porch outside the kitchen. My dad loved backgammon, dominoes, and chess, especially when he was winning. But his patience was starting to ebb with my use of his phone, car, and refrigerator. Every once in a while, before rolling his backgammon dice, he'd ask whether I had a plan.

I'd yet to come up with a good answer.

Neither of my parents did well with uncertainty. They were both always in motion and expected the same from their kids. "Do something constructive!" was my mother's mantra when we were young and bored. She'd followed her own advice as soon as I started high school by returning to college to finish her undergraduate degree, after which she got a master's degree and teaching certificate in special education. She would later spend several years teaching children with learning disabilities at a school in a low-income neighborhood of Daly City, a job that filled her with pride, despite my father's continual protests that it was dangerous to park her BMW there.

Now her bright eyes let me know she'd found an answer to my obvious dilemma.

"I just talked to Sally Weinstein," she said. "She's got a nephew who just moved to San Francisco. She said he's very cute, and he's studying law. She thinks you two should meet."

I bared my teeth into what I hope passed for a smile. Three months earlier I'd left home convinced I was stepping forth into the dawn of my brilliant new future. Now I just needed an excuse to get out of the house at night.

"Sure, sounds great," I said.

My parents had always encouraged me to follow my professional ambition. When I was in high school, my mother even rose early with me to help fold the newspapers I edited. Yet in many ways they'd also communicated their doubt that I'd ever be able to properly support myself, or that my doing so might even be socially acceptable. "I'd really like to see you set up!" my father would often say—his code for married to a nice Jewish professional, like him. Sometimes he skipped the code altogether, urging, "Why don't you just marry a Jewish doctor or lawyer?"

He said this sort of thing all the time, and I'd just roll my eyes, with it never really occurring to me to challenge him about it. My father's frank expressions of anxiety were part of the background noise of my life, which reminds me of that old story about fish.

A big fish swims toward two little fish, greeting them: "Hey boys! How's the water?"

Once he's gone, one fish turns to the other and asks: "What's water?"

The water I grew up in included abundant, delicious, healthy food, the *New York Times* on the kitchen table, tennis at the country club, High Holidays at the Reform synagogue, and a father who had no buffer between his nerves and speech.

The hard part was that I was starting to share his unease. What if I wasted my most attractive years narrowly focused on competing for a job, only to find I'd aged out of the marriage market and condemned myself to poverty?

Mark, the law student, helped calm me down. He was better-looking than Richard: lean from daily workouts at the gym, and with a full head of black, glossy hair. He also had a trust fund and a gorgeous Nob Hill condo, with full-length windows looking out over the city. He picked me up in his convertible Porsche, always opening the car door and paying for meals. I overheard my parents gossiping happily about us on the phone with the Weinsteins.

I didn't go to bed with Mark on my first visit to the condo, but I did on the next four.

"You're beautiful," he told me after the third time, as he held my chin in his hand.

"No, I'm not," I said, turning my face away.

My fledgling conscience was beginning to make me feel guilty about sleeping with Mark when I didn't like him. He smelled like hair products, never made me laugh, and stopped to check himself out whenever he passed a mirror. But the worst was that on the afternoon of our fourth date, he'd asked if I would do his laundry while he studied, and for lack of a good excuse, I agreed. I'm pretty sure that's why, after our next expensive dinner, I grabbed the check and blurted: "Now I don't have to go to bed with you!"

In the moment, it felt like a good joke. The pain in his eyes surprised me.

"I'm just kidding!" I said. And then of course I had to return to his condo with him and pretend I hadn't meant it.

I didn't want to break up with Mark; his attention salved my pride after the breakup with Richard and going out with him seemed better than hanging out at home. So I decided to ask my mother for advice. The next afternoon I caught up with her as she was cooking a batch of date and oatmeal bars. I told her that Mark was feeling stressed and that I might have accidentally offended him.

"Let's make him some brownies!" she immediately replied. Naturally she had all the ingredients on hand. I leaned against the counter, watching her quick, decisive movements. She was never a dawdler like me.

"Tell him you made them!" she said, grinning, as she filled the pan with batter.

Shamelessly, I did. Mark didn't know that I'd grown up believing that a woman's skill at cooking (and sewing and cleaning house and laundry) was a mark of subjugation and consequently rebuffed all of my mother's attempts to teach me. He was touched when I handed him the shoebox lined with aluminum foil and packed with my mother's treats. But I was dejected by my lie—and his readiness to believe it. He had no idea who I was, or who I still, despite my self-doubt, wanted to be.

Although I couldn't have put it into words at the time, what bugged me most about the brownies lie was my willingness to manipulate Mark. I hated that when other women did it. What had stopped me from telling him, like a grownup, that I didn't want to do his laundry, or even see him anymore? For that matter, what had stopped me from getting angry at Richard in London, calling him out on *his* lies instead of telling more of my own?

Lying, playing the victim, massaging egos—those were all necessary tactics for many women of my mother's generation, who weren't financially independent. It was like guerrilla warfare, since they couldn't have won in a fair fight. The man could just stomp off and take his income elsewhere. It so happens that narcissists are also frequently manipulative, and also do it from a sense of weakness. They've grown up assuming they can't express their feelings directly, so they pull strings behind backs so as not to risk being rejected.

Even then, the best part of me didn't want to behave like that anymore. I wanted to be more honest and direct, as nearly impossible as that still seemed.

The next Friday morning I ran into my father in the kitchen as he was about to leave for work.

"Are you seeing Mark this weekend?" he asked, smiling.

"No, probably not. Dad, I'm really not that crazy about him," I said.

My answer surprised me as much as it did him. Only then had it hit me that I'd been keeping things going with Mark for one of the worst possible reasons, namely fear. Of being unlovable, alone, and unable to fend for myself.

But my father didn't appreciate my tiny epiphany.

He slammed down his coffee cup.

"You think I care?" he roared. Again, he'd gone from zero to eighty miles per hour in a heartbeat. "It makes no difference to me! You can take Mark and stick him up your ass!"

I could barely breathe.

"You're insane!" I shouted, and rushed past him to my bedroom, where I wrapped my arms around my chest and squeezed my eyes shut for a moment. Then I grabbed my journal and headed for the front door.

Across the street, after all those years, that big secluded house was still empty. I took my old seat on the edge of the concrete fountain, and for the next few minutes jotted notes on the crazy conversation with my father.

Turning the page, I then compiled a to-do list, a habit that always made big tasks seem less overwhelming. Suddenly there was a lot I needed to accomplish in a short time:

1. Dump Mark.

2. Lose 10 lbs.

3. Gather names and addresses of managing editors at 30 newspapers and wire-service bureaus in cities where I'd like to live. Preferably on the East Coast.

4. Make copies of my best clips from the Newsweek internship & mail them along with letters asking for a job.

5. Leave home for good.

8

Boston, September 1980

That's how it happened that while all four defendants in the Witkin murder case awaited trial for murder in San Jose, potentially facing the gas chamber, I was dragging a carry-on bag through airports and train stations, making my way to drop in on editors of big city newspapers who at most had sent tepid responses to my letters. "I'd be happy to meet with you if you're in town," was about as good as it got.

Having used up most of the money I'd earned in London, I'd had to borrow from my dad. Fortunately, and typically, I was back in his good graces shortly after his last blowup, and despite his continued urging that I focus on getting "set up," he'd handed over the fabulous sum of six hundred dollars with generous repayment terms. The loan paid for transportation to New York, Washington, Boston, Philadelphia, Louisville, and Miami, while I saved on hotels by crashing at the apartments and homes of distant relatives and old friends from college and past internships. These included my mom's third cousin in Miami, plus Sarah, the *Newsweek* secretary in New York, and a reporter I'd briefly slept with while working as an intern at the *Washington Post*.

I'd aimed high when I sent out my thirty letters, dreaming I'd get snapped up right away by a top urban newspaper. I simply couldn't imagine that my Stanford degree and half a dozen cool internships wouldn't push me to the front of the line. Yet I'd failed to account for the bigger picture, the one involving supply and demand. With the economy in a downturn, newspapers were cutting back their budgets even as more candidates applied. In the years since the *Washington Post's* Watergate scoop, journalism had acquired a new cachet. Ivy League grads who might have otherwise gone to law school were lining up to cover city hall. What's more, although I did my best to block the thought from my mind, any editor who checked my references at *Newsweek* would have gotten an earful from my angry former boss.

In newsroom after newsroom, I heard no after no. A few editors said I should send them clips from wherever I landed, although they may have just been trying to be polite. For my part, I had to struggle to feign enthusiasm for the few open entry-level jobs. Many of the big newspapers were creating suburban bureaus to fill special editions with names like "Neighbors." The thought of working for "Neighbors" after my glory days in London and Pakistan made me frantically sad. But getting no job would be much worse. After nine days of strikeouts, I started to panic. It would be humiliating to return to California with no offer.

"How's everything going?" my mom asked when I called her from New York.

"Really great!" I assured her. "I don't have anything solid yet, but tomorrow I'm taking the train to Boston to see about an opening at the Associated Press."

"That's wonderful, dear!"

I wanted her, as always, to think the best of me and not to worry, which is why I didn't tell her that the AP meeting was my last scheduled interview, and that I didn't even want the job.

On the northbound train the next morning, I gave myself a pep talk. Boston might be a fun place to live. My brother Jimmy lived in Cambridge. Wire-service work was relentless and often dull, but the AP had a lot of foreign jobs and a history of fast-tracking reporters to them from big-city general assignment beats.

Five minutes into the interview, the editor said I had a chance.

"I'm looking for someone who'll be a star right away, and you seem like you might have that potential," he said. "Plus your being a woman gives you a good shot. We need to hire more women."

I grinned what I hoped was a womanly grin. "If it helps, I could start next week," I said, adding, as pluckily as I could, "I know I need to pay some dues, and I'm ready to do it!"

He said he'd let me know within a week. Leaving the office, I splurged on a cab to the airport, where I bought a king-sized Hershey's chocolate bar for dinner. I had spent all but fifty-five dollars of my father's loan.

Three days after I returned to California, a letter arrived from the AP editor telling me I hadn't gotten the job. In desperation, I called one of my old journalism professors to get a list of high-quality small newspapers—*really* small ones this time. They paid almost nothing but were feeders for the bigger leagues. I sat back at my typewriter in my old bedroom to crank out another bunch of letters. If this didn't work I was going to have to think about law school.

The next day, however, my mom called me to the phone to talk to John Baker, the managing editor of the *San Jose Mercury*, where I'd sent one of my initial thirty letters but hadn't gotten any answer. The *Mercury* had an opening in San Jose. It was just temporary. Was I interested?

Interested in living in hot, flat San Jose? Thirty minutes from where I'd grown up? Without any guarantee of a staff job?

"When can I start?" I asked Baker.

The *Mercury* was a century-old, family-owned paper that had recently joined with Knight Newspapers to become part of a national chain. It was still a relatively small pond but had a newly ambitious publisher plus lots of extra money from the merger. Most importantly, it had recently opened its first foreign bureau, in Mexico City, and was planning another, soon, in Tokyo. When I learned about that, the embers of my foreign-correspondent dream began to glow.

Baker had a wry, I've-seen-it-all expression that reminded me of Jason Robards playing Ben Bradlee in *All the President's Men*. On my first day at work, just one week after his call, I brazenly told him of my interest in the Mexico bureau. He chuckled and started me out working evenings and weekends on general assignment, meaning I had no beat and no regular hours, but instead was at the mercy of my editors' whims.

I found a small studio overlooking a noisy freeway in a huge apartment complex in the bland but still-affordable city of Santa Clara, and with my first paycheck got the shag haircut and the navy-blue shoulder-padded jacket. My dad offered another loan, which I used to buy a Honda Accord. With monthly installments, I could pay him back in two years.

I can't imagine how I could have gotten started at that job without my father's help. If I'd had any pride I wouldn't have kept taking his money while continuing to listen to my mother complain about him behind his back. As my mother must also have done, I told myself I had no other options. But it wasn't that simple. Despite everything, I still wanted him in my life, and I hadn't stopped loving him.

Over the next several weeks, I threw myself into my new job, eagerly pursuing news-less features about summer carnival workers and graveyard diggers. I wrote daily stories about the construction of a new geothermal plant in Sonoma County, an effort by two hundred and fifty residents of the small city of Cupertino to secede from the municipal government, and plans by the city council in Sunnyvale, another small city, to build a new sewage system. I also took over the routine evening calls to each of the county's several police stations, the pre-internet method of finding out if any newsworthy crimes had occurred. "Hi there, it's the *Mercury*, anything goin' on?" was our robotic greeting.

I racked up so many unpaid hours that the paper's union steward threatened to file for them on my behalf if I didn't. I ignored him, and my strategy succeeded. Three months later, Baker called me at home after work to say my job was permanent.

Only much later would I learn to appreciate labor unions. For now all that mattered was that I was *staff*. No longer just some groupie. I'd earned this all by myself, and it immediately felt even better than I'd imagined.

"The only way you lose this job now is if the publisher gets shot by an irate subscriber, I have a heart attack, and the city editor falls and hits his head and dies," Baker assured me. His apocalyptic riff made no sense until I got to know him better and understood it was at least partly wishful thinking. Baker wasn't getting along well with his colleagues in management, as much as his reporters adored him, and would soon quit to move to Paris, becoming a copyeditor on the *International Herald Tribune*.

"How long before you send me to Mexico?" I asked him, giggling.

"Give it a few months," he growled, but quickly added: "I'm really excited for you. There are good things for you at this paper."

I continued to work overtime, with few friends and no hobbies. I was focused almost entirely on moving up the ladder and move up I did. Within three months, I'd earned a promotion to the criminal court beat. My predecessor, a mild-mannered, sixty-something-year-old—which then seemed impossibly elderly—represented a last vestige of the *Mercury*'s sleepy history, and he knew it: He was headed for early retirement. While showing me the ropes, he ceremoniously handed me the little ledger in which he had meticulously recorded all the upcoming dates for incremental progress in the dozen or so trials he had been following. After a couple of days, I tossed it in the trash. Surely that's what Richard would have done. But probably unlike what Richard would have done, I also threw out the half-empty whiskey bottle I found in his desk drawer.

Richard had strong views about the way one should cover local news. The secret was breaking the rules. Whenever you could get away with it, you had to ignore all those safe, record-keeping stories that few people read, in favor of features with color, emotion, and broader relevance. Your editors would always forgive you for missing a minor story if you grabbed a major one. Another secret: Make friends with the clerks and secretaries, the "little people," as Richard sardonically called them. "I just left my business card everywhere, so if anyone ever got upset about something, they'd know who to call," he'd told me.

Small talk had never come naturally to me but I forced myself to make it and soon had new friends on the beat who were leading me to scoops.

Newsrooms can be heavenly and hellish places for people who crave admiration. There's the thrill of seeing your story in print, and all the compliments you get from strangers for the rest of that day, followed almost immediately by an editor's glance that says: *What have you done for me lately?* Editors praise young reporters by calling them "hungry." I was always scrounging for my next meal.

My best source early on was a public defender named Bryan Shechmeister, who won so many of his cases that other lawyers often came to watch his arguments as if they were tutorials.

One glance at Bryan told you how little he cared about appearances. Balding and a little stooped even in his late thirties, he had a long, frizzy beard and often paired his tweed jacket with a loud plaid shirt. In college, he'd spent several months registering voters in Mississippi, and his long tenure as a public defender, when he could have worked anywhere for much more money, similarly spoke to his convictions.

I first met Bryan while reporting a story about one of his clients, an alleged serial killer who due to an outrageous clerical mistake by someone in the sheriff's office had been accidentally released from jail while awaiting his trial. Delighting in his good fortune, the prisoner had spent two days playing tourist in San Francisco, hanging out at Fisherman's Wharf with a girlfriend before the cops tracked him down and re-arrested him.

Bryan offered me an interview with him, on the condition that I kept it a secret beforehand. He slipped me and a photographer into the jail, and we spent the next hour with his friendly, curly haired client, hearing all about his unexpected weekend of freedom. The story and photograph, which landed on the *Mercury's* front page, accomplished Bryan's goal of humanizing his client, who was nonetheless later convicted of several horrific crimes. From then on, Bryan knew he could trust me. We often met at noon at the deli across the street from the courthouse, eating our sandwiches on the wooden picnic bench outside.

Bryan and I shared a keen distrust of authority, and he led me to several stories that exposed official ineptitude. In one, I described how California's increasingly harsh rape laws were leading rapists to kill their victims, since the penalties for murder were comparatively less of a deterrent. Another story revealed the high number of local verdicts that were being reversed by appellate courts because of misconduct by the DA's office, misconduct that included tampered evidence and bullying of witnesses. That story also made the front page but burned my bridges with most of the prosecutors. A few of them, I later heard, had vowed revenge after I'd named names when discussing some of the most egregious cases.

Fortunately, I still had one loyal and high-level source in the DA's office: the assistant chief district attorney, William "Wild Bill" Hoffman. Tall and white-haired, his thick mustache bristling with fierce energy, he wasn't all that popular either among his underlings, in part since he was known for keeping win-loss statistics on them and for standing by his fifth-floor office window before five in the evening to catch anyone trying to leave early. In the same spirit, he let me know he appreciated my prosecutorial-misconduct story; he thought his minions had it coming.

When Hoffman got bored with his own work, which was often, he used to come by the press office to kibitz, sometimes sidling by my desk to whisper a tip. He once invited me out on a Sunday afternoon to watch him hang-glide off a cliff. I loved the special attention: It felt like being my father's favorite again, without the temper tantrums.

The best of Hoffman's tips concerned a local convicted murderer named Elmo Hatton. In 1956, Hatton had shot down two motorists, complete strangers to him, in a crime he'd told police "felt like a dream." The *Mercury* dubbed him "the dream killer" and a jury found him not guilty by reason of insanity. He spent the next fifteen years in a mental hospital, during which he wrote threatening letters to a series of U.S. presidents. Then, on his release, he dropped out of sight. But thirty-five years later, Hoffman learned that Secret Service agents had arrested Hatton in the Treasury Building next door to the White House. He'd traveled there by bus from San Jose, with a collapsible rifle, fifty rounds of ammunition, and a butcher knife. Hoffman was furious about that; unlike many of his colleagues, he hated America's lax gun laws. That's why he wanted Hatton's story told.

John Baker, the *Mercury* managing editor, decided that "the dream killer" story was worth the investment of sending me to Washington, D.C., to track him down. Before I left, I found and interviewed the San Jose gun store owner who'd sold Hatton his weapon. In D.C., I talked my way into the jail to interview the would-be assassin. My story, which I dictated to the newsroom in San Jose from a phone booth on the National Mall, went out on what was then the Knight-Ridder wire and received prominent play in sister papers including the *Detroit Free Press* and *Philadelphia Inquirer*. My editors barely seemed to mind when I confessed I'd left my wallet, with a three-hundred-dollar cash advance, in the phone booth. They had to wire me more money so I could come back home, but I escaped with only a little light teasing. Same thing, a few months later, when I crashed a rental car into a pole in a parking lot while on another out-of-town assignment.

Grateful as I was for all that tolerance, I still would have left the *Mercury* in a heartbeat for a job at a bigger paper. I was sure that getting a job with the *New York Times, Los Angeles Times*, or *Washington Post* would have felt like the career equivalent of a diamond ring, like proof that I was okay because some man, or men, desired me that much. So in the evenings, long after most other reporters went home, I surreptitiously used the office photocopier to send clips to East Coast editors. As long as I was working this hard, I figured, why not aim higher?

9

San Jose, March 1981

Of the four suspects arrested in Howard Witkin's murder, only Bob Singer would be represented by a private attorney. Bob's wife Judi had borrowed money from her Michigan relatives to hire Bill Melcher, while the other three suspects were assigned attorneys paid by the county. Fortunately for Andy Granger, his lawyer would be Bryan Shechmeister, my public defender friend. Yet as Bryan and I met over turkey sandwiches at our picnic table a couple weeks after he met his new client, he said it would take a small miracle to save Andy's life.

"This one is a heartbreaker," he confided.

I reached into my purse for my notepad.

Bryan had spent much of the previous week in Flint, where he'd interviewed Andy's mother and brothers.

"You can't write anything about this yet," he said, nodding at the pen now clenched in my hand. "But—"

He pushed his sandwich plate aside and reached into his battered leather briefcase to remove a manila file. I smiled as I waited. I loved documents.

Inside the file was a worn white envelope, which Bryan slid toward me across the table.

"You just have to read it," he said.

I put down my pen.

The outside of the envelope was decorated in pencil with a big smiley face, the kind my mother used to draw. Inside was a letter, on white ruled notepaper, from Andy to his mother, telling her how grateful he felt toward the Santa Clara detectives who had flown with him from Flint to San Jose.

"They bought me books and pop and candy out of their OWN money!" he'd scrawled. "God! They both said they'd come up on visiting days. I get real worked up when I think about them. They REALY [sic] care!"

I looked up at Bryan and we both raised our eyebrows and shrugged. Then I picked up the pen to write OTR, for "off the record," before copying down what Andy had written. I didn't know if or how I'd ever use it, but I knew I didn't want to forget it.

It truly was unusual that in all his helpful conversations with police, Andy hadn't once asked for a lawyer or pleaded for leniency in return for his help.

"What's up with him?" I asked. "He seems so self-destructive."

"I've got a theory," Bryan said.

He paused to take a bite of his sandwich before telling me what he'd learned from his interviews in Flint. Andy's mother and brothers had told him that Andy's father had sexually abused him for years.

"When Andy turned sixteen, he finally met his dad with a baseball bat and threatened to kill him. That's when it stopped," Bryan said. "But somewhere along the line, I think Andy got programmed to do what other people thought he should do."

I was so entranced I was forgetting to chew. Did Bryan think this let Andy off the hook?

"Remember, you can't write any of this, not yet," Bryan was saying. "But just look at how Andy said yes to Gary

Oliver, and then said yes to the cops, without ever really thinking about what was good for *him*."

Bryan's sympathy for Andy made him angry at the police, who in his view had unfairly exploited his client's innocence. But he was even angrier at Bob Singer, the accused mastermind, who'd indirectly drawn Andy into doing his dirty work. Bryan was a scholar who often quoted uncommon sources in his arguments, and now he pulled out his own notebook to read me a quote he'd found in the Talmud, the Jewish book of law.

"'To make *another* person sin is *worse than to kill him*,'" he recited. "'To murder a person is only to remove him from this world, but to cause him to sin is to exclude him from the world to come as well.'"

I knew Bryan understood the Talmud was not the California Penal Code, so I wondered how he planned to use this line of reasoning, if at all, in his upcoming trial. Andy's childhood abuse and gullibility probably wouldn't mitigate his crime in the eyes of his jurors. I didn't even think it should, since for whatever reasons he'd become a dangerous person, but I still felt sorry for him.

"Is there any chance Andy could be found not guilty by reason of insanity?" I asked.

Bryan shook his head. "I've really only had one defendant who met that test," he said, and proceeded to tell me about a man who had beat, strangled, and chopped up his father, and then for some reason poured sugar over the corpse's head.

"I could argue that that guy didn't know right from wrong, but Andy does," Bryan said. "He has made that clear every time he confessed. He has repeatedly said that killing Howard was the worst mistake of his life."

Indeed, Andy's remorse had driven him even further than that, as I would learn a few days after our lunch. Bryan, who clearly needed to vent, called me into his office while once again making me promise I wouldn't write about what he planned to show me until he gave his permission.

Closing the door and turning off the lights, he turned on a small TV set to play a video he'd just learned Andy had made at the detectives' request.

The jumpy black-and-white recording had been shot on location at Howard's townhouse. It began with Detective Wayne Britt handing Andy an unloaded BB gun from the cops' evidence room. Plodding in his shackles down the path toward Howard's front door, Andy patiently demonstrated how he had carried the murder weapon under his jacket, *"swinging it with my step,"* he said, to make it less obtrusive.

Britt played the part of Howard, standing where Andy showed him his victim had first appeared. Andy then acted out how he had just been turning to leave, but wheeled around, assumed a crouch, and began to fire.

Despite Andy's many previous statements of regret, he seemed surreally chipper during his reenactment, saluting Britt with a little wave and grin.

"Are you doing this of your own free will, now?" Britt made sure to ask, in his courteous, soft voice.

"YES sir," Andy declared.

"Has anyone made you any promises?"

"NO sir."

"You did it because you want the truth to come out?"

"YES sir."

That's when the video ended. But there was more to the recorded interview, as Bryan told me, shutting off the TV, and reading from a transcript on his desk.

"Britt then asked Andy if he had anything to add," he said sourly, looking down at the page. "At which point, Andy did an imitation of Porky Pig."

"Uh, *yipyibyibyibyibyib*," the confessed triggerman shouted: "THAT'S ALL, FOLKS!"

10

San Jose, May 1981

"Phone call, Ellison!"

My eyes were locked on my computer monitor as I sat in the *Mercury's* main newsroom in San Jose, fiddling with a feature story due later in the week. The story was boring and I didn't know what I could add to fix that, so I was nervously tweaking the sentences, a process known in newsrooms as "polishing a turd."

The receptionist walked over to make sure I heard her. "It's a guy saying he's the 'paper bag killer!'"

"Ha-ha-ha," I muttered into the receiver, expecting to hear one of the more annoying public defenders or DAs on my beat trying to get my goat.

"Thought you'd like that!"

It was Richard, chuckling away, calling from Philadelphia while home on leave to visit the *Inquirer*. I hadn't heard his voice in nearly a year.

I caught my breath and sank back into my chair, pressing the phone to my ear. Two of my colleagues, who'd been talking together in the cubicle next to me and saw me trying to concentrate, turned around and glared. I knew I wasn't widely beloved among the other reporters; my closest newsroom friends were the photographers, with whom there was less threat of competition. In vying with other reporters for our editors' attention, I often felt like I was back home with my siblings, currying favor from our parents. Was it my fault I'd gotten so good at it?

Richard said he'd seen the Elmo Hatton story in his newspaper. "I hear you're really tearing up the court beat!" he added, with what sounded like proprietary pride. "You're doing it like it's never been done, and it's making people stand up and take notice."

In an instant, I all but forgave him for his long silence— just two letters from him since I'd left London. I didn't even mention that I'd only recently discovered one of my paragraphs, *verbatim*, in the story he eventually published on the Kyrgyz nomads. He'd shamelessly stolen it from notes I'd left in his flat. What made his betrayal hurt all the more was that I'd never gotten around to publishing my own version of that story. In my effort to stop dwelling on the past, I'd taken one of his presents, the Pakistani leather purse, to the Goodwill. Two weeks later, I saw it on the arm of a UPI reporter, which struck me as vaguely metaphorical. I'd never had any real claim on Richard or anything he'd given me.

"So what are you doing besides reporting?" he asked.

Rather than give a truthful answer, namely *eating and sleeping*, I dodged. "Oh, not much, what about you?"

He'd moved to Rome, he said, and was living near a piazza with a young Yugoslav woman he'd met in Israel shortly after I left.

"Huh, what does she do?" I asked.

He laughed. "She doesn't do much! She makes things with her hands. She gets high a lot. And she takes care of me."

I pinched the inside of my wrist to try to keep my voice even, as I felt my eyes start to water. *I didn't want to be like that. I could never be like that.* At least my two neighbors had turned back to their computers.

"Wow, that sounds really like what you need, like it would be a lot less tense than it might be living with other people," I managed to whisper. Richard laughed again, sounding touched. My mother might have appreciated how I'd kept my best face on.

We chatted away, slipping back into a conversation we'd begun more than a year ago about Richard's constant hunger to challenge himself at work. He eagerly returned to that old theme, making me suspect his Slavic girlfriend wasn't a great listener.

"I feel like I'm doing the same thing over and over again," he said. "I just have to find a way to make it new ...."

Closing my eyes, I could almost smell the apricot blossoms and taste the whiskey in the permit room and again feel that sense of being right in the middle of where everything important was happening.

We talked for about twenty minutes. It was almost six in the evening when we hung up. As I walked outside to the parking lot and headed toward my car, I felt lighter, happier, like I hadn't felt in months.

Tearing up the court beat. At least Richard hadn't heard about the mysterious trouble I'd been having. The more I'd been treated as a star on the paper, the more I'd been making stupid little errors. Nothing dramatic, mostly misspelled names. The *Mercury's* copyeditors caught some in time to correct them, but others sailed into print, in some cases requiring the published corrections known as "setrecs," short for "setting the record straight." Reading each new setrec gave me the same, excruciating sense of bewilderment. *How did that get there? I didn't do that. Someone else did! I'm too smart for this!*

One recent gaffe in particular haunted me. I'd been sent to Siskiyou County, several hours north by car, to write a feature on an international gathering of the communal Rainbow Family. The angle was how the flood of thousands of free-loving, peace-proselytizing, tie-dyed pot-smokers into the campgrounds near Mount Shasta was upsetting the mostly conservative farmers and ranchers living nearby. At a local diner I found a talkative rancher and quoted him lambasting the hippies, after which, I wrote, he asked me if I wanted to accompany him to "shoot a horse."

The story got great space on the front page, but on the morning it ran the rancher called my editor to complain. "I didn't say 'shoot a horse!' I said '*shoe* a horse!'" he shouted, demanding not only a printed correction but that I personally explain the mishap to his angry sister who worked at the local Humane Society.

My bosses scolded me in a way that showed they were growing less tolerant of all the trouble I was causing. "You're not Shakespeare, you know!" Larry Jinks, the paper's editor, chided.

I promised everyone I'd be more careful. But no matter how hard I tried after that, I kept screwing up.

I called my psychiatrist sister at her home in Denver and told her what was going on. "Do you think I have a brain tumor?" I asked.

I could hear her muffling a laugh as she told me to hold off on the MRI. Her training was old school, and her instinct was to seek a Freudian explanation. "Are you scared of success?" she asked. "Do you think you *want* to screw things up for yourself?"

I had to think that over. Consciously I wanted nothing more than to succeed in journalism, although I felt like a lot was against me. Most of my colleagues didn't like me; my parents didn't understand, and on top of all that was the new zeitgeist. The famous backlash to feminism was just beginning in 1981, the year Ronald Reagan took office promising to restore "family values." The Equal Rights Amendment, which had so recently seemed a sure thing, was headed for defeat the next year. Garter belts, manicures, and high heels were back in style, and magazines were starting to publish stories calling women's professional progress a failed experiment. The changing culture seemed to reinforce my mother's unspoken lessons: that if I ever showed a man that I was smart or ambitious, he'd run away.

So maybe I *was* unthinkingly thwarting my own ambition. I'd thought a lot over the past year about why I'd failed to hold onto Richard when I might have been in love with him. Maybe I'd wrecked the relationship on purpose, so that I could pursue my own career. But now was I trying to wreck my career to make it easier for some man to care for me?

I had to get clear on just what I was trying to destroy, so that I could move forward with the life I wanted. If I could just figure out what that was.

11

San Jose, June 1981

On the morning of opening arguments in the Howard Witkin murder trial, three sheriff's deputies stood in front of a large, new metal detector that blocked the entrance to the courtroom. These days you see metal detectors everywhere—in courtrooms, airports, and government offices—but that was my first glimpse of one.

Sliding my purse along the conveyer belt, I asked the sheriff's deputy manning the machine what was up.

"The cops got a call about the case this morning," he said, keeping his voice low. "Supposedly some guy told them he'd heard about a plot to smuggle a gun in and shoot Bob Singer's wife and his lawyer."

"What? Why?" I asked.

But by then I was holding up the line. The deputy shook his head and motioned me on.

I'd arrived early to make sure to get a seat. I'd expected the courtroom would be packed, and I was right. There were half a dozen reporters, including me, from three local newspapers and three wire agencies, on top of several rubber-necking lawyers with time on their hands, a few retirees seeking free entertainment, and a large contingent of congregants from San Jose's Temple Emanu-El, where Judi,

Bob, and Howard had all once belonged. The synagogue members were divided in their loyalties in the wake of the double-*shanda*, or disgrace, of the Witkin and Singer divorces and subsequent murder. So much so that the trial judge, R. Donald Chapman, had made an unusual ruling during the pretrial hearings, assigning the two factions to separate sides of the room. On the right, Howard's grieving parents sat directly behind the prosecutor, with several other family members and friends behind them. On the left, behind Robert Singer and his lawyer, were the Singer family supporters, most of them smartly dressed women in their thirties, whom I guessed were Judi's friends from her Hadassah years. While taking their seats, several of the spectators traded hostile looks across the aisle.

All of us expected some drama on that first day of trial, but the surprising news of the death threats was enough to inspire a rare appearance by two local TV stations. A few minutes before the bailiff announced the start of the trial, they switched on their lights in the hall outside the courtroom, where Bill Melcher was holding a press conference.

He began by handing out a statement printed on his impressive Beverly Hills office stationery, which cited Bill's "association" with Vincent Bugliosi, the blockbuster bestselling author famed for having prosecuted the serial murderer Charles Manson. The press release confirmed what the sheriff's deputy at the metal detector had told me about the frightening call to the police that morning, and now Bill added new details. Two days earlier, he said, he himself had gotten an anonymous call in his room in the Holiday Inn.

"The caller was a man with a *rough voice*," Bill said. "He warned me that I'd better 'take a dive on Singer.' He said he'd give me big bucks to back off, but I told him there's no kind of money that can make me do that."

I don't remember catching any other reporter's eyes at that moment. We might have exchanged some wondering looks if we hadn't been so busy taking notes.

Bill said that when he rejected the caller's offer, the man with the rough voice said: "In that case, you're a dead man," and hung up.

"And then .... this morning ..." Bill said, his voice slowing dramatically, "While Mrs. Singer and I were on our way to court, we noticed that we were being followed by two men in a white, late-model Mustang."

Although Bill didn't say so explicitly, he was clearly suggesting that these sinister events supported his theory of the motive for Howard's murder—a theory he had already explained to us in detail and which he said he planned to argue in court. According to Bill's version of the crime, Howard was *not* the bumbling, lonely slacker we'd read about in the police reports. Rather, he was a scheming drug kingpin pursued by mob assassins. And apparently now those assassins were pursuing Bill Melcher—and Judi.

It was a truly wild story, and I was starting to suspect it was also one of the worst pack of lies I'd ever heard. Quite likely, Bill was trying to hoodwink us so as to indirectly influence the jury. He didn't offer any hard evidence to support his mob-boss theory, which meant that Judge Chapman wasn't likely to let him elaborate on it before the jurors. But the jurors weren't sequestered. They were free to go home every night, where at least a few of them would likely ignore the judge's warnings not to read the newspapers. That's where we reporters came in.

The problem was that none of us was free to ignore what Bill was telling us. As the defense lawyer in that sensational trial, what he said was automatically news. Plus the metal detector proved the cops had taken that morning's reported threat seriously.

Besides, what if it weren't a lie? We all had just one responsible course of action, which was to check out his story as well as we could before the evening five o'clock deadline.

Over the lunch break, I sought out the prosecutor, Deputy District Attorney Jack Marshall, to show him Bill's press release. Jack was one of my favorite DAs, not least because he was one of the few prosecutors still willing to talk to me after my reporting on the department's misdeeds. He wasn't the kind of lawyer who would bend rules to win a case. Before going to law school, he'd worked as a cowboy in eastern Oregon. He wore a silver saddle-bronc trophy belt buckle and had a crinkly, gap-toothed smile under a nose that listed slightly to the right: the vestige of an old horse-kick. I often saw jurors smiling at him during his long, rambling arguments. Like me, they seemed charmed by his air of sagebrush, honesty, and doing the right thing.

I caught up with Jack in his office. His eyes widened as he read the press release. This was the first time he'd seen it.

Jack planned to argue that Howard's murder had nothing to do with mobs or drugs, and was determined to steer jurors' attention away from the cocaine found in his townhouse, which wasn't likely to generate much sympathy for him. The prosecutor's theory instead was that Bob Singer hoped to indirectly profit from Howard's two-hundred-and-seventy-five-thousand-dollar life insurance policy, which at the time of his murder still listed Judi as the beneficiary. Jack's key witness would be Bob's restaurant manager, the one who'd called police the previous year. Among other things, the manager was prepared to tell the jurors that Bob had been under severe financial pressure when he tried to recruit him to help with the hit.

Now, as he handed back the press release to me, Jack drew a deep, skeptical breath.

"Wellll," he drawled. "I'd think that if anyone had information like this, it would be their civic duty to report it to police."

Another lawyer might have ridiculed Bill's theory. As I quoted the prosecutor's cagey comment in the story I wrote that day, I felt sorry that it paled so much next to Bill's bombast. Even so, I had to appreciate Bill's new dramatic twist. His claims about drug mafias, combined with the reported threat and metal detector, persuaded my editors to assign another reporter to cover the rest of my beat to give me more time to delve into the Witkin murder case. As I did that, over the next few days, I grew more and more intrigued by the story, and, most of all, by Howard's ex-wife, Judi.

Judi had moved to San Jose with her three children almost immediately after Bob was extradited, renting a house in the suburbs, a couple miles from the courtroom. She visited Bob almost every day, arriving at the jail before dawn to be the first in line.

She'd been hard to ignore all through the pretrial hearings, with her loud voice and insistent friendliness, and the way she always stood at Bill's side at his press conferences and whispered to him during the court sessions. Bill had recently informed the judge that Judi was serving as his "chief investigative officer." The day after the news of the alleged phone threat, he told us reporters that she was also going to be his "star witness."

"Her testimony is going to blow this case wide open," he promised.

The next day was a scorcher, the mid-morning temperature already heading into the nineties when Judi walked into the courtroom. Bill walked closely beside her, keeping his hand on her back as if she needed propping up. She smiled down at him as she took the stand and he launched into his initial questions, most of which concerned her children and her marriage to Bob Singer.

They spent the next hour painting a portrait of Judi's motherly devotion and pride in the exemplary family life she had created in the wake of her divorce. Judi spoke lovingly about each of her children, beginning with Daniel, eleven, her first-born son, whom as she confided, she had nicknamed "The Little Messiah." I breathed in sharply on hearing that, recalling how my mother had called me her "Little Savior." Judi then described how she had suffered repeated miscarriages after Daniel's birth and before she and Howard had adopted their daughter, Marie, at age seven. Marie was now fourteen, with long dark hair and a sweet, shy smile. Shortly after she joined the family, Judi unexpectedly got pregnant with her youngest son, Nathan, she recounted. Bob Singer had been such a wonderful father to the three of them, Judi said. He had loved them as if they were his own.

"What was your house like back there?" Bill asked, and Judi brightened, smiling broadly.

"Two-story, four-bedroom, two-and-a-half baths, standard colonial, *super* house!" she answered. I glanced toward the Witkin side of the room to confirm I wasn't alone in being startled by her sprightly tone, which seemed so out of keeping with where the narrative was sure to lead. Nope: Several of the spectators looked just as surprised as I felt.

Judi soon stopped smiling, however, as Bill coaxed her to talk about her marriage to Howard. She told how her early hopes of family bliss had been dashed by her husband's increasing involvement with drugs. She'd first caught Howard smoking marijuana in 1974, six years into their marriage, she said. And over the next four years, he refused to stop or try to get help, to the point where she said she had no choice but to divorce him. After that, Howard's drug use significantly worsened, she said, so much so that every time the children visited their father she worried about their safety.

Then in early 1980, Howard told her that he wanted to take the kids to stay on a houseboat near Yosemite, Judi recounted. This was the plan that had so rattled her during her phone conversation with Detective Britt. Now, with the same harsh tone she'd used then, Judi told the jury how she'd imagined Howard, likely intoxicated, trying to supervise the kids, including their two-year-old Nathan, on a boat. "How was he going to watch that baby and make sure he didn't fall off the side?" she asked. She'd tried to convince Howard to cancel the trip, she went on. Yet when he refused, she filed papers to cut off his visiting privileges. Howard countered by demanding joint custody of all three children. He and Judi had been scheduled to meet in a San Jose civil courtroom on April first—two weeks after the night Howard was murdered.

As Judi told this story, I noticed Jack Marshall leaning forward in his chair. I imagined he must have been wondering, as I was, about Bill's purpose in leading her to elaborate on such an emotional conflict with her ex-husband. We still didn't have any answers by the time court recessed that afternoon, and after I drove back to the main newsroom, my editors agreed with me that we had no news to report. Bill had warned us, however, to expect a "bombshell" when Judi returned to court the next day. Before I left for home, I called him at his hotel to ask if Judi might meet me and a photographer at the courthouse in the morning, to get a picture of her to accompany my story. He seemed happy to agree.

As I parked my Honda in the lot that next day, I saw that the TV trucks were back. I hustled inside the courthouse, where the *Mercury* photographer was already leading Judi to a side door that opened to a small shaded courtyard. Accompanying her were her two older children, Daniel and Marie, whom she'd brought to court for the first time. I followed them.

Judi wore a sheer white blouse with a lace collar. Her pearl necklace gleamed against her tanned chest, and as the photographer snapped away, she gazed downward, seeming so subdued that I wondered whether Bill had scolded her for the previous day's "*super* house!" enthusiasm.

But suddenly I saw her pose in a different light, as something more strategic. As Marie stood off to the side, out of the frame, Daniel moved just behind his mother, his hand on her shoulder and a worried expression on his plump, freckled face. Judi looked like an alabaster Madonna, complete with her Little Messiah.

All they need is a puppy, I thought darkly. I hadn't planned for this. In retrospect, I should have pulled the photographer aside and insisted that he take some candid shots. But I didn't even think of doing that. I don't know why. I just surrendered to the strange inertia I often felt in her presence.

I checked my watch—I had just a few minutes to get back to the courtroom—and caught the photographer's eye to wave goodbye. But on my way to grab a seat, I saw Bill holding court again under the bright TV lights and rushed over to listen. I'd nearly missed his most amazing news to date.

Bill was in the middle of describing how he and Judi had been out together working on the Singer case two days earlier when they decided to order a pizza. Just before midnight, they had stopped at a phone booth in East San Jose, when suddenly a man pulled up alongside them in a new, white Pontiac Trans Am, and shot at them six times.

"Missed us by an inch," Bill said.

Once again, bewilderingly, I can't recall that any of us listening to Bill that day revealed any skepticism about his story. Looking back, I wish I'd been bold enough to ask even one of the many obvious questions that immediately came to mind, such as: *What in the world were he and Judi doing out together so late at night in East San Jose, the most crime-ridden area of town? Why were they ordering a pizza from a phone booth? And why had he waited two days to tell us? Why hadn't he mentioned this at his earlier press conference?*

The answer to that last question would soon be clear. Bill had timed his latest revelation to guarantee that the explosive news would draw extra attention to our reporting on Judi's testimony for the next day's papers. Once again, he was quite likely exploiting us, as we devoured his outlandish claims. But we had the same problem as before. Our editors wouldn't have tolerated any of us sitting on this news. So again, our best and only course was to check with as many other sources as we could to see if his story might be true, knowing we were all going to publish it either way.

Later that day, I called the San Jose police and was able to speak to a cop who confirmed that Bill had reported the shooting, just as he'd said, and also that police had come to the scene and verified that shots had been fired. To my surprise, the cop did not sound at all skeptical about Bill's claim, although nor did he say they were pursuing any suspects. I quoted him in the story that reported the news of Judi's "bombshell" testimony, which she had delivered that afternoon, just as Bill had promised. What she said supported an entirely new theory as to why Howard had been murdered.

Countering what Bill had been telling us up until that day, Judi now suggested that it hadn't been a drug-related crime after all. Instead, she told the jury, she had learned several months earlier that Howard had hired an assassin to kill her and Bob, but that the contract had backfired somehow and had ended in Howard's murder.

This was beyond confusing. If Judi were telling the truth, why had Bill been pushing the drug-boss theory? And why would Howard's supposed murder contract have backfired?

At the next break in the trial, Bill held a second press conference, but with his usual cheerful bombast refused to answer any of our questions. All he wanted to do was to elaborate on what he was now calling his "reverse-hit" theory. A surprise witness had recently emerged, he said: a former jail inmate from Flint who had briefly shared a cell with Gary Oliver, the middleman. The inmate, Bill said, would testify that Gary had told him the truth about the case, that he was originally hired by Howard. "He's going to turn this case on its head!" Bill promised. Certainly that would have been powerful testimony. But the jury never heard it. Instead Judge Chapman called for a two-day break, for reasons he never explained. When the trial reconvened, Bill said nothing more about the surprise witness, and refused to answer our questions about when or if he would appear. "I'll be calling on Bob Singer to testify next," was all he said.

Under Bill's questioning Bob Singer vigorously denied that he'd had anything to do with Howard's murder. He called his restaurant manager a liar and heavy drinker. He acknowledged that he'd gone to the Aladdin Lounge with him but said it had nothing to do with looking for a hitman. Instead, Bob told the jury, they'd stopped in just for a quick drink while en route to another local night club called the Ad Lib, where Bob wanted to watch one of The Onion Crock's waitresses compete in a dance contest. The waitress, as Bob elaborated, was a single parent who suffered from a rare blood disease and had recently been told that she had only six months to live. She desperately needed money for transfusions, and the winner of the contest—determined by the amount of applause received—was to receive fifty dollars. Bob had gone to see if he could help.

Wow, I thought, scribbling in my notepad. How could anyone not see this story for what it was—a clumsy attempt to pluck heartstrings? I looked over at Jack Marshall, who seemed to be having the same thought, as he exchanged an amused glance with his detective, Steve Derossett. But then I looked at the jurors. A few of them were gazing at Bob with what appeared to be like new empathy. Their sympathies had shifted, and I felt a stab of worry as it hit me that some of my reporting—and that soulful portrait of Judi I'd helped arrange—had probably influenced them.

Judge Chapman shared my concern. Two days after Bob finished testifying, Bill stood to deliver his closing argument. But at the lawyer's first mention of his "reverse-hit" theory, Chapman stopped him and sent the jurors out of the room.

"There has been a concerted effort on your part to bring the jury evidence you know they're not entitled to hear," the judge shouted. "I think it's reprehensible that you did this. At what price glory?"

I happily took notes on the rare outburst. By quoting Chapman, I could finally air my own mounting outrage over the way Bill and Judi had been manipulating us. Even so, the rules of journalism obliged me to seek a reaction.

During the afternoon break, I saw Judi sitting on a courtroom bench, whispering with one of her synagogue friends. They fell silent as I approached, smiling, to ask Judi what she'd thought of the judge's accusation. Judi and I were still on good terms—I'd yet to erroneously accuse her of murder and she had yet to sue me.

She inhaled sharply. "Both I and my children have received *several* anonymous, threatening phone calls over the last two days," she said, her eyes on my pen as it raced across the page of my notebook. "I'm appalled at the lack of concern from the police. I walk around frightened and no one cares. The judge doesn't care; the police don't care. No one cares."

I wrote down every word.

Once again, I couldn't ignore what Judi was saying. But from that day on, I stopped believing her.

12

San Jose, July 1981

By the time Jack Marshall delivered his closing argument on July 13, he'd given up on his earlier effort to convince the jurors that Bob Singer had plotted to kill Howard Witkin in the hope of financial gain. Reaching for something stronger to counter Bob's attorney's theatrical claims, he'd decided to focus on Judi's emotional testimony about her custody fight with her ex-husband and her worries about her children's safety.

Slouching over the podium as if leaning on his neighbor's cattle fence, Jack began by reminding the jurors of Bob's "happy years" with his first wife in San Jose, during which he had raised his three sons, worked with his father in the vending machine business, made lots of money, and volunteered at his synagogue.

"There is no indication that at that point in his life, Mr. Singer was other than a good citizen," Jack drawled. "However, as so often happens in life, we come to a fork in the road. And the selection of which fork to take very often changes the entire course and complexion of our lives. And somewhere in 1977 or thereabouts, Robert Singer met Judi Witkin at the temple ... and to make a long story short, the two marriages were terminated and a new one started ..."

I was sitting in the back of the courtroom, as usual, since it gave me the best vantage point to watch everyone's reactions. As Jack warmed to his theme, so unflattering to Judi, of a Good Man Gone Wrong, I heard a happy murmur from the Witkin side of the courtroom. One middle-aged woman smiled and pinched her finger and thumb together in an OK sign.

In the years after the Witkins divorced, Jack went on, Howard "may have been an aggravating force in the life of Judi Singer. And of course, what affects Judi affects Robert ...."

He urged the jurors to picture Bob coming home from work, under pressure from flagging sales at his restaurant. Judi would greet him with her worries—Jack's voice rose, imitating her: "What are we going to do about Howard? His visitation is coming up; I'm afraid to send the kids out. He has a hot tub; he's liable to be smoking dope! What are we going to do? What are we going to do?"

Few emotions compare with a mother's fear for her children's safety, Jack intoned, adding; "Don't we all know that where children are concerned, particularly our own children, the most rational of us will frequently take an irrational stand? To wit: the mother hen and her chicks, the mama bear and her cubs, all the examples we can draw from our animal friends ...."

He went on like this for several more minutes, then paused and walked to an easel in front of the courtroom to draw on a large pad of paper.

"I would like to leave you with ... a symbol or a diagram which I think is the common thread throughout this case—and which is irrefutable, immutable, and cannot be disguised," Jack said.

The marker squeaked as he wrote: "Howard Witkin."

It squeaked again as the prosecutor drew an arrow from Howard's name to that of Judi Singer. From there another arrow pointed to Bob Singer, and then from Bob to Gary Oliver and from Gary to Andy.

"The final arrow from Andy Granger to Howard Witkin completes an *unbroken circle*, ladies and gentlemen," Jack said, tapping the paper with the marker. "And that's what the evidence in this case shows ... the impossible odds ... that those parties could find themselves in that relationship insofar as this crime is concerned other than by premeditation, and deliberation, and design ...."

This was the raw material for my blunder in the story I filed that day, in which I erroneously paraphrased the prosecutor to say that "*Judi and* Bob Singer" had plotted Howard Witkin's murder. For quite a while after Judi sued me, I clung to the belief that all of Jack's talk about an "unbroken circle" and the parties being together in that relationship of premeditation, deliberation, and design had conveyed his belief, even though he hadn't said it, that Judi had been involved in the plot.

In fact, the *unbroken circle* was just one of the potential excuses I'd grasp at as I tried to make sense of my eleven-million-dollar mistake. In 2006, I'd find an even better one, after I was diagnosed with attention-deficit/hyperactivity disorder (ADHD), a neurodevelopmental syndrome that makes people distracted and impulsive. Researchers have shown that the average ADHD brain differs from the norm, both structurally and functionally. We have a built-in, mostly genetic problem with processing dopamine and other neurochemicals that would otherwise help keep us on task. My diagnosis in my late forties was at first a huge relief. ADHD was such a handy, concrete answer to questions that had baffled me for so long, like why I was always running late and losing keys and sunglasses and having clumsy accidents like crashing my bike into the back of a parked car. Yet it almost immediately became clear that while ADHD may have been an explanation—for some things—it wasn't ever going to be a justification. It didn't mean I'd get to stop trying to do better.

13

San Jose, July 1981

Two weeks after Jack's closing argument and five minutes after Bill Melcher handed me the libel suit summons, I took a deep breath, grabbed my purse, and drove over to the Mercury's San Jose headquarters, a low-slung, factory-like building where I had to deliver the bad news to John Baker, the managing editor.

I pulled up a chair in front of his desk in his office, with its glass wall facing out on the newsroom, and pinched the back of my hand again, forcing myself not to cry, as he read the document.

Looking up, he gritted his teeth. "You really blew it this time," he said.

I waited for him to say he was going to fire me. He didn't say that, but what he did say was nearly as awful. He was going to suspend me for three days, he said, adding, "and I'd suggest you use this time to find some professional help. You've got talent, but this behavior doesn't make sense. You need to figure this out."

I nodded. Of course I did. It was just what my sister had been urging me to do, ever since I'd first confided in her about my weird series of mistakes. She had even volunteered to help me find a therapist, but I'd kept changing the subject. I didn't have the money; it would take too much time away from work, and with all due respect for her chosen profession, it seemed way too self-indulgent to sit around whining when literally *billions* of people all over the world had it so much worse than I did. What's more, as we both knew, our mother would take it personally. She felt that airing "dirty laundry" was for people who were weak and self-indulgent, which helped explain why she'd never sought help—or even confided to anyone outside the family—to cope with my dad's abuse. But this didn't stop my brother and sister from going into psychiatry, and over the past several years, as they'd gone through their own psychoanalyses, they'd peppered her with uncomfortable questions. *Did she recall when our dad started drinking? Did she think he had a mood disorder? Did she think* she *had a mood disorder? How many of our aunts, uncles, and cousins might have mood disorders?*

"I used to think I was happy before my kids went into therapy," she had sighed to me on the phone after one of these interrogations.

Still, now, as I listened to John Baker, it looked like therapy might be my last chance to save my job, which meant everything to me.

"Thanks for not firing me," I muttered, slinking out of his office. At an empty desk in the newsroom, out of earshot of the other reporters, I dug in my purse for my little leather address book and called the number of the one local psychiatrist I knew: a Stanford professor I'd recently interviewed for a story about his use of hypnosis in therapy. The story had nothing to do with the criminal courts; I'd heard of him and been intrigued and had written the feature story on my own time. He told me he wasn't seeing private patients but gave me phone numbers for two local colleagues. One was a prestigious veteran while the other was still in training, working under a supervisor.

This was no time for amateurs, so I called the veteran, whom I'll call Dr. P. He answered the phone himself and, to my relief, said he had an unexpected opening the next morning.

The scene in Dr. P's office was just as I'd imagined: the beard, the pipe, and the dim-lit room with shelves full of large texts and African carvings. Over two sessions, three days apart, I told him my history, and under his steady questioning found myself talking not only about my errors at work but also about all my painful relationships with men, from my father to Richard to Mark to a few brief unhappy recent flings.

At the end of the second hour Dr. P summed up his thoughts.

"Your mistakes at work aren't the real problem," he began. "They're like a murderer confessing to a burglary."

He puffed on his pipe.

"Your real problem is that you like to make monkeys out of men," he said.

I didn't say a word in response. It's not as if I didn't know what he meant. Cuckolding Richard in his apartment. Pretending I'd baked those brownies for Mark. Taking money from my dad while siding against him with my mother behind his back.

"You like to make monkeys out of men," Dr. P repeated. "And when you do that, you also make a monkey out of yourself. Because you can have a lot of men, but not a man of your own."

I still didn't respond. Now I was angry. This wasn't about men. This was about my job, which was my life. *I was facing an emergency—didn't he understand that?* And how piggish of him to assume that a man of my-own should be my first priority!

What's more, he was making me sound like a jerk. I liked making monkeys out of men? Did he think I was having fun? Couldn't he see how miserable I was?

Dr. P was still talking. I needed quite a lot of help, he said, and he strongly recommended that I sign up for a minimum of three sessions per week if I didn't want to waste both of our time.

"Anything else," he said, "would be slim pickins.'"

"I have to think about that," I said, although I think we both knew I wouldn't. On top of everything else, the only way I'd be able to afford that many sessions would be with another loan from my father, and that was a nonstarter. I was already late on my car payments.

"I'll call you," I promised Dr. P.

Decades later, when I read what I'd written in my journal after that session, I was surprised by how much Dr. P got right—and also by how little of it penetrated my skull. The more I pictured him sucking on that pipe and reducing me to a caricature and making that stupid slim pickins' comment, the more furious I became. He wasn't just insulting, I decided; he was incompetent. If he'd really wanted me to be his patient, he should have seen how skittish I was and put more energy into building a relationship.

That's how I felt then. Today I better understand two things. One is that a hallmark of people with narcissistic traits, mild and major, is our loathing of anything that seems like judgment. It awakens our defenses, which may include full-on rage, preventing us from even trying to figure out whether any of the criticism may be true. Another thing I've learned is that trust and humility are like muscles. Both need to be strong if you're going to allow someone to help you face the worst of your behavior. Mine weren't yet up to the task.

On leaving Dr. P's office, I reassured myself that therapy would be a waste of time and money, and that even prestigious veteran shrinks were often wrong and most of the time even nuttier than their patients. I could handle this stuff myself. I just had to try harder.

At work, I sought advice from one of my few newsroom friends: Pete Carey, the newspaper's ace investigative reporter. Like everyone else at the *Mercury,* Pete knew about the lawsuit, and although I'd never heard of him making a mistake, he had an air of distraction that made me feel he might understand. He did.

"Just slow down and eyeball every word," Pete coached me.

Slow down? What a concept! But for the next days and weeks, that's what I did, forcing myself over and over again to reread what I'd written, questioning each word, phrase, and sentence before hitting the SEND button.

It was excruciating, but it worked. For the time being, at least, I didn't have another glitch.

Who needs a shrink? I was so grateful to still have a paycheck.

John Baker kept me employed and on the court beat, a decision I figured may have been less because he liked me than to avoid doing anything that might seem like an admission of guilt for having hired such a bozo in the first place. Either way, I was lucky. Without that eleven-million-dollar wakeup call, I might have gone on making small errors until he'd have had to fire me.

Still, Baker didn't have to tell me that I wouldn't be moving to Mexico anytime soon. Having decided that no one on the paper's staff was ready, he was already interviewing reporters from other newspapers. I watched a couple of them swagger into the newsroom: both tall men in their early thirties. One, and I swear I'm not making this up, wore a safari suit.

As if this weren't humiliating enough, I had to keep dealing with the libel lawsuit. For the rest of that summer and into the fall, Judi Singer and Bill Melcher aggressively pursued their case against me and the paper. With each new motion they filed, the newspaper's lawyer would call me into his office to grill me about every interaction I'd had with Judi before I made my mistake.

The lawyer was preparing two arguments in our defense. One was that Jack Marshall, the prosecutor, had all but declared Judi guilty in his "unbroken circle" argument. The other was that Judi had voluntarily become a "public figure" in her husband's case, with her star-witness testimony and constant interviews with reporters, and according to case law would thus have to meet a higher standard to prove libel than if she had been a mere spectator. Specifically, she'd have to find evidence that I'd knowingly or recklessly written something false. Which I hadn't done. Not knowingly, at least. Fortunately, as I kept reassuring our lawyer, I'd never spoken to anyone I knew about my strong feelings toward her, which in the wake of her suit had become even stronger.

Sometimes I felt that I hated her. How could she have jumped on me like that for such an obviously innocent mistake? Was she really so ruthless as to try to profit from my error? Who did she think she was, estimating the value of her reputation at ten million dollars, with an extra one million for "pain and suffering"?

For the next few weeks, I continued to cover the Singer case, despite what was now an obvious conflict of interest. At the same time, I knew I could no longer try to mine the case for drama. My articles now were spare, just-the-facts-ma'am affairs, with no more comments from Bill or Judi. This had become easier to do since the case was winding down and the two of them at least for the moment had stopped manufacturing bombshells.

I tried to reconcile myself to waiting another three or more years for the Mexico job to come open again. In that time, I knew I'd have to find some way to redeem myself with my editors. Meanwhile I stopped sending my clips to other newspapers. No one was going to hire someone in the middle of a libel suit. For the time being, the *Mercury* and I were stuck with each other.

The jurors in the murder case took eleven days to reach a verdict. To no one's surprise, they found Andy Granger guilty of premeditated murder. But they were hopelessly deadlocked when it came to Bob Singer. Gary Oliver and the getaway driver, Tom Maciolek, hadn't yet gone to trial.

An hour or so after the jury's decision, I dropped by Jack Marshall's office, where I found him staring out his window. Jack had kindly commiserated with me over Judi's libel lawsuit, and now I was there to commiserate with him. The deadlock meant he'd probably have to prosecute Bob all over again. And from talking to the jurors, he told me, off the record, he knew just how hard that would be.

The panel had split eight to four, with the four jurors who'd refused to convict Bob having held back mostly due to their doubts about his motivation. They simply couldn't believe that a man like that, law-abiding his entire life, as Jack himself had pointed out, would have plotted a murder for the sake of a two-hundred-and-seventy-five-thousand-dollar insurance policy.

"One of the jurors told me she just couldn't believe Bob could be guilty, considering that nice family of his!" Jack said.

I sighed, all too aware of the secrets nice families can hide.

Driving back to the newsroom, I wondered if I'd still be on the court beat to cover Bob's retrial early the next year. Baker was talking about moving me to cover San Jose city politics in a few months, a move I was resisting. A popular newsroom joke back then was that the difference between San Jose and yogurt was that yogurt had a living culture. I had zero interest in the city, but knew that if it came to it I wouldn't be able to turn it down.

As summer turned to fall, my mood grew darker. I was bored and antsy. No other story on my beat matched the drama of the Singer trial. Nor did any man I met match the excitement of being with Richard in the Himalayan mountains.

I longed to be far from the Bay Area, even as my hopes of jumping to a foreign post or bigger, East Coast paper had dissolved. So when someone told me about a yearlong program at Yale Law School for journalists considering switching careers, I impulsively applied—and was accepted.

I'd told my parents only minimal details about my series of mistakes at work, including the one that resulted in Judi's lawsuit. My father's response was to try to cheer me up with one of his favorite mottos: "When you fall on your ass, ninety percent of people aren't paying attention and the other ten percent are glad!" But my mother understood how mortified I felt and seemed to share my hope that I could change my narrative by switching coasts and careers.

"Yale, wow!" she said on the phone.

We salivated together for a moment. It had been so long since I'd heard that kind of pride in her voice.

"Think of all the great men you'd meet!" she said.

On a visit to New Haven, I strolled past the gorgeous Gothic buildings, fantasizing about reinventing myself, living on the East Coast as I'd dreamed, earning a lot more money, maybe even finding a Yale lawyer to marry and putting my parents' worries to rest. I found an apartment close to campus and paid my deposit to enroll in September 1982. But right before the day I planned to tell my editors, I changed my mind.

I still loved being a journalist. It was the only job I'd ever wanted. I couldn't imagine giving it up.

In January I compiled a new list:

1. Lose 15 pounds;

2. Keep eyeballing every word!

3. Make more friends at work.

4. Sign up for Spanish lessons.

The Spanish lessons had to do with a new, Hail Mary sort of plan, which for the time being I was keeping secret.

14

Cupertino, January 1982

Through much of that hard winter, I had one small consolation, which didn't reflect well on me at all. I felt all warm and glowy every time I imagined that my nemesis, Judi Singer, might be even more miserable than I was.

I'd gotten some surprising news in early January while visiting my friend Dana Priest, a freelance reporter who'd been covering the Singer case for the *Flint Journal* in Michigan. Dana was bright and funny and at least as ambitious as I was. We'd bonded while gossiping about all the strange characters in the case, although I'd mostly kept mum about Judi.

Still, of course, Dana knew about the lawsuit, which is why that night, as we sprawled on the sofa in her rented apartment in Santa Cruz with mugs of chamomile tea, she smiled as she described the story she'd just filed. A couple weeks earlier, just before Christmas, Judi had been arrested for shoplifting in San Jose.

A plainclothes security guard in the home furnishings department at Sears, Roebuck & Co. had reported seeing her pick out a large plastic trash can and fill it with ninety-eight dollars worth of merchandise, including two pillows, four towels, a bathmat, two oven mitts, and some nails. The guard stopped her outside the front door after she tried to leave without paying.

This was the first I'd heard of her arrest. The *Mercury News* hadn't covered it, but the *Flint Journal* was still chasing every blip in the Witkin murder case. And Judi, back in Michigan, was reading every story. Immediately after the report of her arrest appeared, she'd written a letter to complain.

Dana had a copy and showed it to me.

"I have children who need to grow straight and proud," Judi had written. "Children who deserve to maintain some sense of dignity even in the face of the problems confronting this family. How can we comfortably return to Flint now? How can these children return to their schools, sport teams, and friends?"

I shook my head as I read. There she was again, portraying herself as a victim to try to deflect blame. And using her kids to help her do it. "This is *so like her*," I couldn't resist muttering, as I handed Dana back the clipping.

Judi had some nerve, I thought, to twist things around like this. Blaming the messenger when it wasn't the *Flint Journal* that had filled up that trash can at Sears. Ordinary folk would have had some shame and maybe even have apologized for something like this, right? I resented how Judi kept finding ways to let herself off the hook. I hadn't yet confronted all the ways I tried to do that myself.

I tuned back in to hear Dana saying something.

"I am so careful with every word I write about her," she told me.

I grimaced. "Make sure you are!"

We moved on to what I'd come there to discuss. Dana and I had hatched a scheme to kick-start our careers the next summer, when we intended to devote three weeks of vacation and the bulk of our savings to travel to Nicaragua and freelance. That's why I'd signed up for those Spanish lessons. That Hail Mary plan was to regain my editors' confidence and get my dream of becoming a foreign correspondent back on track.

"Nicaragua is a war zone!" my mother had protested when I told her. "Why do you need to go somewhere so unsafe?"

"Oh, Mom, that's kind of the point," I said.

Nicaragua's danger and chaos were key parts of what made it such a great story. Three years earlier, leftist Sandinista rebels had overthrown the U.S.–backed, right-wing dynastical dictator, Anastasio Somoza, Jr. And almost ever since that time, Nicaragua had been besieged by Contras—right-wing rebels, heavily and obviously, albeit supposedly secretly, subsidized by the Reagan Administration. It was a guaranteed front-page story, sure to impress my editors, while it was also the kind of tale that naturally drew my interest: a clear conflict between Latino Davids and a U.S. Goliath. Plus the roundtrip ticket cost just three hundred dollars. After Dana and I made our reservations, I began to sleep better than I had since Judi filed her lawsuit.

While I was plotting my Central American adventure, Jack Marshall continued to prepare for Bob Singer's second trial. Later he'd tell me how worried he was about facing Bill Melcher again with no new evidence with which to arm himself. Early each morning, he'd fret over the case while jogging along the narrow, two-lane roads weaving into the coastal foothills near his home outside Los Altos, just north of San Jose. Often he'd stop by a pasture on his route to stare longingly at the horses, deeply missing his rodeo days. At night he'd returned to his old hobby of playing the bagpipes, one of the few things that helped him take his mind off the case, as much as it annoyed his wife.

There was no mystery about what Jack needed to clinch the case against Bob. The one thing he lacked was a single hour of testimony by Gary Oliver, the murder middleman. Only Gary, Bob Singer's former restaurant employee, could provide the link between Bob and Andy Granger, the triggerman. But Gary, unlike his talkative friend Andy, had stopped cooperating while back in Flint and refused to testify in the first trial. Gary wouldn't help the DA's office without a promise of leniency, which Jack's boss, Chief Assistant DA "Wild Bill" Hoffman, had refused to give him. Jack understood Hoffman's reasoning. Crime was rising in the early 1980s. Voters were fearful, and plea bargains weren't popular.

But what other option did Jack have? Without Gary's testimony, he had only circumstantial evidence to try to portray Bob's motive for murder. Making him all the more anxious were what had become daily phone calls from Geraldyne Witkin, Howard's mother, pleading with him to let her help him somehow with the new trial. At one point, she even offered to pay for a fleet of private investigators to supplement the Santa Clara police. Jack had to turn that proposal down—it had never been done and would be sure to infuriate Britt and Derossett. But he did accept Geraldyne's next idea, which was a paid-in-advance session with a local psychic. This wasn't merely to appease her; Jack had always been interested in what he called paranormal phenomena. Besides, by then he was willing to look almost anywhere for inspiration.

Kathlyn "Kay" Rhea, a former fashion model with long red hair and luminous green eyes, worked out of a two-story home on a wooded lot in Cupertino: then a bedroom community for San Jose, today the gleaming headquarters for Apple. She marketed herself as an expert in "mind-reaching," the sensing of vibrations and auras about distant people and events. Her client list included stock market investors, politicians, and two California police departments, and she had written two books on how to develop psychic skills. In the months before her meeting with Jack Marshall, she had led Stockton police to the corpse of an elderly man who died after wandering away from a Sierra foothills campsite, and had helped Fresno detectives find the remains of two women who had been missing for weeks. A headline in the *Fresno Bee* dubbed her "the Body Finder."

Jack and Detective Steve Derossett arrived at Kay's home on a Saturday morning in early January. She answered the door wearing a low-cut white jumpsuit, looking, Jack thought, like a cross between Dolly Parton and Lucille Ball. Jack could sense Steve's annoyance as they followed her up the stairs to her office. The cop thought this was a lousy way to spend a day off, and as Jack recalled, kept his sunglasses on throughout the meeting.

The psychic led her guests to three stuffed chairs arranged in front of a coffee table, next to a lit fireplace. A large Doberman padded over to sit at attention by her side. Panoramic windows looked out on the green foothills of the eastern Diablo Mountain range. As the morning wore on, Jack assumed that Geraldyne Witkin must have been generous with her advance payment. Kay was in no hurry.

She began by studying two photographs that Jack placed on the coffee table. One, from 1968, was of Howard and Judi as young newlyweds. Judi was smiling, wearing a sleeveless pink gown, while Howard stood behind her, his arms around her waist. He was still slim back then, his hair thick and curly. Both of them looked joyful. The second photograph was Bob Singer's mugshot from 1980.

Kay stared at the pictures in silence for a moment before switching on her tape recorder and launching into a series of observations. A decade later, after Jack let me listen to the tape, I'd understand a few things she got wrong, but also be wowed by all that she got right: things that wouldn't become apparent for years to come.

She began by pointing to Bob, and asking something I'd wondered myself when I first saw him with Judi: "Why in the heck did Judi ever marry him?"

Jack and Steve were silent.

"But I feel that—*sexually*—he produced for her," the psychic murmured, as if speaking to herself. Her voice was raspy and knowing. "There was more of a sexual bond than any mental bond that got things going ...."

"—How bright is he?" Jack broke in, sounding anxious to change the topic.

"Not very bright."

"He's not stupid—"

"Well, but I still don't feel he's that intelligent. "I've seen cases where I'd say, 'Hey, this guy is so smart; he could either be the greatest success in business or the greatest con man ....' But this guy is not that bright. He'd have to commit mistakes ...."

In the pause that followed, I imagined Kay squinting at the mugshot. "... And for some reason," she continued, "Judi had been on his neck about something concerning her ex-husband. I keep feeling that she had hit him over and over again about a problem concerning the ex-husband ...."

So far this was nothing Kay couldn't have figured out by reading the newspapers and talking to Geraldyne Witkin. But I perked up when I heard Jack ask if Judi had known of Bob's plan to murder her ex-husband. By then, I believed her capable of that and more. And it made me bitterly happy to think that Jack might be looking for evidence of her involvement. What if he charged *her* with murder? Bye-bye libel lawsuit, just for starters.

But Kay, to my regret, said she didn't think Judi had any advance knowledge of the murder plot.

"Why is Judi sticking by him so much?" Steve suddenly asked.

"Down inside, she's got some fear of this man," Kay said. "She's faced the fact he just may have done this ....

And, as I said to Mrs. Witkin the other day, I'll betcha ten dollars—he gets sentenced; she's divorced within a couple years. After she's played her role of standing by him."

The conversation turned to Gary Oliver. Jack told Kay how frustrated he was that he couldn't get Gary to testify, and Kay urged him to go back to his boss, "Wild Bill" Hoffman, to pressure him to make a deal.

"I see Singer in prison," she said. "I feel like he'll be convicted .... If Singer walks out, I'm going to throw in the towel."

"Is that on tape?" Jack asked, laughing for the first time that morning.

"You'll get a copy," Kay told him. "When this is over, you're gonna feel that you've done a good job. I can see you turning around and somebody's congratulating you, and you're feeling real good about it .... And I feel Singer in a real dark anger."

Jack sighed loudly and changed the subject to Bill Melcher. He and Steve had puzzled together over the defense attorney's strange behavior, including his press conference about the highly suspicious claim that he'd been shot at in East San Jose. Steve would later tell me that he didn't think Jack really appreciated how outrageous Bill's conduct had been. But Jack had struck up a cordial relationship with Bill, as Jack did with most people, that made him want to give the lawyer the benefit of the doubt.

"Melcher, uh, is an enigma in that, at times, he's a good lawyer, and then he'll do something that I'd consider pretty stupid," Jack said. "Then he'll bounce back and handle something pretty well, and then pull a boner ...."

"What's he built like?" asked the psychic.

"Little shorter than me," interjected Steve, who stood at nearly six feet. "He's got hair I think is dyed blond. *He"* — he must have glanced at Jack—"doesn't necessarily think so."

"He's got darkish roots," Jack allowed. "But it stays pretty consistently the same color. He has a mustache. He's a nice-looking fellow."

"—He's sort of got a little bit of a weasel look to me," Steve said.

Someone turned off the tape at that point. I figured it was time for a bathroom break, or that Kay had got up to make coffee. When the tape resumed, I heard her ask, abruptly: "Does Melcher play around?"

"Well, uh—" Jack stammered. "You're the psychic."

Kay sounded as if she were smiling. "When I put Melcher and Judi together, I think *hmmmm!*" she said.

Jack cleared his throat, and I could sense his discomfort. By then I knew Jack didn't need paranormal help to consider the potentially explosive question of whether Judi and Bill were sleeping together. That business about Judi being Bill's "chief investigative officer," and the way they behaved in court—whispering, laughing, and touching each other's arms—had stirred up quite a bit of gossip by the end of the first trial. I'd been as intrigued as anyone else, but I wasn't ready to take it seriously. Bold as Bill was, I couldn't imagine him doing something that risky, something that might even get him disbarred. Jack seemed to have drawn the same conclusion.

"There are certain people who believe there is something going on between them," the prosecutor now said. "For some reason, I'm one of the few that doesn't really think that there is—"

"—Well, I betcha you're wrong!" Kay broke in, laughing. "I think Melcher just feeds on that. He loves the adoration from the female that he's working a case for."

"That's such dynamite," Jack protested. "I think he's brighter than that."

"Uh, hey. I think it feeds his ego. His ego is just like a furnace that needs constant shuttles of coal," Kay said. "I think he, while he's on stage, I think he will play it. And I'll betcha he does ... I'll betcha a good case of Chivas on that."

I pictured her turning her big green eyes on Jack. "*You see him as being this charming guy that the jury's buying. But I don't think the jury's buying him quite that much."

"I think he wears thin," Jack mused. "If it's going to be a personality contest between me and him, he's gonna have a large jump. But I feel over the long haul, I feel that he will falter, and yet—"

"—Lemme tell you something," Kay broke in again. "Melcher and Judi's situation could be a little *sticky* for Melcher .... It's not gonna be all peaches and cream. Before it's over, it's gonna get sticky for him .... Watch it. Just watch it."

The session with the psychic ran for nearly three hours. As the tape recording came to an end, I pictured Jack and Steve preparing to leave, putting their notepads back into their briefcases, before Kay asked, out of the blue: "Who's the fat lady? Is there a fat lady on the jury?"

The jury for Bob Singer's second trial hadn't yet been chosen, Jack told her. But Kay seemed to have had a sudden insight. She kept insisting that at some point a fat lady would appear and somehow intimidate Bill Melcher.

"There's going to be a time when he's gonna sort of mesmerize the jury," she said. "But something's going to happen. You'll see it."

The tape concluded shortly after that. I imagined Jack and Steve saying their goodbyes and heading out to their car, dejected at having spent so much time for so little useful information. Kay had confirmed a lot of what they already knew: that Bob Singer wasn't that bright, that Gary Oliver's testimony would clinch the case, and even that Bill and Judi shared some sexual chemistry. The only surprise the psychic had in store was her warning about a fat lady. And that made no sense at all on that January afternoon in 1982, although it later would.

15

San Jose, February 1982

Jack Marshall kept his eye out for significantly overweight women all through the jury selection process for Bob Singer's second trial. Yet even in dozens of interviews, he didn't see anyone who matched that description. He tried to put the psychic's warning out of his mind.

Still, Jack was delighted to discover that Kay Rhea had been right about what mattered most to him. Jack had taken her advice to keep pushing his boss, Bill Hoffman, to relent on offering a plea bargain to Gary Oliver, and to his surprise, Hoffman had finally agreed. The DA's office quickly worked out a deal to drop Gary's homicide charge, allowing him to plead guilty to soliciting a murder, with a maximum six-year sentence. Tom Maciolek, the getaway driver, received an even more generous deal, saving the county tens of thousands of dollars it would have had to spend for another trial.

Neither I nor my pressroom colleagues learned about Gary's agreement until the day he testified. Jack had kept it secret, fearing his new key witness might still back out. But Gary had no reason to reject such a good bargain. He appeared in court just a few days after opening arguments, his face pale and his cloud of frizzy hair freshly cropped. Despite Jack's best efforts, he insisted on keeping his sunglasses on throughout his two-hour appearance, but that didn't stop the jurors from hanging on his every word. And his testimony was every bit as devastating for Bob Singer as Jack hoped.

Bob, Gary recounted, had first tried to hire him as a hitman during a casual conversation in the kitchen of The Onion Crock.

"What was your reaction?" Jack asked.

"At first I thought, you know, it was just a joke. But then I realized he was serious," Gary mumbled.

Jack walked Gary through the story of his journey with Andy from Flint to Santa Clara and back again. On his return to The Onion Crock, Gary testified, Bob congratulated him on the "good work" and began paying him as he had promised.

"And how much did he pay you?" Jack asked.

"Five hundred dollars, in cash, each week," Gary answered.

"Thank you," Jack said, his mouth twitching as if he were suppressing a smile. There it was: the missing link. The case would be all downhill from here.

Indeed, Bob Singer's second trial was moving along much faster than his first. Mostly this was because Bill Melcher was spending so much less time cross-examining Jack's witnesses.

Dana, the *Flint Journal* freelancer, and I were both struck by this. Bill had poured so much energy into the first trial. Yet suddenly now there were no more exciting press conferences, no wild reports of death threats or of being followed in sports cars, and no theatrical testimony from Judi. At very least, we'd expected Bob's lawyer to attack Gary Oliver. But Bill seemed strangely lethargic, letting the damaging testimony go nearly unchallenged.

As I'd later learn, Bill had good reasons to be phoning it in. Mainly he was under enormous financial pressure. Shortly after the end of the first trial, Bob and Judi had run out of money and stopped paying him, after having reimbursed him for only a small fraction of his costs. He'd been charging them a steep hourly rate not only for his work in the murder case but for Judi's libel suit, her defense of the shoplifting charge, and his representation of her in an arbitration case with Howard's parents, who were fighting her efforts to prevent them from visiting their grandchildren.

Bill had trusted his clients to pay him when they could, but now he was behind on the rent for his Beverly Hills office and on wages due to his investigator and his secretary, Leslie Bennett. While working in San Jose, Bill had left his office in Leslie's care, which as he'd tell Jack Marshall, who told me, was making him increasingly nervous. It wasn't just because Leslie was upset about not being paid. Bill told Jack that he suspected she was having some sort of personal crisis. She was drinking on the job, he said, and had put on so much weight that Bill, behind her back, had started calling her "Fat Leslie." He told Jack that he planned to fire her as soon as the Singer case ended and he had time to find a replacement.

What Bill couldn't have foreseen was how his cruelty toward her was about to backfire. Leslie Bennett—just as Kay Rhea had predicted—was the "fat lady" who would bring about Bill's downfall.

Bill did make one final effort for his client. On February 25, 1982, just a few days before closing arguments were scheduled, he called the "surprise witness" who had failed to appear in the first trial, to support his "reverse-hit" theory.

Mitchell Henderson was a convicted small-time sex offender who had briefly shared a cell with Gary Oliver in Michigan. He testified just as Bill had promised he would: that Gary had confided to him that Howard Witkin had originally hired him to kill Bob Singer. Henderson quoted Gary as explaining the mystery of Howard's supposed motive. "'If you take Bob,'" he said Gary told him, "'I can get my kids and I get some insurance money. And if I be lucky, you know, I even get my wife back.'"

Jack's cross-examination was brief and to the point, his bemused expression telling the jury how little he thought of Bill's "surprise witness." Under the prosecutor's questioning, Henderson admitted, among other things, that he'd failed to appear in the first trial, after Bill paid him to fly from Michigan to San Jose, because he'd cashed in his ticket and skipped town. That explained why the judge had called for that mysterious two-day break.

On the day that Henderson testified, Judi once again brought her two older children, Daniel and Marie, to the courtroom. As the bailiff was about to lead Bob back to his cell, the kids leaped up and ran toward their stepfather. But before they got within a few feet of Bob, Howard's grieving mother, Geraldyne Witkin, bolted from her seat and screamed, "Don't hug your father's murderer!"

I kept watching and taking notes as Geraldyne remained standing, sobbing and refusing to leave, until Bob was escorted from the room. It was the last day of his trial.

Around five thirty that evening, I'd filed my story on Henderson's testimony and was about to drive home when I got a call from the bailiff. The trial had ended less than four hours earlier but the jury had already reached a verdict. I shouted the news to Dana, and together we ran across the parking lot from the county offices to the courthouse.

I took a seat in the third row, on the left, where I had a clear view of Judi and Bob's faces.

This time the jury found Bob guilty of three of the four charges against him: first-degree murder, conspiracy, and the special circumstance of murder-for-hire. They acquitted him only of the second special circumstance—that he had killed for financial gain. Once again Jack had failed to convince jurors that Bob had any financial motive.

I kept my eyes on Judi as the foreman said his first "Guilty." Immediately her shoulders began to shake and tears rolled down from behind her large sunglasses. Bob slumped in his chair.

It looked like acting to me; I couldn't believe they were that surprised. Across the aisle, some of Howard's relatives also wept, in this case from sorrow and relief.

The next step, as the judge explained, would be a hearing at which jurors would listen to character witnesses for Bob to help them decide whether he should be executed or spend his life in jail. But then there was another unexpected delay.

I got a call the next day from our police beat reporter who'd heard that Bob Singer had tried to commit suicide. Several months earlier, a jail doctor had prescribed him an anti-depressant, Elavil, and he'd hoarded a supply of three-hundred-and-fifty pills, which he'd pretended to swallow, in an envelope tucked under his mattress. At seven in the morning on the morning after the verdict, he'd gulped down his entire stash.

By the time I learned what Bob had done, he'd fallen into a coma. I wrote a short story about his attempt for the next day's paper. Four days later, I wrote another story on what doctors described as his near-miraculous survival. As the jail warden explained it, Bob had inadvertently saved himself by taking so much of the medicine at once. The pills stuck together, delaying the absorption of the drug into his bloodstream.

Bob appeared at his rescheduled penalty hearing just one week after that bungled attempt. He looked pale, thin, and exhausted.

Over the next three days, Bill Melcher called half a dozen witnesses, including Judi Singer and Bob's rabbi, to talk about what an upstanding citizen Bob had been when he lived in San Jose. When it came to Jack Marshall's turn, he didn't call for the death penalty explicitly, but did urge the jurors to consider the effects of Bob's crime not only on his dead victim but on Andy Granger, Gary Oliver, and the getaway driver.

After less than a day of deliberating, the jury handed Bob a life sentence, sparing him from San Quentin State Prison's Death Row. For my story on that decision, I quoted the foreman, who suggested they'd felt some sympathy for him. "He was a simple man," he said of Bob. "He was easily led, and I think he *was* being led ... There was evidence that most of his life's decisions were made for him. And he wasn't very bright. Nobody bright would have hired his own employee as a hitman."

Just before Bob was led off to start serving his sentence, the trial judge, John McInerny, said he wanted to give him a chance to come clean, for the sake of Judi's children. "You say you are innocent, and they apparently believe you," the judge said. "If you let them grow up still believing this, and if it not be true, then there is a possibility they will grow up to be embittered and disillusioned adults. Should that occur, only you would profit from it, and it would be a tragedy. Not today, not tomorrow, maybe not even next year, but someday, before irreparable damage is done to them, give them the credit for loving you enough to earn your trust. I implore you to tell them the truth—the *real truth* about your complicity in this matter, so that they may be at peace with you, themselves, and society ...."

The judge stopped talking and looked expectantly at Bob. But Bob simply stared at the floor.

As Dana and I left the courtroom, we saw Bill Melcher and Judi Singer encircled by reporters again, out in the hall. Judi looked utterly different from the weeping wife who'd watched Bob be convicted. She was smiling more broadly than she had for several months. I noticed she'd fastened a pin to her tote bag, which said "Urban Cowboys Do It with Spurs."

Bill, also smiling, was passing out a press release, which announced that Judi now planned to attend law school and eventually join Bill's legal practice. "She has uncanny aptitude in this area, an intensely inquiring mind, and a present knowledge and *understanding* of the law that rivals most lawyers," the statement said. "She is extremely intelligent and multitalented and society will be well-served by her entry into the profession."

According to the statement, Bill and Judi planned to work together to expand his law practice nationally, "with particular emphasis in criminal law, medical-legal law [sic], entertainment, sports, and libel and privacy litigation." But first, the two intended to write a book on the "intensely intriguing undertones of the Singer case." Movie rights, Bill added, were being sought by "a major studio."

I looked around the circle of my colleagues, noting all the slack jaws. In a trial full of outrageous behavior, this was a new peak. I could only wonder what Bob would think of it all when he read my story on that press conference, as he surely would, in his prison cell.

I wouldn't find that out for several more years, when I talked to Bob in person for the first time. During that interview, Bob would also show me evidence of how hard Judi was working to manage his feelings, even while announcing her plan to practice law with Bill Melcher. Shortly after moving back to Michigan with the kids, she mailed him a greeting card, preprinted as "A Report Card to My Husband."

"You know I love you and I'm yours *for keeps*," Judi wrote on the inside of the card. Then, answering the prompts, she gave Bob high marks for "shares his feelings openly" and "always remembers our anniversary with a gift. Especially when I tell him not to." She added up his score, and in the space marked, ENTITLES YOU TO, wrote: "Anything you want whenever you want it!!!"

Two months after Bob got his report card, Judi filed for divorce. In a subsequent letter, she told him that this was for the sake of her children. It wouldn't be fair for them not to have a father figure in their lives. She had to get them back into some semblance of a normal life.

Bob agreed to all her terms. In the divorce settlement, Judi Barnett—her maiden name—was awarded all the household furniture, her checking accounts, and their new Buick. The settlement also explicitly noted that neither party would have any further interest in any life insurance policies owned by the other.

16

Managua, Nicaragua, June 1982

On the flight to Miami en route to Managua, I opened my journal to take stock. I couldn't have been more ready for the next three weeks, I wrote. My passport was tucked into a money belt around my waist; a tiny bandage on my deltoid marked where I'd gotten my gamma globulin shot, and my backpack was crammed with printouts of background material—mostly other reporters' articles and typed notes from interviews I'd done on the phone for the past week with U.S. experts on Central America.

"What more could I possibly need?" I wrote, before scribbling my answer: "Confidence. Calm."

Was it just my imagination, or were most of the hit songs of the early 1980s about triumphing over obstacles? "Eye of the Tiger." "Another One Bites the Dust." "Chariots of Fire." "We Got the Beat!" All their lyrics seemed to speak directly to me, my happiness veering close to mania as I traveled ever farther away from Judi's libel suit and my constant worries about my mother.

My father had just had a health scare—a small tumor on his parotid gland. I'd gone down to be with him for his surgery, during which he was sweet and grateful, but within days of the danger having passed he'd careened into another bad patch. Once again, he was drinking too much, driving unsafely, yelling at my mother, and throwing furniture around. She told me on the phone that she was scared he'd hurt her. She had begged him to get help, she said, but he wouldn't.

"What should I do?" she'd asked me, two days before I left.

"Put your foot down," I'd told her, as I'd so often said before. "Come stay with me. Insist he see a psychiatrist." I recommended that she learn about Al-Anon and offered to go to a meeting with her. She said she'd let me know. I printed out information about alcoholism and mailed it to her. She promised to read it.

I couldn't sleep on the night after her call, worrying about the two of them brawling. But the next day, as usual, she told me that all was fine. He'd apologized. She'd accepted it. It hadn't really been that big a deal.

Now I looked over at Dana, leaning back in the seat next to me, her eyes closed, and tried to breathe in some of what I imagined was her God-given tranquility. I was convinced that most people I knew were having a much easier time all around than I was. I consoled myself with the thought that the cost of calling home more than once or twice would be prohibitive, as my mother would surely understand.

Over the next three weeks, I filled my head and notebooks with quotes from interviews and press conferences and my first impressions of the steamy capital city, its streets still torn up from a decade-old earthquake. In his last years in power, Somoza had not only tortured and murdered dissidents but siphoned off the humanitarian aid that flowed in after Managua was flattened to fill his Swiss bank accounts. The city had never been rebuilt, so people gave you directions by telling you to turn left where there used to be a bank and then right where there used to be a post office.

One of the few intact oases from the heat and traffic jams was the five-star Intercontinental Hotel, where the top-tier reporters and foreign dignitaries stayed. Dana and I, paying our own way, headed instead to a cheap pension called Casa Fiedler, owned by an elderly German woman who kept a photo of her late husband, in Nazi regalia, on her mantel. Each morning we'd take a cab to the Intercon to splurge on the dollar-fifty breakfast buffet in the high-ceilinged lobby with its wicker chairs and potted palms. While picking at our boiled yucca and scrambled eggs, we kept a casual lookout for the two—count 'em!—celebrity New York Times reporters, both males, of course, striding past in their starched white guayaberas, reminding us of what a huge story we were covering. Managua was crawling with reporters of all kinds: big-leaguers, farm club members, and lowly freelancers like us. We ran into each other at solidarity demonstrations, where we drolly mouthed the line from the Nicaraguan anthem—"We fight against the Yankee, enemy of humanity!"—and in the evening debriefed over iced cacao drinks at Antojitos, an outdoor restaurant next to the Intercon.

Everything was new and exotic, and I felt competent and heady, hailing taxis, arranging interviews, and ordering coffee in my ugly Spanish accent. "Now I'm back on my feet," I sang to myself, "Just a man and his will to survive!"

I reported six long stories for the *Mercury*: all newsy features with flexible-enough time pegs so that I could finish writing them once I returned home. For our Sunday magazine I was preparing a snide look at the hundreds of lefty American sympathizers—"Sandalistas," as they were called—who'd come to Nicaragua as volunteers and witnesses. Toward the end of the piece I briefly described a pair of freelance reporters whom Dana and I had met in the Sandinista government pressroom. The two were on assignment for *Pacific News Service*, a small, ultra-liberal news agency in San Francisco, and had been shocked to discover that two other freelancers, illegitimately claiming *they* worked for PNS, had nabbed their credentials the previous week.

The two uncredentialed PNS reporters were Jim Evans and Jack Epstein, both from the Bay Area. Jim was a longtime journalist and surfer who spoke fluent Spanish and was tall and fit and blue-eyed. Jack had a bushy black beard, thick glasses and muscular arms from his previous job hauling mailbags at the Oakland post office. Before that he'd spent two years in the Peace Corps in Brazil and Panama. When he wasn't on the road writing freelance stories for a hundred dollars apiece, Jack lived in Berkeley, in a small room he called "the crawl space" in the back of a rented apartment he shared with a friend. After that first meeting, Dana and I kept seeing the two of them at press conferences. They always seemed frustrated about something.

One afternoon the four of us and another reporter we'd met shared a small taxi, pooling resources to do a story I'm still pretty sure was my idea, although Jack insists he and Jim thought of it first. We were headed to interview Orlando Tardencillas, a nineteen-year-old Nicaraguan who'd recently embarrassed the Reagan Administration. U.S. officials had accused the Sandinistas of spreading revolution throughout Central America, and were therefore overjoyed when Tardencillas, who'd been captured in El Salvador, agreed to tell the Washington press corps that he'd been sent there by his government. Once he got in front of cameras, however, he announced that he'd previously confessed under torture and that he'd in fact traveled to El Salvador on his own accord. On his return to Nicaragua, Tardencillas had been welcomed as a hero, but no U.S. reporter had yet talked to him there.

On the way to Tardencilla's new office at a government youth organization, I sat on Jim's lap in the front of the crowded cab. Jack, in the back, was telling a long story about how he and Jim had been dissed the previous week by one of the *New York Times* reporters. They'd run into each other on the tarmac of a tiny airport in southern Honduras as both were headed for a large refugee camp. The *Times* reporter was traveling on an army helicopter, while Jack and Jim had to hitch a ride on the back of a garbage truck. They arrived at the camp after several hours, muddy and smelly, after which the *Times* reporter had the gall to ask if they'd seen anything interesting on the way. But Jack took a vengeful delight in describing how he'd then seen the *Times* guy, in his crisp khaki trousers, duck into the bushes and come out a moment later with his pants, as Jack said, all *"ferpishta,"* a word I recognized as derived from the Yiddish *pish,* for urine.

Laughing, I turned around to give Jack a closer look. His Yiddish wisecrack made me feel at home, but in a good way.

Still, I'd told Dana before we left that the last thing I planned to do on our trip was get involved with some guy. We were there to work, *punto final.* Nor did Jack seem all that interested in me, beyond our joking friendship.

Tardencillas was waiting for us, as we'd hoped. He was slim and bespectacled and smart, reminding me of my brother Jimmy, and his story felt just right: the triumph of a David against a clumsy, immoral Goliath.

The four of us collaborated on a few more stories, including interviewing Herty Lewites, the tourism minister, for a sardonic piece on the delights of travel in the war-torn country. It was so cheap to fly around inside Nicaragua that Dana and I took Lewites up on a few of his suggestions, spending a couple days exploring the white-sand beaches of the Corn Islands, off Nicaragua's east coast, and then one night in the forested northern mountains.

In Matagalpa we stayed at a resort called the Selva Negra, in the middle of a coffee plantation. A sudden loud rainstorm struck just after dinner. I'd drunk too much coffee before going to bed, and ended up staying awake long past midnight, listening to the wind. When I finally fell asleep, I dreamed about my mother in a way I hadn't done for several years. Once again, she was locked high in a tower, and I was trying to save her. But this time I could hear her singing, which in the dream became the saddest sound I'd ever heard. Waking up, I pulled my thick woolen blanket over my head so as not to wake Dana with my crying. Apparently there was nowhere on earth I could go to escape my mother's need for me nor my frustration that I couldn't help her.

During my last few days in Managua, I found myself recalling what Dr. P had said, and wondering whether I'd been wrong to have run away from his blunt invitation to understand myself better. On the plane home, I opened my journal and wrote down a new plan. Just one item this time. After I got back, I was going to give therapy another try.

17

Dr. Y stopped me as I was heading out his office door.

"Kathy, excuse me! Can you come back here for a minute?"

"Sure," I said, turning around.

This was weird. In the six or seven weeks that I'd been seeing him, Dr. Y had never let a session run past fifty minutes. Instead, at the end of that time, he'd quietly click his ballpoint pen, signaling me to stop talking.

I wondered what might be wrong. *Had my check bounced again?*

I waited for him to tell me.

Dr. Y was the psychiatrist in training whom I'd previously decided was too much of an amateur to be of any use. But that was before my nightmare in Matagalpa made me rethink my resistance to therapy. I'd since signed up with him for three sessions a week.

This was just what Dr. P had recommended, although except for Dr. Y's bushy beard, dim office lighting, tasteful bookshelves, and couch, he couldn't have more different than his stern predecessor. He had kind eyes and a subversive laugh, and at our first meeting introduced himself as a "crazy Irishman."

Considering his relative inexperience, he'd offered a steep discount that made all those sessions affordable, as long as I didn't eat out or buy any new clothes. As a resident, he reported to a more experienced supervisor, which reminded me of the cheap haircuts I sometimes got from trainees at my local hair salon. Although in this case the supervisor was Bruno Bettelheim, the world-famous Austrian psychoanalyst. Such a deal!

Most importantly, Dr. Y never once compared me to a murderer, as Dr. P had done, although he also never treated me like a victim. He insisted that I follow his rules, including paying on time and giving him twenty-four-hours' notice to cancel a session, which he said he'd assume I'd do only for good reasons. He also challenged me every time I tried to paste a smiley face on the childhood secrets I'd started to tell him, by offering excuses for my parents or speaking in what he teased was my "mellifluous voice."

"Is there anyone in your life that you can cry with, or get angry at?" he asked at one point. No, there wasn't, I had to admit.

Early on, he offered a diagnosis: anxiety stemming from "insecure attachment," a term that refers to an infant's failure to form a strong bond with his or her mother. Insecure attachment, as he explained, can lead to failure to trust others and a bottomless need for reassurance, symptoms I had to acknowledge were familiar, even as I later learned they can also be narcissistic traits. After noticing how keenly I'd watched his face, adjusting my behavior to suit his reactions, he asked me to lie on his couch, where I could only monitor the ceiling. His strategy, as he'd explain to me many years later (after I'd more or less graduated and was free to ask him questions), was to behave as much as possible like an ideal parent: attentive, limit-setting, and able to see me for who I was instead of as a way to meet his needs.

For a long time, I didn't appreciate what a gift this was. Instead, I felt embarrassed and impatient and continually talked about quitting. In the early 1980s, "talk therapy" was growing more popular but was also the target of endless jokes and insults. In 1976, the journalist Tom Wolfe, writing in *New York Magazine*, had dubbed the 1970s the "Me Decade," lumping in and dismissing everything from primal scream sessions to marriage counseling as fomenting narcissists by inviting them to indulge in their favorite pastime: "Let's Talk about Me!" In 1979, the historian Christopher Lasch published his bestseller, *The Culture of Narcissism*, which carried a similar message. My ironic dilemma was that in order to recognize and deal with behavior I feared might be narcissism, I had to commit to a process that these hip authorities were condemning as narcissistic. I did it anyway, albeit in awkward fits and starts. Somehow I knew I'd needed to find someone I trusted enough to call me out on my behavior, and by that March morning when Dr. Y stopped me from going out his door, he had my faith.

I'd already improved under his care. My stories from Nicaragua had helped get me back in my editors' good graces. I hadn't made another mistake since the Judi Singer debacle and was happy to learn that she and Bill Melcher hadn't filed any new motions or responded to ours for several months. The newspaper's lawyer had recently told me he planned to file a motion to dismiss the case on the grounds that they were no longer pursuing it. That wouldn't be the best kind of victory—complete exoneration would be better—but I'd take it.

I'd handed in a memo listing several more stories I could do in Central America, including one on a group of Nicaraguan Contra rebels who'd been training with their AR-15s in a San Jose garage. They'd contacted me after seeing my stories in hopes of getting me to understand their side and had invited me to visit their supposedly secret camp on the Honduran border. This time my editors agreed to front my expenses.

I was also beginning to be a lot less lonely. Almost every other day I was talking on the phone with Jack, the freelancer I'd met in Managua, and who was now back in Berkeley. He'd invited me over for dinner that weekend in the apartment he shared with his friend, and I was already starting to rethink my plan to focus entirely on work instead of men.

There was still a lot of work I had to do with Dr. Y. While I hadn't made another mistake in a story, I constantly feared that I would. Each time I let go of a newly written article, I felt as if tiny claws were clutching my intestines until the next day, after I saw it in the paper and no one had called to complain. Had I really been trying to sabotage myself or just carelessly screwing up? Either way, I didn't trust that my friend Pete's guidance to "eyeball every word" would be enough to keep me out of trouble.

I'd also come around to agreeing with Dr. P's suggestion that I needed to better understand how I was treating men, and also had accepted that this might have something to do with the way I grew up.

Dr. Y and I had just spent another fifty minutes excavating painful memories from my early adolescence on the morning that he stopped me at his door. I couldn't figure out why he was smiling. I raised my eyebrows.

"Don't you know what you just did?" he asked.

I shook my head. *Not a clue.*

"You locked my door as you were going out. You've done this twice before. Do you not want my other patients to be able to come see me?"

Now it was my turn to smile. *Of course I hadn't been doing that. That would be ridiculous.* "Of course I haven't been doing that," I said, looking down. "That would be—"

My thumb was still poised on the lock.

He held my gaze.

"I just don't believe I did that," I said.

I didn't mean it rhetorically. Even with that evidence, I couldn't accept that it had happened.

Over my next four years of sessions with Dr. Y, that moment in his office with my thumb on the lock would repeatedly remind me of the puzzling power of my subconscious. My brain's pilot had left the cabin, just as it had when I wrongly accused Judi Singer of murder. What other crazy things was I doing that I wasn't yet aware of, for reasons I didn't understand?

I *did* understand why I was locking Dr. Y's door. He was right about me not wanting him to see other patients. Part of me—the part still recoiling from the painful work of baring my heart—wanted to run from his office, never to return. Meanwhile, a considerably larger part wanted to move in for back-to-back sessions, seven days a week. This was the beginning of the magic of "transference": the way a patient redirects strong feelings for other people, mostly parents, onto the therapist, in the process of trying to heal childhood wounds. Soon I'd find myself dressing up for my sessions and daydreaming about running into Dr. Y at a party.

It would still take a long time for me to stop second-guessing the process and canceling our sessions whenever work got in the way. When I did show up, I dithered, alternately blaming my parents for the trouble and pain I was in and blaming myself for not being able to move on, already, since my problems weren't all that serious.

How could I lie there whining, I asked Dr. Y, when billions of people throughout the world were simply trying to survive amid poverty, hunger, and war? This had often been my parents' refrain whenever my siblings and I would complain about anything from homework to hunger. "You think *you've* got problems?"

Even in our privileged enclave of Hillsborough, there were plenty of sordid tales that made my family's troubles look tame. In 1974, when I was a junior in high school,

Patty Hearst, who'd lived around the corner from us, was kidnapped by the Symbionese Liberation Army and joined in their crime spree. In 1983, my tennis-playing orthodontist and his beautiful young wife were murdered and their college-aged son tried for the crime. Years later, a wealthy real-estate developer friend of my parents I'd fondly remembered for the fabulous eggnog at his holiday parties would be indicted for having sex with child prostitutes whom he paid in cocaine.

"This just feels so selfish," I said one morning that summer, about six months in. "Compared to most people in the world, I'm really lucky. I love my parents; and whatever problems they had, they *doted* on me ...."

I'd already heard Dr. Y gently sighing during the times I'd gone on about the starving masses, but this seemed to push him over the edge.

"I grew up in East Oakland," he interrupted. "My mom was a sixteen-year-old high school dropout and my dad was a drug addict who went to prison soon after I was born."

I wriggled around on the couch to stare at him. *Shrinks weren't supposed to talk about themselves like that, were they? Aren't they supposed to be blank slates? What would Bruno Bettelheim think?*

What he'd said about his parents also came as a surprise. I'd pictured them as an Irish version of my own: possibly crazy, but at least outwardly conventional and well-to-do. He'd gone to Stanford, just like I had, after all. How had he done that?

"—But here's the thing," Dr. Y was saying. "I think I had it easier than you, because those issues were all obvious. On the surface. And consistent."

I didn't answer. I wasn't convinced that what he'd said was true, and it also made me nervous. He'd stepped out of line, I told myself. He didn't know what he was doing.

A few more months would pass before I'd understand the truth: that Dr. Y's kindness had frightened me, and that I'd been looking for a reason to distrust him, and that seeing him as an amateur again seemed like a good one. In the meantime, I conveniently got so busy that I had to skip several appointments.

I was seeing a lot more of Jack, after that first dinner at apartment in Berkeley. He'd hosted me and eight other friends on his softball team, the Fleet Feet, preparing a feast of feijoada, an elaborate Brazilian pork and black bean stew. Afterward we caravanned to Red Vest Pizza in El Cerrito to hear a bluegrass band called the Good Ol' Persons. From that night on, I'd love watching Jack with his friends. They'd circle around him as if he were a campfire as he told stories from his years of adventures in Latin America. He'd written a travel guide, "Along the Gringo Trail," which had become a cult classic for hip low-budget travelers, although one reviewer carped that he'd skipped over tourist centers like Acapulco and Mazatlan while devoting several pages to topics like how to chew coca leaves and how to treat parasite infestations. Jack and I saw each other as friends for a few weeks before we got closer. After that, I spent most of my weekends in Berkeley, joining in the late-night poker games with his buddies and cheering for him at his Fleet Feet games.

Around the same time, I was promoted to the San Francisco bureau, where I'd share an office with Susan Yoachum, a talented reporter and new friend. Within a few weeks after I arrived, we began to collaborate on an investigative series about human rights abuses by the city's police force. Our first story started by describing a cop who was notorious for swallowing bullets with tequila and for having more than two hundred lawsuits filed against him—and who had just been promoted.

After the series ran, we heard that some of the cops were referring to us as "Yoachum and Smoke'um." My car was towed for no good reason, after which Dianne Feinstein, then the city's mayor, called us into her office to chew us out for forty minutes for hanging out the dirty laundry of her hard-working department.

I'd moved to a new apartment, a converted room in a large house in the Haight-Ashbury district, which meant that continuing to see Dr. Y three times a week would add twenty-four hours of driving each month to my overloaded schedule. Plus, really, what more did he think we could accomplish?

"Psychotherapy seems like a racket, like the goal line is constantly changing," I complained. "Didn't Freud say the point was to transform hysterical misery into common unhappiness? Wouldn't you say I'm there?"

Dr. Y laughed. "I think you can aim higher," he said. But he added that if I did intend to quit, we should at least taper off. Toward the end of that year, we dropped down from three weekly sessions to two, many of which I canceled when work got in the way.

18

Khartoum, Sudan, December 1983

There was no way I was going to stay at the Hotel Arafat, I told my new boyfriend, Jack, on our first night in Khartoum. We stood in the middle of an empty street at one end of the Victory Bridge, which spanned the White Nile. It was a few minutes after midnight. A pair of rats scuttled across the unpaved sidewalk and in between the legs of a donkey nibbling trash. A warm breeze smelled of urine. "There is no way I'm staying at the Hotel Arafat!" I repeated, more loudly this time, since Jack was walking away. As if he expected me to follow. Which I didn't, at least just then, intend to do.

Jack had no problem with the Hotel Arafat. He appreciated that it charged only ten dollars a night and didn't seem to mind that we'd be sharing a bathroom with six strangers. He hadn't even flinched, an hour earlier, after the toothless doorman in the dirty jalabiya showed us what would have been our room, and I pointed out a bloodstain on a pillowcase.

I wanted to stay at Le Meridian, which was clean, with a pool, and had armed watchmen out front, all of which struck me as a pretty good deal for eighty-five dollars a night.

After all, our plan was to stay in Khartoum for just one day—two at most. The very next morning we were scheduled to meet with representatives of the Eritrean

People's Liberation Front, who planned to sneak us across the northern border. The EPLF was one of two rebel groups that had been fighting for the past twenty years to break away from Ethiopia. Over a recent meeting at a diner in Oakland, their U.S. envoy had offered us the tour of their sophisticated network of underground base camps. We'd be the first U.S. journalists to see them, he promised.

This was it: genuine war reporting. And just the kind of story I loved. Although in this case the Goliath wasn't the United States but its archrival, the Soviet Union, which was backing Ethiopia's cruel bombardments intended to crush the rebellion.

Jack had set up the trip. One of his buddies from high school had connections with the EPLF from his days in the Peace Corps in Ethiopia. There was sure to be goat meat and Soviet air strikes: the same sorts of things I'd been relieved to avoid three years earlier, when Richard left me behind in Pakistan while he traveled to Afghanistan. But this time I was ready. For starters, unlike Richard, Jack had welcomed me along, treating me like an equal. This kind of thing was just one of the reasons I'd fallen in love with him over the past ten months.

Jack was dramatically different from any man I'd been involved with. He joked that he was my parents' worst nightmare: "a Jew without a job." He was eleven years older than me but had much less formal work experience, mostly limited to that stint at the post office, on top of his two years in the Peace Corps, a couple factory jobs, and a gig selling homemade candles on Telegraph Avenue.

None of that worried me then. He had so many other extraordinary qualities, beginning with the fact that he was one of the least narcissistic men I'd ever met. He had a healthy sense of self-esteem but was unfailingly kind and never seemed self-absorbed. I raved about him to Dr. Y, who concluded, approvingly, "He's comfortable in his own skin."

Jack never seemed to mind my ambition, and never once suggested I do his laundry. His mother, a violinist for the L.A. Philharmonic, and father, a movie-theater manager who fed their kids when she was working, had brought him up right that way. Most of all, I loved being with him. He introduced me to bossa nova, with Gilberto Gil and Tom Jobim providing the soundtrack of our courtship. He made me laugh harder than I'd done since passing notes with Lucy Goldstein in our fourth-grade Spanish class, and I no longer had to pretend I was having a good time in bed. I felt something new with Jack, which I guess boiled down to *safe*. So much so that to my surprise it had occurred to me what a great dad he'd make, even as he'd assured me more than once that he shared my lack of interest in children. "I can barely be responsible for myself!" he said.

I'd looked forward to spending the next three weeks with him for months as we'd planned our trip. The *Mercury News*—the paper's name had recently changed—wasn't fronting expenses but had given me extra time off and promised to run the stories if they were good, while I was also free to freelance for other publications. I was excited to finally be starting out but also petrified. Marie Colvin— the courageous *Sunday Times* war correspondent who'd be killed in Syria in 2012—I wasn't. I'd never been this close to actual war and was starting to dwell on the fact that we were about to trust perfect strangers to keep us safe. Plus, who knew what parasites lurked in the East African desert? I'd signed up for these risks with my eyes open. This was the life I'd dreamed of for so long. But was it really too much to expect to spend one night in a room with clean sheets and no rats?

"It's a false economy to risk being robbed or getting rabies or dysentery!" I needled Jack.

Instead of answering, he fished in his backpack for his travel guide. Walking over to a streetlight, he squinted at the pages.

"You're a cheap penny-pincher!" I said.

He looked up. *"You're a bourgeois Jewish Princess!"*

We scowled at each other for two more seconds and then both burst out laughing. My worries about rat bites paled next to a longer-lived fear that was delightfully ebbing—that if I ever showed anger toward someone I loved, he or she would disappear. I took a particular joy in calling Jack rude names.

"Let's look at one more place," Jack said. "The Nile Palace. Three dollars a night. You can't beat that!"

At the Nile Palace, we still had to share a bathroom, but only with four strangers, and I didn't see any blood on the sheets. All the better, since we ended up staying there for nearly a week, waiting, increasingly nervously, for the EPLF to overcome a series of mysterious logistical issues in the way of our starting our trip. We spent some of the time reporting a story on sharia law, which had just been imposed by Gaafar Nimeiry, the authoritarian president whose picture hung in every shop and home. Unwisely, we lingered too close to edges of a mob gathered outside a dusty stadium to watch authorities chop off the hand of an alleged thief, until government guards thwacking leather belts chased us away.

Each day I found new reasons to detest Sudan, so much so that by the time our EPLF contacts finally told us it was all clear to leave for Eritrea, I was less nervous about trusting our safety to the rebels than thrilled to be checking out of the Nile Palace. On the other hand, for the first several hours that night, as I rode in the front seat of the jeep that drove us out of Khartoum, I found it hard to take my eyes off the three bullet holes in the windshield. Our minders had earlier casually informed us that just a week earlier a Swedish journalist riding in my seat had been killed during an ambush with the rival guerrilla faction. On top of that, I was coping with some new intrusive thoughts about tapeworms and conjunctivitis.

Just after midnight, we crossed Sudan's northeastern border on an unmarked dirt road with empty desert all around us. The stars were brighter than any I'd seen outside of a planetarium. The jeep jolted along a trail that wound around groves of prickly pear cacti, following the "Tokar Road" supply route—the EPLF's Ho Chi Minh trail through Eritrea's western lowlands. The sand below us looked like silver dust.

"How are you doing, peach of my life?" Jack whispered from the back seat.

I reached back to hold his warm hand and began to give myself over to the electric spell of the novelty and sense of mission involved in reporting on life-or-death struggles in a strange, new country.

We always traveled by night, to avoid Soviet MIGs, but even in the dark there were lots of things to see. One evening we spotted a troop of barking baboons as they clambered up a rocky mountain; the next morning, just before sunrise, after I slipped out of our underground shelter to pee behind a cactus, I looked up at the sudden jingling of bells to see a camel caravan of men in flowing white robes, advancing toward me out of nowhere.

Our young, English-speaking EPLF guide, Fesseha, who had quit his university studies in Asmara to join the revolution, proudly showed us around the rebels' underground shelters, supply sites, and even a three-hundred-bed hospital, all expertly camouflaged from Soviet reconnaissance planes. Between destinations, we drove for as much as seven hours at a time over the rocky desert. Sometimes we picked up hitchhikers, often wounded fighters lacking an eye or a limb. Each night we ate pasta or stewed goat that sometimes still had hair clinging to the skin.

I took scores of photographs: pieces of MIGs on the ground, women with brilliant orange headscarves and big gold hoops through their noses. We kept meeting rebels who, like Fesseha, were risking their lives to fight and work in the desert. At the hospital, we interviewed one young woman who'd been taken captive by Ethiopian soldiers, who had shot her five times and poked out one of her eyes. Her doctor was worried the nerve damage in her hands would prevent her from being able to use her crutches. When Jack asked what she planned to do next, she laughed and said, "It's obvious; I'll keep on fighting." As I listened to her I again felt wretched about all the hours I'd spent complaining to Dr. Y about my petty suburban childhood traumas. What a wimp I was.

Along those same lines, after four days in the desert, I was ready to turn around. My notebooks were full; I was grimy and tired, and I hoped we might still avoid getting strafed. But Jack was having the time of his life, so I only suggested it two or three times. "Think about it," he said that night, as we scooched our sleeping bags close to each other in the hole in the ground that served as a dormitory. "We're in a *rebel stronghold*—just like in Pancho Villa's time!"

We spent several more days with the rebels, touring a refugee camp, visiting underground classrooms, and photographing Soviet tanks and missile shells near the earth-and-stone trenches guarding the front lines at a hill-town called Nakfa. On our last night, we met with a high-ranking EPLF commander, Sebhat Efrem, over lasagna and crème caramel served on fine china in a bunker outfitted with a doily-covered sofa. Efrem, who would later become the young nation's minister of defense, told us of the rebels' plan to form a model democracy once it took power, comparing their long struggle to Vietnam's thirty-year war of independence.

The rebels would go on to win their war after another seven years, although that model democracy didn't materialize. Isaias Afwerki, one of the founders of the revolution, took power in 1993 and didn't let go. Eritrea's regime became notorious for corruption and human rights abuses including torture, extrajudicial executions, and forced labor. One U.S. ambassador called Afwerki "unhinged" and "narcissistic."

It's not always true that long-suffering Davids create narcissistic personality cults and try to out-Goliath the Goliaths as soon as they get the chance. Nelson Mandela never behaved that way, even after 27 years in South Africa's prisons. Still, the aftermath of the revolutions I saw up close in Eritrea—and alas, also in Nicaragua, whose beleaguered rebel rulers also turned self-celebrating and repressive— sometimes seemed like a cruel retort to that Martin Luther King, Jr., line about the arc of the moral universe bending toward justice. This looked more like entropy.

After traveling back to Khartoum, Jack and I flew to Egypt for a few days of vacation. We sailed down the Nile and drank sugary mint tea and played dominoes in cafes in Cairo. Then, as we'd planned, we parted ways. Jack wanted to spend more time traveling, but I'd used up all my vacation time and had to get back to work. Unlike Jack, I also *wanted* to get back to work. Vacations made me nervous; I much preferred structure, deadlines, and completed tasks.

The *Mercury News* organized my photographs and stories on Sudan and Eritrea into a series on the Horn of Africa that ran on the front page for two days. I also sold feature stories to the *London Sunday Times* and the *Washington Post*. A *New York Times Magazine* editor I'd pitched to consider a story on our trip asked me to send him a detailed proposal. I was floating. The *Times* magazine had worldwide readership and unsurpassed prestige. Writing this story would be worth every ounce of the hard work it would take.

When Jack called from Tel Aviv after my first week home, I told him the good news about the *Times*, and he told me all about his travels, how he'd made his way through the Sinai desert, newly under Egyptian control, into Israel with plans to head from there to Cyprus and from there, by boat, to Italy. The story went on and on.

I pursed my lips.

"But when are you coming home, so we can do the magazine piece together?"

He paused. "I'm having a great time. And I don't know when I'm going to get the chance to get back here."

"What do you mean? You don't know when you'll be back?"

Despite what I knew and even—sometimes—appreciated about Jack's ability to live in the moment, I couldn't fathom why he wouldn't seize *this* moment to advance his career, not to mention mine. Plus, didn't he miss me at all?

I didn't ask, and he didn't tell.

All that next week, I came home from work late each evening to the empty apartment to listen to my bossa nova tapes and weep. I woke up early each morning to work on the *Times* proposal, sending it in with just my name on it. For the rest of each day, I waited for a card or phone call from Jack. But after that one call from Tel Aviv, another two weeks passed without a word. It was just like waiting for Richard in his apartment in London. I started to fume.

Then, on a cold Thursday night in mid-January, I went downtown to hear a lecture by the journalist I.F. Stone, one of my heroes. On my return home, just after ten, I was slowing down to drive into my apartment's garage when a man ran up to my car. I'd let my guard down after three weeks of hypervigilance in Africa and hadn't locked the car door. The stranger burst in, pushing me aside and thrusting a hunting knife against my neck.

Whenever I'd thought about how I'd react in this sort of situation, I'd imagined myself being calm and self-controlled, choosing just the right psychologically attuned words to help me escape uninjured. Instead, I screamed into the mugger's ear: "*Please don't hurt me!*"

Hysteria may have been the right play, though, because somehow I got out of the car with my apartment keys, leaving behind my purse and one sandal, and raced inside, where I double-locked the door. Impulsively, I called my parents, waking them.

"Did you call the police?" my father asked.

I must have been in shock. I hadn't yet thought to do that.

"Don't stay in that apartment!" my mother chimed in. "Do you want to come here and stay with us? You have to change your locks!"

Now I felt on familiar ground. I forced myself to calm down so that I could calm them down.

"I'll be okay," I assured them, smiling by the time I hung up. After all those months of spilling their secrets to Dr. Y, I sometimes feared they wouldn't pick up the phone when I called.

Two days later the police found my car parked in the lot of a nearby supermarket. I changed my locks, as my mother had advised, and talked the apartment manager into getting an automatic door for the garage.

A few more days passed with still no word from Jack. One of my editors told me he'd heard that Richard was getting married to an editor in New York. That night I dreamed that Jack was a tortoise: impossibly old, wizened, barely able to move. I awoke aware that my subconscious, previously Jack's loyal fan, had begun to root for me to move on.

A few days after I got mugged, the *Times* editor who'd asked me to send him a pitch called to say the proposal I'd slaved over wasn't going to fly. He loved the story, he assured me, and I'd done a great job with the proposal, but his bosses had nixed it. They had only recently discovered that a story they'd published a year earlier on the Khmer Rouge in Cambodia had been fabricated by a twenty-four-year-old journalist who had never gone to Cambodia. He'd even plagiarized a passage from Andre Malraux's novel, *The Royal Way*. As the editor explained, his bosses were now simply too wary about trusting freelancers.

But I wasn't a freelancer, I argued. I was *on staff* with a newspaper.

He said he was sorry.

Later that week I got a postcard from Jack, which he said he wrote while drinking cappuccino and watching boats glide by on the Ponte Vecchio in Florence.

I caught a cold that flared into pneumonia.

I blamed Jack for all of it: the mugging, the failed proposal, and the virus.

Of course I was being ridiculous. Jack had every right to linger in Europe; he hadn't broken any promises to me and reasonably didn't assume I expected he'd protect me from muggers and disease. But his "I'm OK, You're OK" take on relationships was new to me, and my first reaction was to hate it.

A couple days after I recovered, I was invited to a party in a fancy apartment in San Francisco's Marina District. Everyone there looked young and bright and successful. I spent two hours on a sofa drinking martinis with a dapper blond man who told me all about his plan to make partner at his firm within three years. He asked me to dinner the next evening, and I happily accepted.

The next day I sent a letter to Jack in Italy telling him I didn't want to see him again. I couldn't trust him, I wrote. I promised myself I'd find a tolerable breadwinner to marry or else reconcile myself to living alone.

Men stink, I told myself. No exceptions.

For good measure, I canceled my next two scheduled appointments with Dr. Y.

19

San Francisco, February 1984

On a foggy afternoon two months after I returned from Eritrea, a thick package addressed to me arrived at the San Francisco bureau office of the *Mercury News.* The return address listed the sender as "The Voices of Truth."

Inside was a set of documents that answered one of the most scandalous questions dogging Bob Singer's murder trial: namely, whether Judi Singer and Bill Melcher had been having an affair. Someone had photocopied fifteen cards and letters that were so explicitly amorous as to rule out any doubt that the affair had taken place.

The package included a typed note to me, saying the "Voices" had been following Judi's libel suit and thought I'd be interested in the letters.

Well, yes.

This was stunning news, putting Bill Melcher and Judi in the worst possible light. How could Bill, in love with Bob Singer's wife, not have been conflicted over defending his client from the death penalty? And what a liar Judi had been by posing as such a devoted, loyal wife.

Alone in the bureau office, I put my feet up on the desk and spent the next hour reading, gasping, and laughing in unapologetic delight. Judi's suit had been the most humiliating setback of my life and had certainly cost me the

Mexico job. But this sure looked like the end of it. How, after all, could a judge value Judi's reputation at millions of dollars after reading lines like these:

You are so very easy to be with. Easy to talk to, laugh with, listen to, be quiet with, sleep with, be naked with, dress with, eat with .... And loving you is the most glorious duet of all: Touching, holding—skin on skin, mouth on mouth— quiet, frantic, peaceful, abandoned, giving, demanding, gentle, fierce—and always knowing when and what is right. We even make fuck, cock and cunt sound like endearments. (Did I actually write those words?) Lying together in such peaceful contentment that we're able to drift into sleep with you still inside of me, touching me like I've never been touched before .... That's not just sex, baby ....

Judi's missives spanned the length of her romance with Bill, from its flirtatious beginning in the summer of 1981 to its apparently sour end the next year. They began with a series of colorful greeting cards, featuring pictures of raccoons, turkeys, and frogs. Judi, as I noted with a brief tightening in my chest, had embellished several of the cards with a little smiley face, just like my mother—and Andy Granger—liked to do.

In one of her notes, Judi thanked Bill for books he'd given her, remarking that his "Posture is Power" article was "super ... I was particularly interested in the theory of strategic use of space around the jury.... establishing a 'sensitive spot' for 'smoking-gun' moments." In another, she offered her husband's attorney an "exclusive on my body." In yet another, she joked that she had told doctors at the Stanford University Medical Center that she needed her "Melcher Miracle Injections."

Judi even tried her hand at a limerick, writing:

There once was a Princess from Flint.

She had in her eyes a big glint
For a Cowboy named Bill
Who gives her such a thrill
When he's near, she feels like a mint ...

Well, that explains the Urban Cowboy pin, I thought.

The letters contained several references to Bob Singer's two murder trials. In one, Judi made fun of Jack Marshall's references to mother hens and mama bears.

"My darling, as our "Animal Friends" might say," she began:

You make my

quill quiver beak blister
hump hatch hindquarters heat
wings wiggle paws prickle
hooves howl antennas [sic] activate
tail tingle haunches hustle
antlers atrophy snout sparkle
trunk thump pouch puff.

Judi's mischievous tone vanished, however, as her letters continued through the spring of 1982, during Bob's second trial. At one point, after Bill returned from a family vacation in Hawaii, she reproached him for not sending her "even a rotten postcard." In another, she begged him not to quit Bob's case, assuring him that she had raised twenty-five-thousand dollars in promises of cash.

"The last couple of weeks have been among the most difficult weeks I've spent in my life," Judi wrote, adding:

I have pushed, shoved, and begged people in order to raise whatever funds possible. I have swallowed much, lost all remaining traces of my pride, and basically laid myself wide open ... I am at a total standstill. No one has cash .... I have no place to turn .... It is YOUR case, you know. It goes without saying, too, that you can try this case again with one hand tied behind your back. It would not be flattery for me to tell you that we consider you the finest criminal mind available to us anywhere .... Who else could possibly attack these creeps on the stand as you do—with real insight into what you need to get out of them?

"Please know that everyone here is counting on you," Judi pleaded:

So many times, you've said, "Just leave it to Uncle Bill"—and we all have .... You know how impossible it would be to replace you—no one else is as good, and no one even adequate would look at this with us still owing you so much money.

We need you—more than you can ever imagine. Please know that I've done everything possible and a little bit of the impossible too. I feel debased and dirty and I have no more to offer—unless you're interested in book rights, further time waivers, or a large percentage of the *Mercury News* "winnings" ....

On reading this last line, I loudly cleared my throat. I'd been skimming over everything that showed how pathetic and desperate Judi had become, but I stopped at that line about *Mercury News* "winnings." There it was: proof of how coldheartedly she had been trying to take advantage of the newspaper, and my stupid error, to try to make a profit. Did I need any more evidence of her depravity?

Despite Bill's agreement to stick it out through Bob's second trial, what looked like the nadir of his relationship with Judi was documented in a letter dated October 10, 1981, four months before the trial began. Judi, who'd so long managed to maintain such admirable poise, let loose some unladylike rage.

She began by complaining that Bill had cancelled a plan to spend the night with her in San Jose. "Suddenly ... you've got to keep on 'working,'" she wrote, adding:

That's bullshit and we both know it .... Give me more credit and some other reason, Bill—that one, and the uncaring manner in which it was delivered, were too much for me to swallow ... Are you trying to reject me so continuously that I finally start destroying us too? Would it be that distasteful to spend the night here ... is it that unpleasant and unfulfilling ...?

Your choice, each time you need to make one, seems to be against any nurturing of the joys of Bill and Judi. I feel rejected .... I also feel cheap and debased. I am a valuable person, my friend .... Yet, you've assumed the posture of making me feel valueless—as a person, and most particularly as a woman .... Couldn't you just join me in grabbing good times together whenever we can? Please stop fighting me ... I do still get 'breathless' close to you ... together we're an amazing team."

I gathered up the letters and walked down the hall to the photocopier, where I made copies to send to our lawyer and the city editor in San Jose. This certainly seemed like important news, assuming we could verify the documents and maybe also identify the "Voices of Truth." An affair between Judi and Bob Singer's lawyer, while he was supposedly trying to save Bob's life? *Talk about making monkeys out of men!*

I wished I could write the story on the letters, although I knew I had to hand it off. The documentary evidence aside, anyone who knew about Judi's suit against me could have assumed I was too involved in the story to be neutral about this new development. And they'd be right: Every time I thought about Judi's name on those pages I felt joyful, as if watching the sun burst through clouds. How often is any hidden truth revealed that clearly?

20

It took more than two years of regular appointments with Dr. Y before I could talk meaningfully about my mother. And as soon as I did, I felt like a miserable snitch. Every time I said something unflattering, I'd remember her girlish voice on the phone, the way she always encouraged me to tell her my problems, and how she'd tell me hers, and how she'd cry over stories she'd just read in the *New York Times,* about prisoners in crowded cells at Rikers or flood victims in Bangladesh. Many who knew my mother believed she was too good for this world. Most of the time I did, too.

So why was I suddenly having dreams in which she appeared as a flying vampire bat?

"Or a ghoul ...." I muttered, supine on Dr. Y's couch, rolling my eyes to his ceiling.

"What's a ghoul?" he asked, before providing his own answer: "A ghoul is a consumer of human flesh."

I shook my head. *No! My mother was an angel, a martyr, not a fiend.*

I would need more time for those nightmares to make more sense, but I already suspected they had something to do with the strong emotions I'd had while reading Judi Barnett's love letters to Bill Melcher. I couldn't stop thinking about those letters or talking about them with Dr. Y. They vividly revealed a secret side of Judi that was so contrary to the upstanding synagogue-fundraiser-devoted-mom image she'd carefully cultivated. On the page, Judi was grandiose, furious, and desperate, reminding me of my mother's fury, to which I was so often the sole, secret witness.

Under Dr. Y's patient questioning I now tried to remember what my mother had been doing at times when my father was at his worst. I pictured her pouring him a glass of vodka and then catching my eye, signaling her disapproval of his drinking. I recalled how even when she acted like his victim, she'd snipe at him with muttered complaints.

I also heard her voice, over all those years, asking me to sit next to him at dinner when he was drunk and surly, to try to cheer him up, and to forgive his tantrums because he was having problems at work, or worried about one of his boys, or "going through a phase." I remember how scared I'd been that he'd erupt again and hurt someone if I didn't do as she asked.

I knew what my mother would say about this: that my memories were all wrong, that I was too sensitive and maybe a little crazy. After almost every session with Dr. Y I felt the need to go back to my journals to remind myself of what was true. I was also fact-checking on the phone with my psychiatrist brother Jimmy.

Jimmy and I talked for more than an hour on the evening after the "ghoul" session with Dr. Y. Lying on the sofa facing my large picture window in San Francisco, I watched the foggy sky over Golden Gate Park turn first pink, then purple as he told me how his own psychiatrist, an Austrian immigrant, had to coax him to look beyond our father.

"'*Vere* is your *mutter*?'" he imitated him.

"So where was she?"

He paused, then finally said: "She's like The Shadow."

Jimmy liked a lot of arcane stuff, but this time I knew what he meant: It was a reference to an old radio program. "The Shadow?" I asked. "The one that goes: 'Who knows what evil lurks in the hearts of men? The Shadow knows!'"

"He could read minds, right," Jimmy said. "But he also had this other superpower. He could hypnotize other people so they wouldn't see him. He'd say: 'I have the power to cloud men's minds.'"

Neither of us spoke for a minute. Then I laughed softly, although I didn't explain why. I'd always thought *I* was The Shadow. Not the superhero, but that clingy figure from the Robert Louis Stevenson poem. When I was in elementary school, and already unusually anxious, I'd follow my mother around so closely that she sometimes teased: "I have a little shadow that goes in and out with me!"

It didn't make me any less clingy. Whenever she got angry with me—or, as she'd call it, "disappointed"—all her light and warmth would vanish, leaving me frantic. I was so scared I'd lose her for good that I couldn't bear to let her out of my sight.

But now I considered this business of clouding minds. So many times in Dr. Y's office I'd gone blank when I tried to remember certain scenes from my childhood, even scenes I'd recorded in detail.

"It's really frustrating how much I can't remember," I told my brother, not for the first time.

"Maybe you dissociated," Jimmy said. "When you get really stressed, you can sometimes just detach, like leaving your body. You might not even form a memory of what happened."

Had this become a habit? I thought about all those mistakes at work and that unsettling moment when Dr. Y caught me locking his office door. I shut my eyes. I hated to think I could be that much out of control.

Jimmy could tell I was crying and waited on the line. But it was nearly midnight on the East Coast. He had to get up early for work, and this wasn't easy for him either.

"We can keep talking about this," he said softly.

All life on Earth began in water. But more than half a billion years ago, after a long, slow evolution, a pioneer sea creature left its familiar habitat to step onto the land.

I also needed to evolve before I could leave the water I grew up in, or even to understand what it was. It was only after that night on the phone with Jimmy that I seriously asked myself that question in the story about the fish, namely: "What's water?" What was my mother's true nature? Was she a narcissist? Had she made me into one? Why was I always so quick to feel like a victim? And why did I keep comparing my mother to Judi Barnett, when the two were so fundamentally unalike? My mother would never have forgiven me for linking the two of them together. Not in a million years would she have shoplifted or committed adultery. Still, aside from their superficial similarities, the two of them clearly shared at least one crazy-making habit: of pretending things were fine when they so obviously weren't.

On the morning after that phone call with Jimmy I told Dr. Y that I believed my mother had recruited me to help preserve our family's destructive status quo, in which my father was always the bad guy and she was always the victim.

"She makes a monkey out of him, and I hand her the bananas," I said.

"Doesn't it make you feel angry at her?" Dr. Y asked.

My mind went blank again. He waited until I found the words.

"I still can't really feel angry," I said.

My mother depended on me, and I needed her, too. Getting angry at her might mean I'd lose my usefulness as her daughter, and I suppose I also wanted superhero powers. But now I wondered: Could these feelings I didn't want to feel have led to my error in the story about Judi Singer?

Sigmund Freud has often been quoted as saying "There are no accidents," even though as far as I can tell, he never put it in those words. Instead, Freud argued that errors in speech, writing, and reading tend to have meaning, delivering messages from the subconscious. There's that joking definition of a "Freudian slip": "When you mean one thing but say your mother." But had there really been a message behind my slip? Had I smeared an innocent stranger because I couldn't bear to accuse my own mother with a crime—specifically that co-conspiracy in the beating of my brothers? Or was my error only about Judi? Perhaps I had simply subconsciously decided that she had been involved in her husband's murder, and written it that way?

One thing seemed clear: My subconscious wasn't pleased with Dr. Y's increasingly blunt questions. That night I had a vivid dream in which a tall, obese sheriff was threatening me with a tiny gun. Dr. Y was neither tall nor overweight, but we both laughed when I told him about it, after which he asked, unnecessarily: "Who's the sheriff?"

"Yes, this does kind of make me hate you," I said, laughing with him, mostly out of sheer pleasure in my trust that my anger wouldn't make him disappear.

The sheriff image gave us a lot to talk about over the next few weeks. Among other things, it demonstrated how I'd come to look at most men, including my father and Dr. Y, as both threatening and impotent.

For the next several weeks I stopped looking for excuses to cancel our appointments. I also forced myself to pay closer attention to my parents when we were together, taking mental notes as if I were reporting a story.

I was in full reporter mode on the early summer evening that my parents next picked me up in San Francisco to go out for dinner. My mother, as usual, arrived with gifts: a casserole dish full of stuffed peppers she had cooked that afternoon and a new silver belt she thought I'd like. Strapping myself into the back seat of my dad's BMW sedan, I noted the pressure in my chest after his lurching left turn onto Divisadero revealed he'd had a drink or two before they'd left Hillsborough. He seemed irritated about something but didn't say a word as he careened toward Pacific Heights.

We were bound for a cozy Italian restaurant that my mother had read about in the *San Francisco Chronicle*. From the back seat I could see she was wearing a brand-new diamond ring, a special gift from my dad, she told me proudly, to celebrate their upcoming anniversary. The two-carat stone protruded from its thick, white-gold band without a hint of subtlety.

My father dropped us off at the restaurant's front door before veering away to park the car.

"He's in a pretty bad mood, isn't he?" I asked.

"*You* think so? *I* don't think so!"

The moment he reached our table, he flagged down a waiter to order a martini.

"Oh, Ellis," my mother stage-whispered. "Do you really need it?"

He ignored her.

I couldn't think of anything to say.

"*Kathy* thinks you're in a bad mood!" my mother said suddenly. "And I agree."

I cringed in my seat, but my father didn't respond. Instead, he jerked his head toward the kitchen.

"Why's it taking so long?" he asked no one in particular.

He caught the eye of our waiter, a slim, tall man in his thirties, who hustled over to our table.

"What's a guy gotta do to get a drink in this place?" asked my dad, as if he'd invented the line.

The waiter grimaced.

"It's on the way—" he said, turning back toward the kitchen.

"HEY!" my father roared, grabbing the waiter's wrist. He never could tolerate disrespect. But the waiter didn't give him a chance to say so. He shook off my father's hand, sputtering, "You will NOT touch me!" and walked off.

The three of us sat in silence again. I realized I was shaking, as the sound of my father shouting reminded me of all the other times I'd felt that helpless.

But then it hit me that I wasn't eleven years old anymore, and that while there might have been all sorts of explanations for my father's behavior that night, it still wasn't justified.

I turned to my mother and said, "Look, I'm getting a cab home. You're welcome to come with me—"

"Go ahead!" my father bellowed.

"Do you want to come along?" I asked my mother again, forcing my voice to stay low.

She kept her eyes on her plate.

I heard nothing from either of my parents for the next two weeks.

This was a record for me and my mother. In the past I'd always talked her out of the silent treatment within a day or two. This time, despite how much I missed her, I fought the impulse to seek her forgiveness. We were playing chicken, and I won. Sort of. On a morning when my mother knew I'd be at work, she finally broke her silence, leaving a message on my answering machine.

Her voice was shrill.

"You *left me* there to deal with all the—shit!" she said.

I stared at the machine.

She'd come out of the shadows.

21

San Francisco, January 1985

The first time I saw Imelda Marcos was at a rally of several hundred of her supporters in San Francisco in 1982. Tall, regal, and glittering with diamonds, the Filipina strongwoman, wife of the archipelago's dictator, Ferdinand, sang songs in Tagalog to the enraptured crowd of loyalists wolfing down free pizza and chicken adobo in a ballroom at the St. Francis Hotel. The walls muffled the clamor from outside in Union Square, where hundreds of protesters waved placards and shouted: "Marcos is a U.S. puppet!" But Imelda must have heard them on her way in. She paused between songs and whispered throatily into the microphone: "Marcos is not a puppet. He is a puppy dog!"

I had only just begun to pay attention to the story unfolding in the Philippines on that spring evening when my editors assigned me to cover Imelda's visit, but the basics were enough to seduce me. Imelda and her husband, Ferdinand Marcos, had been treasured U.S. Cold War allies since 1965, when Ferdinand first took office with the lovely Imelda as his first lady. Yet in the subsequent two decades, the so-called "conjugal dictatorship" had steadily become more repressive and corrupt, inspiring the first cracks in the alliance. Imelda's visit to California was an attempt to shore up support.

Opposition in and outside the Philippines continued to grow all the same, however, and barely one year after that charming diplomatic offensive, the Marcoses tested the limits of U.S. support when government henchmen gunned down a leading opposition activist, Benigno "Ninoy" Aquino, on his arrival at the Manila airport after a long U.S. exile. Over the next two years, the news from the Philippines became increasingly more intriguing, to the point where in the spring of 1985, already bored in the San Francisco bureau, I made another Hail Mary pass and typed up a memo to my editors, urging them to consider a series of stories that would look more closely at the Marcoses and their links to the United States. I attempted to justify my role with the thin argument that there were a lot of Filipinos in the San Francisco area.

What I didn't know then was that the *Mercury News* had already started work on a series of stories that within another year would make history in the United States and the Philippines. The newspaper had recently opened a bureau in Tokyo, hiring as its chief a veteran foreign correspondent named Lew Simons. Lew had excellent sources in Asia and was starting to scout rumors that the Marcoses and their cronies for years had been siphoning money out of the country and into overseas bank accounts and real estate, especially in the United States and Canada. Soon after the Aquino assassination, Lew and his editor, Jonathan Krim, resolved to try to document these investments. Jonathan brought in Pete Carey, the paper's star investigative reporter, to join the effort.

Once I found out about the project underway, I nervously waited to hear if I might be part of it. I had some reasons for hope. My recent reporting trips to Central America and Africa had impressed my editors, while, to our huge relief that year, a judge had dismissed Judi's libel suit on the grounds that she had stopped pursuing it. It felt as if someone had loosened a band around my neck.

The Philippines investigation, if the paper took it on, would be legally sensitive, with no room for blunders. Knowing that made me even more happy when, a few weeks later, I was pulled onto it. For an unspecified time, which would turn out to be more than six months, Lew, Pete, and I would be freed from our assigned beats to focus entirely on the Philippines.

Lew developed and tracked leads in the Philippines and other parts of Asia while Pete and I made contacts with Filipinos in San Francisco, San Jose, and Los Angeles. We shared leads and hunted for evidence from sources and documents of financial and real-estate holdings by the Marcoses and their top enablers and cohorts, who had concealed much of the information via shell companies, frontmen, and overseas relatives.

By early February of 1985 our search widened to Washington, D.C., and New York City, as Pete and I checked real estate records and met with lawyers and State Department officials. In San Jose, a secretive high-level Marcos fixer who'd gotten wind of the project approached us and offered to be our "Deep Throat." He met with us in a small, spare office that had no sign on the door, and to our amazement agreed to provide information about his bosses' investments on condition that we keep his name out of the paper.

Among other things, the fixer led me to a San Francisco attorney who was also in the business of hiding assets for the Marcoses and friends. He insisted on meeting me for lunch at the Commercial Club, a plush private men's dining room in the Financial District. After his third gin and tonic, while he tried to play footsie with me under the table, he boasted that he held fifty-million dollars' worth of Filipino-owned property in his name, which he could sell at any time, if he wanted to. "I just wouldn't," he said, "because they trust me." I smiled at him encouragingly while moving my chair just out of reach, and at my first opportunity ran to the phone to share his information with Pete.

Our "Deep Throat" also helped us track down another paper millionaire, this time in New York City, where Imelda's private secretary, Vilma H. Bautista, was listed as the registered agent for two luxury condos. When Pete reached her on the phone, she readily confirmed that she worked for Imelda yet politely claimed to know nothing about the condos. "There are so many names; there are so many phone numbers," she told him, adding, "This could be another Vilma H. Bautista!"

Pete and I cackled together about these encounters as we worked late into the evenings in the San Jose newsroom. It was almost always fun, even though we sometimes argued so loudly that other reporters dubbed us "The Bickersons," a reference to a 1940s radio comedy about a squabbling married couple.

In his rumpled plaid shirt and with his wild, contagious laugh, Pete was the trustworthy antithesis of my image of men as sheriffs with tiny guns. We worked together as equals, appreciating each other's talents and cheering each other on, although I privately feared I could never match his skills. Long before most newspapers realized the benefits of mining databases, Pete could have taught classes in how to do it.

Early on, Pete tracked down our Rosetta Stone—perhaps the only document existing to name either one of the Marcoses as owning a U.S. property. It was part of a sealed lawsuit concerning a dispute over a thirteen-acre waterfront estate, known as Lindenmere, in Center Moriches, New York, and it said that Imelda owned that property along with several New York City buildings.

Seeing Imelda's name on that page gave me the same jolt as reading Judi Barnett's illicit love letters. I was also impressed that it was Imelda, rather than her husband, who was now exposed as a primary actor in their financial scheme, even as she had so scrupulously built up her image as Ferdinand's innocent arm candy. This, too, reminded me of Judi.

The feminist activist Gloria Steinem famously called Marilyn Monroe a "female impersonator," a term that also seemed to fit the Filipina first lady. Imelda put a lot of work into maintaining her doll-like image, wearing traditional gowns with butterfly sleeves, with her hair, face, and nails always flawless. One of her gaggle of women friends, the so-called "Blue Ladies," told me she routinely woke after midnight each night to reapply her makeup.

Our opposition sources painted a sinister image of the woman behind this façade, insisting that Imelda's property purchases and notorious binges of spending on handbags and shoes were the least of her sins. Imelda, they said, was the evil power behind the Marcos throne: a hard-liner responsible for many of the atrocities against dissidents over the years. The Marcoses had reportedly murdered and "disappeared" more than thirty-two hundred political opponents, while torturing and jailing tens of thousands more. The mutilated bodies of dissidents were dumped in public places to spread fear.

Imelda was also rumored to have lobbied her husband to give the orders to murder Ninoy Aquino. She and Aquino had dated in their twenties, but he'd jilted her and she'd hated him ever since, our sources said.

After Pete discovered the Lindenmere document, our editors realized our series might be a good candidate for a Pulitzer. Other newspapers were starting to chase the story, but we were far ahead. Our stories were scheduled to be published early that summer, and we felt sure they would have impact both in Washington, D.C., and Manila.

Every so often, Pete and I speculated about our chances to win that top prize, and what we'd give to have it happen.

"I'd let someone chop my little finger off if it made any difference," I told him. "Although I'm not sure if I'd give an index finger." On the other hand, I thought, a person could probably live a fine life without an index finger.

Even without the possibility of big awards, the Philippines series was by far the most exciting project I'd ever been involved in. I threw myself into the work every day, so much that it surprised me when I later looked back at my journals to find how little I'd written about Ferdinand and Imelda Marcos compared to all the pages about Dr. Y and Jack.

Jack had never received my angry breakup letter, or so he said on his return from his travels in early 1984. My resolve to stop seeing him had quickly faded in the rare pleasure of his company, and we were soon back to spending most of every weekend together, either in his Berkeley crawl space or my apartment in the Haight. We lay together in his bed or mine on Sunday mornings, reading the *San Francisco Chronicle* and *New York Times*, brunched at the Homemade Cafe diner in Berkeley, took walks in Tilden Park, and went to matinees.

Every once in a while I'd catch myself thinking that I shouldn't necessarily rule out babies. That was ridiculous, of course. Jack still wasn't interested in ever having children; I still didn't feel any irresistible tug, and I was doing all I could to build a career that would make motherhood all but impossible.

On the other hand, I was nearly twenty-eight and had been trained to meet deadlines. Soon I'd have to decide where I wanted my life to lead. I didn't want to be a mother to please my parents or conform to some antiquated social convention. But I also didn't want *not* to be one out of a lack of self-confidence or fear, or a blind determination to do the opposite of what my mother had done. I intellectualized ad nauseam about this essentially non-intellectual decision because deep down I still had no idea what I felt.

"What gives someone the confidence to have a child, anyway?" I nagged Dr. Y. "Why would someone like *Judi Singer* be able to, while I can't even imagine it?"

Judi, despite everything, had always seemed so proud and fulfilled by motherhood. I envied what I supposed had to be her patience and faith, when I couldn't even keep houseplants alive. The patience-and-faith problem had become a central topic in my sessions with Dr. Y, although at that point I was still mostly complaining about why I doubted I could ever write a book.

"You may not be ready right now," he said. "That doesn't mean you never will be, if that's what you want to do."

As much as I'd grown to trust Dr. Y, I questioned his confidence that one day I'd know what I wanted, and that more conversations with him would help get me there. I seemed to be backtracking more than ever. As much as I loved spending time with Jack, I kept hearing my mother's voice asking why I hadn't gotten a more prestigious job or had babies, like my sister had done—while in medical school. And if I did want babies, shouldn't I be investing my time in recruiting a more eligible mate, one who earned a good living, truly wanted to be a dad, and hadn't left me to get mugged while he was drinking cappuccinos on the Ponte Vecchio?

"Right, so Jack is like the *San Jose Mercury News* of boyfriends, isn't he?" joked Dr. Y.

Awful as it is to remember that today, he had a point. Because even while spending all that happy time with Jack I was also still seeing the lawyer I'd met while he was on the road. Like the way I'd gone back, as soon as the lawsuit was over, to using the *Mercury News'* photocopier to send copies of my stories to more prestigious newspapers.

I never failed to miss Jack when I was with the lawyer, but I told myself, in my mother's voice, to keep an open mind. The lawyer was smart, witty, and wealthy, and seemed to be falling in love with me. He was also chivalrous in a way Jack never was, always picking up the checks and opening the car door for me. A lot of the time, Jack wanted me to drive. I pictured vacations with the lawyer in nice hotels in Mexico, with our two perfect kids playing in the sand, along with a nanny or two. I'd be reading a novel under an umbrella, not a worry on my mind. I didn't tell Jack or the lawyer that I wasn't seeing either one of them exclusively; they just assumed that was true. The lawyer was particularly easy to fool: he worked so many weekends that he didn't seem to mind that I also had so little free time.

Our investigative series: "Hidden Billions: The Draining of the Philippines," was published in June 1985, and, just as we'd hoped, it made waves. Newspapers in Manila reprinted our stories on their front pages; major U.S. newspapers followed our leads, and lawmakers in the U.S. and Philippines launched investigations. Now I was reporting mainly on the fallout from our revelations. Over the next year, I'd make eight trips to the Philippines to cover the rapidly building, newly energized opposition to the Marcoses. In the fall of that year, under pressure at home and from his U.S. patrons, Ferdinand Marcos called for an early presidential election on February 7, 1986. His opponent would be Corazon "Cory" Aquino, the widow of the slain activist. Marcos was confident that the so-called "snap" election would confirm his popularity—even if he had to steal thousands of ballots in the process.

While Marcos was scheming in Manila, I finally, out of the blue, got the break I'd dreamed of for the past five years. The Metro editor at the *Los Angeles Times* called to offer me a job in the newspaper's San Diego bureau. He flew me down for a full day of interviews, including lunch at a chic downtown restaurant. That night I stayed at the five-star Omni Hotel, at the *Times'* expense, drinking minibar champagne in a bubble bath.

"I can just see it," I told Dr. Y on my return.

What I saw, specifically, was me on the terrace of a house with a view of the ocean. I'd be spending a lot of time on the beach while also throwing myself into work, earning a lot more money, and telling sources that I worked for a newspaper known and respected throughout the world. The Times had more than a dozen foreign bureaus, as the Metro editor had reminded me. Maybe instead of Mexico City I could report from Beijing or Jerusalem.

In the year since I'd walked out on the dinner with my parents, leaving my mother to deal with "the shit," she and I had gradually settled back into our old, warm relationship, including talking on the phone every day. She didn't want me to move away, she said, but she sounded excited as she described her friends' response to news of my prestigious offer. "I'm so proud of you!" she told me.

On the morning after that call, I phoned the Metro editor to accept. For the next ten hours I remained convinced that getting hired by the *Los Angeles Times* would make me happy.

But that night I couldn't sleep. All I could think about was everything I'd be giving up by leaving the Bay Area. Jack didn't want to move. He'd grown up in Los Angeles but loved living in Berkeley. I'd also have to stop reporting on the Philippines, a story that was getting bigger and better all the time. I'd be saying goodbye to San Francisco and the apartment I adored. And I'd be leaving Dr. Y, who said he thought I still had important work to do.

He reminded me that working for the *Los Angeles Times* wasn't going to magically fill my empty insides or settle the questions of whether I'd ever be able to have a healthy marriage or know if I wanted babies or to move beyond daily reporting.

"I think you should stay here," he said. "I believe in you. And I am committed to this process."

Once again, I turned around on the couch. It sure seemed like he was once again stepping over the line. And as I'd learn from Dr. Y many years later, that's also how Bruno Bettelheim saw it. He scolded his supervisee for yielding to his "countertransference"—getting emotionally entangled with a patient. By that time, however, I'd decided that the ends justified the means. I needed his unorthodox push. Turning down the *Times* would be completely opposed to the way I'd lived my life up to that moment.

Two days later I called the *Los Angeles Times* editor to say I couldn't take the job after all—at least not just then. I blamed it on the Philippines story, which was partly true. The project might win a Pulitzer; how could I duck out now?

He sounded surprised and annoyed. He wasn't used to being turned down by farm-club reporters, and up to that moment I'd seemed nothing but thrilled by his offer. "I have no doubt of your talent, but I do have some questions about your stability," he told me frostily.

That stung as much as he meant for it to do, but I figured I might as well make the most of it. When I told my editors that I'd turned down the *Los Angeles Times*, I got a raise and another promise that they'd seriously consider me for the Mexico job when it reopened in another year or two.

22

San Jose, August 1985

The *Mercury News* editors, with the caution they had shown
ever since Judi's lawsuit, waited several months after
receiving Judi's love letters to publish excerpts of them, and
only did so then after they'd become part of a larger story.
In the spring of 1984, around the same time as I received
my "Voices of Truth" packet, Bob Singer got his own set of
photocopied letters, along with this note:

We are not writing you to cause you distress: we are
writing you to enlighten you to the TRUTH. Are you aware
of the torrid love affair between your attorney and so-called
friend, Bill Melcher, and your wife? Ask them about their
sexual activities .... Ask them about waking up with each
other in the morning, while your ass stayed parked in jail ....
After all, you do have a right to know the truth about your
wife and her lover—your attorney. The attorney who was
supposed to be your "friend." Some friend. Fucking your
wife. Fucking you over ....

Bob immediately wrote to Bill Melcher to demand an
explanation. Bill responded just as quickly, telling Bob that
he'd also received copies of the letters, which he swore were
fakes.

"We both (you and I) developed enemies in some rather unlikely places during and immediately after the trial," Bill wrote. He added that he'd reported the matter to "federal law enforcement agencies," who were planning a "sting" to trap the sender, "and, due to this, they are maintaining strict secrecy."

Bob didn't reply. His trust in Bill had finally disappeared. What's more, once he got over his outrage at the proof of his wife's unfaithfulness, he suspected Judi's letters might be helpful to him, as he prepared an appeal of his murder conviction. With support from his father, Bob had hired one of San Francisco's most celebrated defense lawyers: Patrick "Butch" Hallinan. Hallinan was the son of a local legend: Vincent Hallinan, a defense attorney who had run for president in 1952 for the Progressive Party. With a brashness that apparently ran in the family, Vincent Hallinan had also sued the Catholic Church for fraud, demanding that it prove the existence of heaven and hell. In the 1960s, Patrick Hallinan had made his own name defending activists including Eldridge Cleaver and the Soledad brothers.

Bob sent Judi's love letters to Hallinan, who immediately recognized their value. He filed a motion contending that Judi and Bill's affair had created a conflict of interest that deprived Bob of his right to effective legal counsel. Consciously or unconsciously, the defense attorney's judgment had been compromised, Hallinan argued. He might have purposely avoided investigating the murder for fear of turning up something harmful to Judi or her relatives. He might even have schemed to lose the case in order to eliminate his rival. And even if none of this were true, Hallinan wrote, Bill had betrayed his client with his adultery and lies, adding, "Mr. Singer would have sent Mr. Melcher to hell in a bucket if he had known he was sleeping with his wife."

In fact, Bill Melcher was *still* lying to Bob. He knew who'd sent him and Bob those photocopied letters, under the alias of the "Voices of Truth." He'd recognized the vengeful tone of the note that had accompanied his packet.

"It is time, finally, for sweet, SWEET RETRIBUTION," it read, adding "Be prepared to lose sleep .... The worse you feel, the better we feel."

Bill knew he'd made some enemies over the years. But as he'd later acknowledge in court, there was only one person who hated him this much. He figured that the "Voices of Truth" mastermind had to be Leslie Bennett, the secretary he'd fired in 1982—and the one he called "Fat Leslie." Just as the Cupertino psychic had predicted, a "fat lady" had shown up to intimidate him.

Soon after receiving his "Voices of Truth" letters, Bill Melcher wrote to Leslie, addressing her as "Fatso" and threatening to report her to the police. She never answered him, but nor did she drop her campaign. A few weeks later, she also revealed her identity to Bob Singer's lawyers.

Fay Imamura, a junior lawyer in Patrick Hallinan's office, had scheduled what she had assumed would be a routine interview with Bill Melcher's former secretary to collect background information on him, when Leslie surprised her by sliding a package across the table between them. It contained yet another set of copies of Judi Barnett's love letters.

Leslie told Fay that she had known Bill planned to fire her in early 1982. While Bill was in San Jose for Bob Singer's second trial, she took the opportunity to prowl through his desk drawers in hopes of finding something she might one day use against him. She couldn't believe her luck when she found the letters.

She used the office photocopier to make several sets of copies, and a few months later, after Bill demanded she turn in her keys, she began to plot her campaign.

Bill was unfit to be a lawyer for reasons that went beyond his love affair with Judi, Leslie told Fay. She'd watched him treat his clients terribly, calling them "assholes" and sometimes even hiding in his office to avoid meeting with them. He had also fallen out with his legal associates. A spat with his famous colleague, Vincent Bugliosi, led to Bill having to leave their shared office suite, but before he did, he'd vandalized the room, defacing a painting with liquid typewriter correction fluid, drawing lines depicting a man urinating.

Leslie told Fay that she felt afraid of Bill's reaction if she were to accuse him in public. Still, if they truly needed her, she said, she was ready to testify.

Six more years would pass before I'd be able to reconstruct these events. By then I'd also be curious about Jack Marshall's reaction when he first read Patrick Hallinan's petition and realized that the Singer case was coming back to haunt him, after two trials and four years.

When I spoke to Jack in 1991, he compared the experience to a scene from his all-time favorite movie, *Zulu*. The 1960s film tells the story of how undermanned British forces in South Africa in the nineteenth century tried to defend their mission from Zulu warriors. In the movie's climactic scene, after a couple hundred British soldiers have been fighting off thousands of Zulu warriors for an entire day, the Zulus have finally retreated, leaving the besieged British to tend their wounded. But then one of the officers, played by Michael Caine, looks up toward a nearby ridge and sees the silhouetted ranks of a new, enormous, advancing horde.

"Oh my God," says Caine.

"Oh my God," Jack told me he said to himself, as he scanned Hallinan's documents, alone at his desk.

Propping his head in his hand as he read, he tried but failed to find a reason to stay calm. As he neared his fiftieth birthday, Jack had prosecuted twenty murder cases, winning all but a couple of them. Never before had an appeals court reversed one of his convictions. Yet now he feared his good record would be ruined for reasons beyond his control. If an appeals court accepted Patrick Hallinan's argument, the DA's office would either have to try Bob Singer for murder for a third time or release him.

Patrick Hallinan had done his work well. The petition carefully detailed major differences in the ways Bill Melcher had handled Bob Singer's first murder trial versus the retrial that began after he'd started his affair with Judi. He'd spent six days and called twenty-three witnesses during that first trial, compared with two days and five witnesses in the second.

The motion included copies of Judi's cards and letters plus a five-page declaration by Bob Singer, written earlier that month from his cell in San Quentin. Bob's tone was characteristically self-pitying. After once again insisting on his innocence, he complained of how he'd been victimized by his lawyer. Bill had "stunned" him, he wrote, during the second trial, when he advised him that neither he nor Judi should testify. Bob had gone along with that, he wrote, because he trusted Bill completely. "I placed my fate and my life in his hands." Only after learning of the affair did he understand Bill's betrayal. "I believe he and Judi may have wished to see me convicted," he bitterly added, "or even put to death."

Jack Marshall knew he didn't have to answer Bob's petition himself if he didn't want to. He'd recently been promoted to homicide team leader and was mostly supervising other attorneys. At the same time, however, he felt like this was still his case. His personal Zulu horde.

He dutifully cleared some time from his schedule, but each time he sat down to work on a response to the petition, he was overcome by lassitude. The legal challenge posed by Singer's petition was theoretically fascinating but Jack soon realized he'd rather do almost anything than research it. No sooner would he sit down with a book but he'd be picking up his phone to call a friend or colleague or wandering down the hall on vague scouting missions for coffee or pens or notebooks. He was also repeatedly distracted by other attorneys in the office who kept dropping by in hopes he'd let them read Judi's letters.

After three weeks of this, Jack had to admit he needed help, and recruited a young deputy, Lane Liroff, to share the work.

The two prosecutors soon agreed that if they wanted to keep Bob Singer in jail, they'd have to forge a new, pragmatic relationship with their former opponent, Bill Melcher. And Bill was only too eager to join forces. Within a week of their first meeting, he supplied his new allies with a thirty-nine-page memo outlining his view of the case.

Bob Singer, Bill now declared, was indeed guilty of plotting Howard Witkin's murder. And Bill would be only too happy to provide evidence to show it. Just to start, he could show them Bob's signature on an invoice for a Western Union money transfer that had been sent to the triggerman, Andy Granger. Under his previous assumption of Bob's innocence, Bill had paid for a handwriting analysis that he expected would help exonerate his client, he said. But the expert confirmed the signature was Bob's.

Furthermore, Bill wrote, during Bob's second trial Bob and Judi had paid for his "surprise witness," Mitchell Henderson, to lie for Bob on the stand. Bill claimed he didn't know about the payment until after Henderson testified.

Most importantly, the attorney insisted he'd never had an affair with Judi. He described the allegations as a purposeful ruse, something Judi and Bob had planned all along. If Bob were convicted, they could use the presumed conflict of interest as their "fail-safe" option, he claimed. And Judi, he said, was fully capable of carrying out such a deception. Ignoring the fact that he'd touted her, three years earlier, as an "extremely intelligent and multitalented" future law partner, Bill now described Judi as "vicious," "conniving," "manipulative," and "an accomplished liar."

Bill's disclosures shocked the prosecutors. Neither of them had ever before seen a lawyer so eager to betray his clients' trust. But they had to ignore their revulsion, since to win their case they had to do their best to protect his reputation.

Their written response to Patrick Hallinan's petition made no mention of Bill's allegations. Their argument, instead, was simple: Judi's love letters to Bill weren't enough to prove that an affair had occurred. And even if it had, there was no evidence that it had compromised Bill's professional behavior.

To their disappointment, however, the appellate court disagreed. The justices stopped short of overturning Bob's conviction, but sent the case back to the Santa Clara County Superior Court for a hearing on an unprecedented question: Had a love affair robbed a convicted murderer of his right to a fair trial?

23

Manila, February 1986

While San Jose prosecutors struggled to stave off a third murder trial for Bob Singer, I was repeatedly yanked back to the Philippines. More than once I left for home after a three-week reporting trip only to be sent back again, just a few days later—and once, even the next day—after the story took another surprising turn.

That's how I found myself running through the halls of Malacanang Palace in the humid early morning hours of Tuesday, February 25, 1986. Less than three hours earlier, Ferdinand and Imelda Marcos, with their children and entourage, had been whisked off to Guam in a U.S. military helicopter, ending their twenty-year rule.

In the two weeks following the "snap" presidential elections, which Marcos unsurprisingly claimed to have won, international monitors exposed his massive attempted fraud. Factions of the military deserted to support Cory Aquino. Hundreds of thousands of protesters clad in yellow, the opposition color, rallied in the streets as Aquino called for a national strike. U.S. congressmembers again voiced their concern.

I'd left San Francisco with Jim Gensheimer, a *Mercury News* photographer, late the evening of February 23 for what we assumed would be a fourteen-hour nonstop Philippines

Airlines flight. But the plane stopped in Honolulu where we were told we couldn't go on because of "the political situation." Jim and I were stuck for about twelve hours, as we tried to figure out if any other airlines would take us, until our PAL flight finally took off. Just before we landed, the pilot announced the news about the Marcoses fleeing the palace. "We have a new president: President Cory Aquino!" he added. Several passengers applauded, and I wanted to join them. It just seemed like such a clear, rare triumph of good over evil.

On our arrival, Jim had to wait for his equipment at the baggage department. I ran on ahead, grabbing a cab and arriving at the palace just as a crowd of sweating, rifle-bearing soldiers was entering the grounds. The soldiers seemed panicked and confused. A couple times they asked me what I was doing there but then got too distracted to follow up.

Other soldiers had just finished clearing out tens of thousands of celebrating Filipinos and most likely also some Manila-based reporters who had poured into the white colonnaded mansion immediately after the Marcoses' departure. Some were still hanging around outside, lighting small bonfires on the lawn and spearing frogs in the ponds. The sumptuous palace was a mess, with documents strewn all over the floors, and some still stuffed in a paper shredder. I knew I had limited time before I'd get kicked out too and was scribbling notes as fast as I could, while picking up whatever papers looked interesting, although I failed to find anything newsworthy. I knew both my editors and I would be miserable if another reporter got to them first, and indeed we gnashed our teeth the next day, after the *Washington Post* described a document that had been "tucked in a drawer" containing handwritten receipts showing Imelda had spent the equivalent of forty-nine-thousand dollars in a single day at various antique shops in a northern province.

Jim, the photographer, met me after a short time, and before we got kicked out managed to document evidence of some of the Marcoses' most jealously guarded secrets: the president's failing health and the couple's extravagant lifestyle. A hospital bed, four cots, and several trays of drugs and medical supplies lay in a hidden room that clearly had belonged to the former president. I also saw a dialysis machine and diapers in the master bedroom.

"It's a gold mine!" I babbled, showing Jim around.

Still, somehow we and other reporters missed seeing what would later become the biggest news sensation of all. Some weeks after Cory Aquino took office as the Philippines' new president, government officials would reveal that while inventorying Imelda's quarters, they had found what at first reports were three-thousand pairs of designer shoes—an estimate later scaled down to just over a thousand—in addition to five-hundred black brassieres and five shelves of brand-new Gucci handbags. When I returned to Manila later that year with *Mercury News* photographer Karen Borchers, we got permission to spend a couple hours in those rooms. Karen photographed several tall shelves stacked with the extravagant footwear: a standing parade of sandals, pumps, and boots, in every imaginable color and texture, including leathers, suedes, snakeskins, and rhinestones. My favorite was a translucent plastic sandal with a three-inch, battery-powered flashing heel.

I couldn't help but think of my mother as I walked past the rows and rows of the all brands she fetishized: Ferragamos, Bruno Maglis, Oleg Cassinis. She couldn't hold a candle to Imelda as a shopper. But both of them sure loved those trophy shoes.

The continuing revelations from Imelda's closets were another chance to peer behind an audacious facade. It was just like reading Judi Barnett's love letters. Imelda had kept her mask on to the very end, and while *Rolling Stone* magazine had recently described her as "crazy as a rat in a coffee can," I wondered whether her goofy frivolity had been an act, and a good one.

Three months earlier, she had summoned me to the palace for an interview in which she promised to answer all the charges in our series. Diamonds sparkled on her neck and wrists as we sat facing each other at a small table. Behind her was a life-size portrait portraying her stepping out of a clamshell, swathed in mist, a la Botticelli's *Birth of Venus*. "Money has never been my obsession," she told me, with a straight face. "All I ever wanted was a little home with a little picket fence by the sea."

She dismissed the reports of her property holdings as "character assassination," assuring me that "whatever little modest wealth we've had has been put into the Marcos Foundation to serve deprived children who want a better education."

When I pressed her about the Lindenmere estate, Imelda simply shook her head with a sweet smile. She urged me instead to consider the Philippines' strategic importance to the United States, after which she spent the next twenty minutes of our forty-minute interview sketching a map to bring her point home. Ignoring my increasingly anxious attempts to change the subject, she slowly and laboriously drew the Philippine archipelago as if it were in the center of the world, surrounded by nations whose names she patiently recorded: China, the United States, Indonesia, Pakistan, Uruguay, Argentina, and Brazil. As she continued drawing, over my protests—India, Canada, South Africa, Libya—I realized that our interview was over.

We ultimately did get the goods on Imelda and Ferdinand, however, as the Pulitzer judges confirmed the following April of 1986. Ours was the first Pulitzer won by the *Mercury News* in its 135-year history. Other reporters toasted me and Pete and our editor Jonathan Krim with champagne and then pushed us into the fountain in front of the paper's main office. Our editors celebrated with a manic spending spree, hosting several dinner parties and booking the four of us (including Lew, flown in from Tokyo) at the Algonquin Hotel when we flew to New York to accept the award. New York's U.S. Representative Stephen Solarz read a statement in Congress declaring that we'd contributed to "the triumph over tyranny" in the Philippines. Half a dozen newspapers and TV stations called to interview us. Emails and calls came in from literary agents urging each of us to write a book.

The *Los Angeles Times* editor called me to apologize for having questioned my stability—the award having apparently confirmed my sound mental health—and offered me another job. *Time Magazine* flew me to New York and proposed sending me to head their bureau in Atlanta. In New York, I met with a literary agent who encouraged me to write a book about Imelda.

That last idea enticed me. Maybe I was perversely drawn to narcissists. But I also wanted to know more about what makes people behave that atrociously. Unsurprisingly, Imelda had had a miserable childhood: a depressed and manipulative mother, a father who was less successful than the rest of his clan. While she wasn't dirt poor, she grew up thinking of herself that way, which she compared to being naked—"Every drop of rain you feel. A little of the wind that blows, you feel." She'd certainly be fun to write about, with her colorful quotes and excesses, but she also seemed to offer a useful cautionary tale about how destructive insecure people can be.

I met with the literary agent for two hours at her luxurious home office near Riverside Park, after which we agreed that she would send me a contract. Later that evening I went to a party with Sarah, my old Newsweek secretary friend, where we ran into Jimmy Breslin, the famous *New York Daily News* columnist, who had just won his own Pulitzer Prize for commentary. "When you go back to your paper you can really bullshit 'em now," he coached me. "Be real snotty." I'd always thought that winning a Pulitzer would magically give me that kind of confidence and was surprised to find it didn't. This made more sense when I later learned that many scientists believe there are two kinds of narcissists: "grandiose" and "vulnerable." You find the grandiose traits in people like Kim Kardashian and Donald Trump, who seem convinced of their own wonderfulness. The vulnerable ones are just as needy of attention but are sneakier about it (some experts even call them "covert"). One researcher told me he saw vulnerable narcissists as similar to George Costanza in the *Seinfeld* TV series: thin-skinned but with low self-esteem. Granted, personalities aren't black and white, and some people swing from grandiose to vulnerable on a regular basis. But if I truly was narcissistic, I knew I was a lot more like George Costanza than Donald Trump. I couldn't imagine George or I ever pulling off "snotty." And while the prize opened doors, it didn't make me a better negotiator or even help me choose between all my new options.

The literary agent's contract arrived in the mail five days after our meeting but stayed unopened on my desk for the next three weeks. The *Los Angeles Times* job I'd been offered was no easier to deal with: The editor wanted me to run its bureau in San Bernardino, reporting on a smoggy, bland stretch of Southern California known as the Inland Empire. A *Mercury News* editor in whom I'd confided tried to show me what a bad move it would be by printing out a San Bernardino story from that day's wire-service reporting. It described how a truck full of chickens had capsized on the highway. "The Inland Empire!" he snorted.

Jack and I drove down to explore, making widening circles around the office to see where we might want to live before agreeing there was nowhere. After turning this job down, I suspected I'd never hear from the *Times* editor again, and I was right.

When I broached a move to Atlanta, my new literary agent sneered: "They fry their coleslaw there!" Jack simply said, "Gag me." It wasn't just that he'd become a Bay Area snob. He couldn't think of what he would do in Georgia. I counteroffered the editors at *Time*, suggesting they put me in their San Francisco bureau, but they turned me down. "You sound pretty sticky," the managing editor said.

It was painful to turn these jobs down. I still longed for the status of a staff job at a big-name newspaper or magazine. But the *Times* editor had a point. Despite myself I was getting sticky—or rather stuck on Jack—to the point of doing something previously unthinkable: prioritizing a relationship over my career. The fact that I was still cheating on Jack with the lawyer I'd met when he was on the road seemed beside the point.

My editors were also doing their best to convince me to stay. They gave me another raise and said they'd send me to the Tokyo bureau that summer to fill in for Lew Simons who was taking a leave to write a book on the Philippines revolution. After that I could have three months off to write my own book. And after that it would be less than a year before the Mexico City job came open again. They assured me I had it in the bag this time, and I believed them.

24

Tokyo, July 1986

I'd been in Tokyo for almost a month by the time the hearing on Bob Singer's appeal got underway in San Jose. Santa Clara County Superior Court Judge Robert Foley was seeking answers to two explosive questions: whether Bob's wife and lawyer had truly had an affair, and if so, whether it caused enough of a conflict of interest to overturn Bob's murder conviction.

I eagerly read every story on the hearing as soon as the back issues of *Mercury News* arrived at Lew's apartment in the tony, leafy Omotesando district. A couple times I also treated myself to a call to the reporter covering the case in San Jose, in search of details that hadn't made it into the paper.

I couldn't stop thinking about the drama playing out in California, despite how much more I had to occupy my mind that summer. Japan was holding congressional elections; there were riots in South Korea and continuing turmoil in the Philippines, where the new president, Cory Aquino, was fighting back against a series of military revolts. I had carte blanche to explore the region, and Jack was right there with me, making me thankful for the flexibility that came with his lack of a job. He arrived in Tokyo a couple weeks after I settled in, and already knew his way around and even spoke a little Japanese from his earlier travels, when he had taught English in Kyoto. We challenged each other to find interesting feature ideas and fun places to go on my time off. In Kyoto we stayed at a traditional inn, or ryokan, with tatami mats and bamboo floors with openings that looked down on a pool stocked with koi. On South Korea's Cheju Island, we picked out eel from a tank to be barbecued. I put the lawyer in San Francisco out of my mind.

I wasn't proud of my continuing obsession with Judi Barnett's squalid story; it was simply irresistible as the tale took its most outlandish turn to date. It seemed amazing that Judi and Bill, who had lied so audaciously and repeatedly during Bob Singer's trial, might finally be forced to own up to their dishonesty in public.

My editors and our readers were also keenly interested. Despite competition from a lot of extraordinary news that year—from the nuclear meltdown in Chernobyl to the Exxon Valdez oil spill in Alaska to the secret White House plot to sell weapons to Iran to raise funds for Nicaraguan Contras—the paper ran thirteen detailed stories on the soap-operaish special hearing.

Bob Singer's lawyers had called Judi Barnett as their first witness, and I couldn't wait to learn what she would say. She had fought hard against having to appear, and for a full year had managed to delay the hearing, hiring a Palo Alto attorney to argue that her testimony wasn't needed, was unfair to her children, and might even be dangerous, considering the "threats" she'd received, and the fact that she had been shot at in East San Jose during the first trial. But at last she had run out of arguments. Judge Foley ruled that she had to testify, and now her dilemma was clear. She'd either have to admit to the affair and humiliate herself in public or deny it and possibly destroy her former husband's last chance for freedom.

At my desk in the Tokyo bureau office, I studied Judi's picture on the front page of the local section. She was wearing her signature strand of pearls over a tailored silk blouse and blazer and looked a lot older than the last time I'd seen her, four years earlier. She'd gained some weight and her former neat blond bob had grown out into graying, shoulder-length waves.

Barely fifteen minutes into her testimony she confirmed that the affair had occurred. It began toward the end of Bob's first trial, she said, and resumed during his retrial, and ended after he was convicted.

Judi was once again a splendid witness for her husband, even while admitting she had cheated on him with his lawyer. She readily acknowledged having written all of the fifteen cards and letters in the "Voices of Truth" package, and willingly explained matters such as how, when she addressed Bill as "NJO," it stood for her pet name for him: "Nincompoop J. Owl." Bill, she testified, was partial to owls.

When asked about why she'd had the affair, Judi played the victim more extravagantly than ever before. Bill, she told Judge Foley, had been her "life preserver." She'd embarked on the affair with her husband's attorney because "I was alone and frightened and vulnerable and scared. And I didn't have anybody to take care of me, and I was taking care of everybody else."

Bob's lawyer, Patrick Hallinan, grinned with apparent relief at Judi's candor, as the *Mercury News* story noted. He'd had a handwriting expert waiting outside the courtroom, ready if needed to confirm that she had written the love letters. Now that wouldn't be necessary.

For the DA's office, however, Judi's admission was a terrible development. Deputy District Attorney Lane Liroff tried his best to chip away at her credibility, pressing her on details such as when the affair had begun. After his first few questions, Judi began to sob.

"Please understand the way we were living—and how difficult it is to remember these kinds of things," she said.

"I will if I can first understand, who is 'we'?"

"Bob, me, the children."

"How were we living at that point?"

"Under the most possible stress that people can live under. Exposed to things that we had never been exposed to before. Forced to deal with things that we had never had to deal with before. Fear for the future. Fear for Bob's health and safety."

In what seemed like an attempt to minimize the importance of the affair, Judi testified that she had only spent the night at Bill's San Jose apartment a couple of times. But Bob's lawyers next called a witness who contradicted her. This was Judi's daughter, Marie, now nineteen, whose appearance was a surprise. She had run away from Judi's home in Michigan earlier that year to live with her boyfriend in Arizona, but Bob's lawyers had tracked her down and convinced her to agree to try to help him.

Judi in fact had spent most weeknights away from her kids so as to be with Bill, Marie testified. "I was the live-in babysitter," she declared.

Despite being just fifteen years old at the time, Marie had been responsible for waking her brothers and getting them off to school, supervising their homework, cooking them dinner, and getting them to bed. She'd been tired, and her schoolwork had suffered, she acknowledged, but added: "You know, as an oldest child, when things go bad for the family, you do what you have to do."

I figured Bill Melcher was done for at that point, but I'd underestimated him. As the next day's newspaper described, he had his own surprise waiting on the day he took the stand, and it was a doozy. He couldn't possibly have had sex with Judi, he testified—because he was impotent. He'd had a vasectomy in 1978 and had been involuntarily celibate ever since.

The picture that ran with the story on Bill's testimony showed Patrick Hallinan, Bob's attorney, with his forehead on his desk. He had slammed his head down with a *thwack!* the reporter noted, at the moment he understood Bill's drift. Hallinan already thought the worst of Bill. He'd told reporters that he should be disbarred for his betrayal of his client. But this was a new outrage: Bill, he felt, was now insulting his intelligence.

Over the next three days, as the *Mercury News* reported, Hallinan methodically sought to expose Bill's dishonesty. He called on one of the lawyer's former friends, who testified that Bill had told him details about his affair with Judi— the same affair that Bill had just denied under oath. He then spent several hours badgering Bill about his claim that he was impotent and thus couldn't have had the affair.

"How long after that operation did you find that you could not get an erection?" Hallinan demanded.

"Immediately," said Bill.

"And ever since that period, that condition has persisted?"

"That is correct."

"And when did you file a malpractice action against the Kaiser facility for the condition that resulted as a result of your submission to a vasectomy?"

"Patients can't sue Kaiser," Bill protested. "They must go through arbitration."

"All right, sir. When did you file the arbitration?"

"I did not. I never intended to, and I never will."

"You were distressed by the fact that you could not get an erection after this office surgery, weren't you?"

"No."

"You didn't find that a disturbing matter?"

"No."

Five years later, after I read the hearing transcripts, I asked Jack Marshall how he'd felt while watching his star witness be systematically destroyed. His answer surprised me. On the one hand, he said, he felt justifiable dread about his case, and even some pity for Bill, who by the third day of testimony looked "mauled," as Jack put it, adding, "his hair no longer lay straight; he seemed to be limping; he even seemed to have shrunk."

Yet Jack confessed he had also taken a connoisseur's enjoyment in Patrick Hallinan's performance. As someone who had cultivated his own courtroom persona, Jack couldn't help but admire the hint of a brogue that crept into Hallinan's voice, giving the California native an air of a young James Cagney. He caught himself wishing there'd been a jury to hear him, imagining how that might have inspired Hallinan to even greater theatrical heights.

My own favorite part of the hearing came when Hallinan accused Bill of lying to police during Bob Singer's first trial, when Bill claimed that he and Judi had been shot at by strangers in East San Jose. I had always regretted that I couldn't disprove that at the time, when I suspected Bill was manipulating me and other journalists to get his theory of the case into print. Hallinan summoned a San Jose cop to testify that the police had never believed Bill's story, that they'd even briefly considered charging him with filing a false police report, but let it go because they had more important cases to deal with. The lawyer then called Judi back to testify about the incident, after getting the DA to grant her immunity from her past perjuries—most recently including using the shooting story to try to get out of appearing at the hearing.

Bill, as Judi now revealed, told her he'd needed to do something dramatic to counter the strong testimony against Bob Singer. She described how Bill had smuggled a gun through the metal detector at the Los Angeles airport by hiding it inside two aluminum pie-baking pans, and how she'd watched him stage the alleged attack on a deserted street corner in San Jose. "We drove by in my car and he shot at the phone booth," she said. On cross-examination, Judi insisted she hadn't wanted to go along with the sham. "It wasn't just illegal; it just wasn't right," she said. But Bill had convinced her, she added, after which "I lied to the police because Bill told me to. I did everything Bill asked me to do during that time."

"—I'm sorry, ma'am," Lane Liroff interrupted. "And this may sound familiar. But if Bill told you to jump off a roof, would you have done that?"

"Probably."

The San Jose hearing was originally scheduled to last just one week, yet dragged on, with several interruptions, into October, after Hallinan asked for time to locate two witnesses. These turned out to be a pair of highly credentialed doctors, both experts on male reproductive health, who, after reviewing Bill's medical records agreed that he couldn't possibly have been impotent in 1981, given that he had sought treatment around the same time for "fissures" resulting from intercourse and for a sexually transmitted disease.

Faced with this decisive testimony, the prosecutors still made one last, pathetic effort to prop up their case. I winced as I read how they called Bill's wife, Denise Melcher, to confirm his absurd story. A petite, brunette bank teller, she held her head high as she walked to the witness stand, as the *Mercury News* reported. Despite the couple's repeated efforts, she said, her husband was "unable to have an erection," she insisted, although she added, smiling: "We haven't given up trying."

Judge Foley took another six months to issue his ruling. By then I was back in my apartment in the Haight, on leave from the newspaper to work on my unauthorized biography of Imelda Marcos. As I read the report of his decision, I could see why he needed all that time. He had neither legal precedent nor even any professional standards to guide him. Unlike medical doctors and psychiatrists, lawyers had vigorously fought against limits on their sexual conduct, and in 1986 not a single state bar association had established one, despite precedents far more outrageous than Bill's dalliance with Judi. In 1980, for instance, the Beverly Hills celebrity divorce lawyer Marvin Mitchelson was charged with raping two former clients. A state victims' compensation board found the women sufficiently credible to award them fifty-six-thousand dollars for medical care and counseling, but the Los Angeles District Attorney's office said there was insufficient evidence to prosecute Mitchelson, and the California bar took no action to discipline him.

In this context, Judge Foley's ruling wasn't surprising. While he agreed with Bob Singer's lawyers that an affair had taken place, he said they hadn't shown that it had undermined Bill Melcher's legal performance. In other words, there would be no third trial for Bob Singer. His 1982 murder conviction would stand, to the great relief of the prosecutors, Jack Marshall and Lane Liroff. They could finally put the Singer case behind them.

I was also more than ready to stop thinking about Judi, Bob, and Bill. Around the same time that Judge Foley released his ruling, my old dream was finally coming true. In October 1987, I'd be heading south as the *Mercury News's* new bureau chief in Mexico City.

25

Tecate, Mexico, August 1987

"Do you ever talk to Mark?" my mother asked. She seemed to be trying to sound casual as she asked about the young lawyer she'd tried to set me up with seven years earlier. "Ugh, no!" I answered, making no such effort. We both laughed. We were walking arm-in-arm toward the dining room at Rancho la Puerta, a "wellness retreat" on four thousand acres outside the Mexican town of Tecate, which had become my mother's favorite place on earth. "It's Shangri-La!" she trilled, as our shuttle bus from San Diego arrived two days earlier, and we stepped down to hand our bags to friendly white-uniformed attendants and breathe in the scent of lavender and sage from the gorgeously landscaped grounds. She was treating me to a week of yoga, Pilates, mountain hikes, spa treatments, and gourmet vegetarian meals as a luxurious farewell gift two months before I moved out of the country. I took care of the logistics, the reservations and flights, and carried her bags through the airports.

While we never explicitly discussed it, we both knew the biggest luxury for my mother at her Shangri-La was a week away from my father. It was a week in which she could relax her nervous vigil over his erratic drinking and driving and boorish behavior, and offer an opinion, even finish a sentence, without being interrupted. After the first day there, her eyes shone and she looked several years younger, an effect beyond the power of any aromatherapy facial.

We slipped into our old roles as each other's confidantes during breakfasts under the acacia trees on the outdoor patio and during morning walks through desert canyons. Several other women approached us that week to gush over how much they envied our mother-daughter bond, and I felt privileged to bask in her undivided, loving attention. After just a couple days, she opened up more than ever before about her continuing frustrations with her marriage, how hard it was to live with my dad, and how much she hated his drinking. For the first time, she agreed with me that he was an alcoholic, although she seemed to have trouble even saying the word. She made a joke of it, with a comic stutter: "a-a-alcoholic."

Why, I asked yet again, couldn't she leave him? Even for a night? She insisted she couldn't, while refusing to say why. What if she saw a psychiatrist about it? Could she get *him* to see a psychiatrist? Had she thought about going to an Al-Anon meeting?

I kept throwing out ideas. She promised to think about them. I knew she wouldn't.

It seemed all the stranger that she would still be pressing me about Mark, implying I should follow her in choosing a man for his income potential: a choice that was obviously making her so unhappy. By then she'd met Jack several times, and had always been nice to him, yet all that summer she pouted whenever his name came up. "Do you think you'd need to support him if you two got married?" she asked on our third evening, as we sat on our private patio at twilight, sipping Chardonnay she'd brought for the trip. "Don't you want someone you can lean on?"

Yes of course I did, but by then I knew how differently we interpreted that phrase. Her question made me think of the feminist crusader Elizabeth Cady Stanton, who in 1890 wrote: "No matter how much women prefer to lean, to be protected and supported, nor how much men desire to have them do so, they must make the voyage of life alone." I agreed with Stanton up to a point. I didn't want or need a man to protect me, and I was determined that I would always be able to support myself. But the time I'd spent with Jack had raised my hopes that I could be accompanied and even supported on my own voyage.

On our return from Tokyo the previous year, he'd surprised me by announcing that he planned to go back to school and get his teaching credential. The "Jew without a job" was looking for a regular paycheck! Then when I learned I'd be going to Mexico, he surprised me again by negotiating a job at the American School in Mexico City. I hadn't yet told my mother that he planned to join me there as soon as he graduated in early 1988. I knew how much she'd still prefer I marry someone like Mark and stay in the Bay Area, my life merged with hers.

It had taken a crisis for Jack and me to commit to our plan. In the fall of 1986, just a few months after Judi was forced to admit her adultery in that degrading public hearing, I'd confronted my own infidelity in the privacy of Dr. Y's office. I often felt that year as if there were two parallel investigations unfolding: one delving into Judi's awful bad behavior, the other into my own. I knew I loved Jack but hadn't stopped sleeping around, primarily although not exclusively with the lawyer I'd met three years earlier.

The more time I'd spent with the lawyer, the worse I'd felt, and not only because of the guilt about Jack. As I'd gotten to know him better, he'd become a lot more critical, finding fault with things I said and did and wore. When I complained, he criticized me for being defensive. He told me he loved me and wanted to see more of me, but I'd feel wretched for days after every date. Maybe he was right, and I was overreacting. Maybe his critiques were good for me, a healthy challenge, like an aerobics class that leaves you exhausted and in pain, whereas with Jack's unconditional love I'd never grow. I couldn't be sure.

I expected that Dr. Y would sympathize with me, considering how much I was suffering, excruciatingly unable to abandon either option. Yet as session after session went by in which I treated him like my confessor, telling him how awful I felt about lying even as I continued to do so—he started sighing again.

"If you keep this up you might never be able to feel real love, only anger," he finally warned. Then he suggested a brave plan: I should write letters to Jack and the lawyer, admitting to every lie I'd ever told them. "Leave nothing out," he said, "and then if you end up with one of them you'll know he loves you for who you really are."

I nodded as I listened, much like I'd nodded in my interview with Imelda when she was drawing her absurd map of the world. I assumed that Dr. Y knew as well as I did that there was no way I'd do that. Why would I trust that someone would love me if he knew how awful I was?

At our next session, I told Dr. Y that I'd gone to New York for a weekend with the lawyer, telling Jack it was for work.

"He doesn't suspect anything," I muttered.

"You mean he wouldn't think you're that untrustworthy?"

I looked around at him and made a twisting-knife motion with my hand, to show how he had injured me. Which I guess was what pushed him past those professional boundaries for a third time.

"Watching you with all this has been like watching someone sitting on the railroad tracks," he burst out. "I can't just not say anything."

I was silent. He sounded livid. This couldn't be kosher.

"Jack is *good for you*," Dr. Y said. "You just have to let Jack be Jack."

For a moment, I imagined Oriana Fallaci—assuming she'd give a damn—rolling over in her grave. I'd supposedly structured my life to be as free as I could from men making decisions for me, and here I was listening to a man telling me whom I should sleep with. How was this different from joining a cult?

Even so, I listened. I told myself his advice was like training wheels, a safety measure until I was able to ride on my own. And I didn't do *everything* he suggested. I never wrote that confessional letter to Jack and the lawyer. But I did call Jack and tell him that I'd been seeing someone else. Then I drove to his apartment to Berkeley to talk it out. For some reason we decided to do our talking at Brennan's, one of his favorite dives. Both of us were crying as we left his apartment, and both of us headed for the passenger seat of my car, waiting for the other person to drive. *This is just what's wrong with the relationship*, I fumed to myself, although I knew it might also be part of what was right. Committing to Jack meant I'd have to give up that fantasy, which I'd secretly shared with Judi Barnett, that someone bigger and stronger would take the wheel. Even if it ensured I'd remain a passenger.

I drove. In the dark bar, Jack told me he was angry and that he'd need time to forgive me, but that he loved me and that if I stopped lying to him he'd try. I said I'd try too. That evening I left a cowardly message on the lawyer's answering machine, telling him I was in love with someone else. I never heard from him again.

I couldn't tell my mother any of this, as I joined her at her Pilates class or jumped around in the pool with her during water aerobics. She wouldn't have understood, much less approve. She also would have been rooting for the lawyer, and I didn't want to get her hopes up for nothing.

For similar reasons, I also didn't tell my mother how worried I'd become about moving to Mexico that fall. Like the proverbial dog that finally catches a car, I'd been stunned by getting what I'd always thought I wanted. Only now that my dream was coming true could I look past the gauze of adolescent fantasies to realities I'd managed to ignore. If I'd been honest with my mother about how just how scared I was, she would have tried to talk me out of going.

I had no friends in Mexico City, didn't speak Spanish as well as I'd pretended, and would need to obsessively track events throughout the region so as not to get serially scooped by a crowd of more experienced and probably more talented competitors. Plus part of the job involved covering wars in El Salvador and Nicaragua just as our readers' interest in those drawn-out conflicts was fading, which meant I might be risking my life for back-page stories.

"Millions of Mexicans are trying to come to the United States, and my daughter wants to go in the opposite direction!" my father had announced to a table of dinner guests earlier that summer.

His comments were getting harder to laugh off. The next afternoon in the newsroom I let my nerves get the better of me.

"Chuck, look at this!" I called to Chuck Buxton, my future editor. He ambled over to my desk to look over my shoulder at the computer monitor.

The *Chicago Tribune* was reporting on a new study that found that sixteen-thousand-five-hundred tons of toxic particles fell from Mexico City's sky every day. People were streaming into hospitals suffering from conjunctivitis, digestive problems, and hacking coughs. Some patients treated for schizophrenia were found instead to be suffering from lead poisoning.

"Wow, that's pretty bad," Chuck agreed with a shrug. *He* wasn't moving there.

"Chuck, the U.S. Embassy is giving its workers in Mexico City two years' credit toward retirement for every year they spend there!" I told him the next day.

He shook his head. That wasn't going to be in my contract. What *was* in my contract was a stipulation that I'd have to pay back my moving costs if I stayed in the job any less than one year. When I later asked Chuck if the paper would pay for air purifiers in my new office, given another report that said people were finding dead birds on their lawn, birds that had apparently fallen from the sky and out of trees after breathing too much of the smog, he said: "Kathy, I can't make it go away!"

All this made my stay at my mother's Shangri-La all the more wistful. This was a place where rich ladies came, mostly at their husbands' expense, to tone their bodies and ease their minds. A week in that desert oasis made me feel as tan and pampered as my first sight of Judi Singer, six years earlier, and I was only too aware that marrying Jack might put these luxuries permanently out of my reach. As I watched my mother dressing for our next delicious healthy dinner, patting La Mer cream under her eyes and donning her Eileen Fisher slacks and Ferragamo sandals, I pictured myself with a hacking cough and lead poisoning, wearing rags and trapped in a scene of desolation straight out of *Mad Max*. Going to Mexico was my choice, I kept having to remind myself. So was committing to Jack. Plus I no longer had any doubt that Shangri-La, that supposedly permanently carefree Himalayan kingdom, had never been more than fiction.

26

Hillsborough, California, April 1990

On February 27, 1990, about six weeks before Jack and I got married, I made yet another clumsy mistake, although this time it wasn't in print. While reporting on presidential elections in Nicaragua, I was running after Violeta Chamorro, the country's newly elected leader, but failed to look where I was going and fell into a manhole, shattering my knee. I'd always assumed that if I ever got hurt on the job, it would be from something more glamorous, like being kidnapped or shot or stepping on a land mine. Making matters worse, Chamorro, who had recently had knee surgery, was using crutches at the time. I could easily have paid more attention and still caught her.

Two of my colleagues helped me get to a clinic, where a doctor wearing a blood-spattered apron handled my leg and told me nothing was wrong.

"Camina, camina!" he ordered. Walk, walk!

I limped back to my hotel room and filed my last story while anesthetizing myself with Flor de Cana rum. Three days later I flew back to California, where my parents, looking stricken, picked me up at the airport and took me to their friend the orthopedist. Once again, in a pinch, I ran to them for support, and they were there for me. The orthopedist said the bone was too fragmented for surgery and put my leg in a cast.

I was home a lot earlier than I'd planned, with Jack stuck at work for the next two weeks. It made no sense to return to Mexico, so I settled in to wait for the big day. In the afternoons I worked on a freelance piece from a recent trip to Cuba that would run in the *Atlantic*, and after dinner played backgammon with my father. He was once again back in his Jekyll mode: drinking less, peaceful, and affectionate. He had bonded with Jack over an all-you-can-eat ribs dinner several months earlier, and having deemed him a mensch, to my delighted surprise had stopped nagging me to marry a doctor or lawyer.

Jack and I had been having a great time in Mexico City. Two years earlier, he'd moved into the small white house I'd found to rent in Coyoacan, an artsy neighborhood with cobblestone streets where Frida Kahlo had once shared a home with Diego Rivera. Two blocks from us, purple jacaranda trees surrounded the ancient Plaza Hidalgo, with its restaurants and wandering musicians.

Jack was teaching journalism and history at the American School, while I traveled all over Mexico and Central America, finally learning enough Spanish to interview government officials about border conflicts, interest rates, and the drug war. Sometimes when Jack had time off from school we traveled together and he freelanced. I hadn't made a single mistake, or at least not one that I knew of. We'd made some good friends among the other correspondents and adored our Mexican landlords, a young family who invited us to their country home in Tepotzlan. We'd even adopted a puppy, a Samoyed we named Clea, after the faithful blond character in Lawrence Durrell's *The Alexandria Quartet*. The smog hadn't been the nightmare that I'd feared, at least not most of the year. Quite often, I'd catch myself thinking that my dream as a thirteen-year-old had come true, and that it was even better than I'd imagined.

I'd been the first to bring up the subject of marriage. We'd been together seven years, and while Jack had always said he didn't need the government's approval to be faithful, I suspected it might help me do that. That's why, one afternoon, as we were arguing about our future on a beach vacation near Tulum, and he, in exasperation, said, "What do you want me to do, ask you to marry me?" I said yes. We've since had many romantic moments that have made up for that.

I hadn't seen Dr. Y since I'd left for Mexico in the fall of 1987. At our last session, he'd assured me I'd gotten what I'd needed from him. Sometimes I believed that, too. He had shown me, in real time, how much of my behavior I'd been blind to, and helped me, through lots of practice, strengthen my self-monitoring system so that I didn't—to paraphrase the bumper-sticker—believe everything I thought. It seemed as if his gentle voice had been permanently installed in my head, reminding me to pay better attention, to make more of an effort to listen when other people were talking, and to think twice before sending a nasty email or telling any kind of lie. On top of all that, I'd grown more patient, at least enough to finish the book on Imelda, which was published in 1988.

Not that there weren't lapses. If I close my eyes today and listen, I can still hear the sound of the AP photographer I met on my first trip to San Salvador swearing at me for five minutes straight after I called his hotel room to check a fact at three in the morning. I worried that I could still behave blindly, and thoughtlessly, and sitting there in Hillsborough, all but immobilized by that cast, my worries focused on the upcoming marriage.

Four years had passed since I'd heard anything about Judi Barnett, but with all that time on my hands she popped into my thoughts. I had lied, like she had, and been disloyal, and had exploited people, while blaming my behavior on others or telling myself I had no other option. What if all that time with Dr. Y really hadn't changed me?

These were the doubts that drove me, one week before the wedding, to make an appointment at a mikveh, a ceremonial bath normally more familiar to Orthodox Jews rather than those like me who'd been brought up with the barest minimum of rules and rituals. The mikveh is mostly used by women to purify themselves for their husbands before their marriage or after their periods. Some feminists object to the ritual's implication that only women are unclean. But for me this wasn't about blood, but rather about making a clean break with my past.

I found a bath in San Francisco where a bemused attendant in a flowered cotton headscarf stood by as I wriggled around to submerge as much as I could while keeping my thigh-length cast out of the water. It felt nothing but awkward until I was back on my feet, on the crutches, and wrapped in a thin, worn towel. The attendant stopped smirking and recited a quiet Hebrew prayer. All will be fine, I told myself, and meant it.

Two days later, on a lawn facing the Pacific, outside an inn near Mendocino, my psychiatrist brother and sister played Vivaldi's "Winter" on violin and piano as I hobbled, flanked by my parents, down a path bordered by blue and yellow wildflowers. Jack was waiting under the chuppah, wearing one of the only two sports jackets he would own for the next thirty years.

Someone had tied a big white bow on one of my crutches. Handing them off to a bridesmaid, I leaned against my husband. I've been leaning on him, and he on me, ever since.

27

"Hello?"

At first, Judi Barnett's voice sounded unusually relaxed, considering the phone had rung at nearly eleven at night.

"Judi!" Bob Singer greeted her heartily. "How are you?"

A pause.

"I'm fine!" Judi answered, now a little more warily.

"Good! What's cookin'?"

"*Who is this*?" Judi demanded. Her voice had grown cold.

Bob had been picking up steam, but this cut him short. He sucked in his breath and asked:

"You mean, after all these years, you don't remember my voice, huh? This is your ex-husband."

Bob and Judi were talking again—on a secretly recorded call—because of yet another unexpected development in the 1980 murder case. This time the twist was explosive. After nearly a decade in prison, Bob had surprised the DA's office by finally owning up to his role in the crime, but also saying that Judi had made him do it. Judi, as Bob now claimed, had pressured him to hire the assassins and plotted with him to carry out the job. Meaning, among other things, that my stupid mistake back in 1981 had accidentally hit on the truth.

Bob now had a big incentive to help trap Judi. In early August 1991, an appellate court had overturned his murder conviction, overruling the San Jose judge's decision that Judi's affair with his attorney hadn't undermined his defense. Bob's lawyers offered him as a witness against his former wife in return for a plea bargain that would reduce his sentence of life without parole.

Deputy District Attorney John Luft, who now had charge of the case, was eager to prosecute Judi. He pictured her as an iconic villainess, a black widow like Kathleen Turner in *Body Heat*.

"A first-grader could see it," Luft told his supervisor, Jack Marshall, who had initially balked at reopening the case that had haunted him for more than a decade. "An estranged wife with a compelling personality. She lures a family man away from his home—and then, when he's totally dependent on her, she makes him do her dirty work!" The scenario had made Luft feel something like sympathy for Bob, who struck him as hopelessly henpecked.

Luft made Bob take a lie detector test, and once he passed it Jack Marshall agreed to go ahead. If Bob continued to help them and didn't tell another lie he'd be eligible for parole in another three years. His late-night call to Judi was his first chance to prove his worth.

As I later listened to the recording of the call, I tried to imagine Judi's reaction to hearing Bob's voice for the first time in five years. While Bob was serving his life sentence she'd worked hard to establish a new life for herself and the kids back in Michigan. They lived in an apartment in West Bloomfield, a wealthy suburb of Detroit, their expenses mostly paid for by Howard Witkin's trust. But Judi had recently gotten her first paying job, as a part-time property manager. She'd enrolled her two sons in Detroit Country Day School, one of the nation's most prestigious and expensive private schools. Daniel joined the football team, and Judi attended every game, wearing a T-shirt reading, "I'm a Country Day Mom." A call from her ex-husband in prison didn't belong in this tableau.

Bob told Judi he was calling from the hospital where he was being treated for back pain, and that his doctors had let him use the phone as a favor. In reality, he was sitting in a spare county office, chained at his ankles and wrists, while being coached by John Luft and his investigator, Sandy Williams.

Sandy could see Bob's knuckles turning white as he grasped the telephone receiver. She smiled and nodded at him to egg him on. She and John Luft and Bob had practiced together for half an hour before he made the call, after which Sandy had unscrewed the mouthpiece of the telephone set on which she planned to listen in, so that Judi wouldn't hear her breathe. From time to time, when Bob seemed at a loss, she scribbled suggestions for him on a yellow legal pad.

Bob told Judi that the date for his trial had been moved up and that he'd be going to court in the third week in August—in other words, in one more week.

"You know, I got, I got two ways to go on this, Hon," he said. "I'm just letting you know .... The DA is looking for me to make a deal and you know what that means. They're looking to take the life top, the life without, off of me. That means I'd have to do another five to eight—"

Judi indeed knew what Bob meant. Her last trace of composure disappeared.

"—Oh, shit, you don't," she interrupted. "No, we'll get you out. That's ridiculous—"

Bob kept going. "—Because you know what they want," he said. "They want you. I mean, they've come point—point out blank, they want you. And they want to know what your involvement in this is and how, uh, you threatened all kinds of shit on me, that if I didn't do this, what you were going to do."

There was a brief silence, after which Judi said: "Let's go to trial. Your attorneys are very confident, very confident." On hearing this, Sandy nodded happily at Bob, giving him a thumbs-up sign. She caught John Luft's eye and the two exchanged smiles. Of course they'd hoped that Judi would be more explicit. But as John Luft would later tell me, *o*missions can often be just as good as *ad*missions, and any reasonable juror hearing that tape would have to wonder why, if Judi *weren't* guilty, she hadn't stopped Bob in his tracks and demanded to know what he was talking about.

As if realizing she'd slipped, Judi tried to change the subject. She'd heard Bob had remarried his first wife, Joan, she said. "Are you happy?" she asked.

"Uh, no," Bob responded, his voice dull, before turning back to his script.

"The only thing I got left is the truth," he said. "Think I ought to tell them the truth—uh, you know, about, uh, your involvement ...? Do you think you could handle it if I did?"

There was silence for a moment. Then: "Bob, go to trial," Judi urged. "I think you should go to trial. Your attorneys are confident. I think you should go to trial."

She made another effort to divert his attention, with news about her kids. Her son Daniel had been diagnosed with diabetes but was faring well after a couple of bad years. Marie had left home and Judi hadn't heard from her for weeks. Nathan was fourteen, doing fine and planning to accompany her to California for Bob's upcoming trial. "It's very important for him to see you," she coaxed, and then abruptly asked, "Who's paying for this call?"

"Uh, the hospital."

"Impossible!" she said.

Bob shot Sandy a nervous look before again going on the offensive.

"You know, for so long, I've been sitting on this thing, uh, justifying, uh, what I did, and, and, and whether honestly, if we did the right thing eleven years ago—" he began.

"—Go to trial, Bob," Judi interrupted, this time more forcefully. "My testimony will be the same as in the first trial."

Bob talked over her. "How are we gonna get out of this? You know, you got me into this mess. Now, I, I, I, I thought I—"

"Bob. Go to trial."

"Do you think it's gonna work? Do you think what you're gonna say is gonna get me out?"

"Bob, go to trial. Go to trial .... I don't like this conversation. I don't like what, what, what, I don't like any of this. Go to trial—"

Bob's voice sounded nakedly desperate as he made one last effort.

"Honey, did I do the right thing eleven years ago?"

"Bob, I'll have my attorney talk to your attorney tomorrow, OK?" Judi said, and they said their goodbyes.

Three days after that call took place, Bryan Shechmeister, my old friend from the public defender's office, learned what was in the works and called me in Mexico. We'd kept in touch over the past four years, during which we'd often joke—at least I thought it was a joke—about collaborating on a book about the Witkin murder case. Now he sounded serious.

"Judi is going to be arrested any day!" he said. "It's time!"

Judi's arrest and trial for murder would offer closure for the last chapter, we agreed. But Bryan then told me we probably wouldn't be working together after all. He had just been diagnosed with a brain tumor and didn't expect to live more than another year.

I'd taken the phone onto our bedroom balcony. Now I stood biting my lip as I gazed at the red-tiled colonial rooftops surrounding our *cerrada*, a closed-in alley with homes on both sides. I could easily think of so many other people who deserved to die from a brain tumor. Not Bryan. He had two young sons. He was such a great guy. "Isn't there anything more you can do?" I asked dumbly.

"No," he said. "So just get up here because I've got all the records you need: the transcripts, the arrest reports, pictures, you name it, and I really want to talk to you about all of this while I still can."

The murder case was connected to the most embarrassing moment of my life. In that moment, I wasn't tremendously enthusiastic about jumping back in. But it seemed to have been decided. My next home leave was scheduled in another three weeks, and I promised Bryan I'd visit him then. And by the time I got to California, I knew I did want to go ahead. I was still oddly compelled by Judi's story, and now was also enticed by the prospect of better understanding how these seemingly ordinary people—upper-middle-class Jews who might have been my own relatives—could engage in such appalling behavior. In theory, I would have loved the opportunity to hold up that kind of magnifying glass to my complicated parents. In practice, I was still too bound by our family taboos to even question them closely about their childhoods.

With a lot of help from Bryan that fall, I wrote a proposal to tell the story of the murder and decade-long delay in finding its true author. I sent it to my New York agent and was stunned by how quickly I got a contract from a big publisher, with an advance that would cover my time off from work and travel expenses. Another surprise was that my editors agreed to a second book leave. Three months ought to be enough, we all agreed. I had a habit of sometimes underestimating how long things can take.

28

Flint, Michigan, August 1991

It was long past midnight on Wednesday, August 28 of 1991, by the time Sandy Williams staggered off the American Eagle connecting flight from Chicago at Flint's Bishop Airport. Beside her strode two businessmen, carrying her briefcase and files.

Sandy was wearing just one shoe. She carried the other, a broken, blue, high-heeled Capezio, in a crumpled airsickness bag. Her bare big toe was bleeding through her torn nylon stocking; her tailored blue suit looked as if she had slept in it, which she had, and her long blond hair, normally pinned up in a neat chignon, fell loose about her shoulders. She also smelled faintly of champagne.

The three Michigan cops waiting for her at the gate had wondered what to expect when they heard that San Jose was sending a female investigator to help them snag Judi Barnett. Their first sight of Sandy may have confirmed their worst suspicions, until they learned that her condition was the product of professional zeal. Earlier that day, she had been rushing to meet a judge to get his signature for Judi's arrest warrant when a bailiff swung open the courtroom's large steel door, slicing off the top of her toe.

I loved hearing this story over pizza with Sandy, as I noticed how much we both liked to sprinkle our slices with hot chili flakes. Her sliced toe reminded me of my broken knee in Nicaragua. We both may have been a bit impulsive. Sandy had been rushing for good reason. The sensational news that Howard Witkin's ex-wife was being charged with his murder, a full decade after the crime, had yet to hit the Michigan newspapers. But Sandy suspected Judi had already somehow found out and left town to avoid arrest.

She'd been calling Judi's apartment in West Bloomfield for the past three days, but no one ever picked up. She had also tracked down a number for Judi's office, where a receptionist said Judi hadn't come to work that week, and that no one knew where she had gone. Sandy next called Judi's haberdasher father, Bob Barnett, with a ruse. Posing as a Michigan police officer, she said she was trying to contact Judi about a stolen wallet Judi had reported. Barnett told her that neither he nor anyone else in the family knew where Judi was. She had left town suddenly, he said, taking her fourteen-year-old son, Nathan along. Only her lawyer knew their whereabouts.

Hearing that, Sandy decided she had to get to Michigan on the double. She figured she didn't even have time to see a doctor about her foot. As she boarded the plane, a flight attendant did a double take at her gory, amateurishly bandaged toe and insisted she sit in first class. Sandy happily settled herself into the large seat by the window, and when the flight attendant passed by with the free champagne, she couldn't bring herself to turn it down. She was in a lot of pain.

The Michigan cops dropped Sandy off at her hotel at around two in the morning and returned five hours later to head to Judi's apartment. Rain pounded at the windows all day long, as the four cops walked silently through the empty rooms, scooping up potential evidence to take back to headquarters. The apartment was fastidiously clean, with a big walk-in closet that held Judi's many dresses and skirts and several pairs of shoes dyed to match. No clues there, but on the bedside table they found a yellow legal pad with some scribbled notes. One of the Michigan investigators whistled in surprise when he saw it, and they smiled as they read it together. Sandy tapped her finger on the name, "John Luft," and then on the date, "August 14"—the day Bob had entered his plea bargain. A scribbled sentence explicitly confirmed their suspicions about the reason for Judi's absence. "California wants me," it read. Left on the kitchen table was a torn-out section of the newspaper listing want ads for northern-state resort rentals. In a rare lapse of her usual discipline, Judi had left compelling evidence to back up a charge of fleeing arrest.

Sandy tracked down Judi's lawyer, Richard Goldstein, and demanded an explanation. Goldstein insisted his client wasn't a fugitive. Rather, he said, she merely needed a couple of days to prepare herself to face the police. He promised to help arrange her surrender when she was ready.

None of the detectives took this well. They grumbled among themselves about Judi's apparent sense of entitlement. Was Goldstein really asking them to wait around for Judi to turn herself in at her convenience? When she might have been taking advantage of the extra time to flee the country? They responded by ramping up their search, alerting Customs officers on the U.S. and Canadian sides of the border as well as officials at every major air carrier at the Flint and Detroit airports. They also sent press releases to local TV stations, including photos of Judi and a toll-free number to call for tips on where she might be.

The following Tuesday, September 3, 1991—a full six days after Sandy's arrival in Flint—Goldstein finally called the detectives to say he planned to keep his promise to arrange Judi's surrender, assuming they agreed to her conditions. She didn't want any news reporters present, and also insisted that police fax Goldstein a list of items found in their search of her apartment.

The cops' irritation at these new demands escalated to outrage. They agreed to try to keep the media away but told Goldstein they weren't about to trade in investigative information. The search warrant list was now a sealed record in any case. Judi would have to wait for her arraignment to see it.

Judi's lawyer wasn't pleased but agreed to go ahead. Just before two in the afternoon the next day, the detectives watched as Judi's eldest son, Daniel, who was now twenty-one, drove up to Goldstein's office. He stayed there for the next three hours, during which time the cops and Judi's lawyer again conferred by phone. When Daniel returned to his car and drove off, Sandy Williams and a Michigan cop followed him, a maneuver that accomplished Judi's goal of eluding the press.

After all the long drama leading up to Judi's arrest, her surrender, as far as Sandy was concerned, was downright disappointing. At 5:05 p.m. the cops met their fugitive at the Flint State Police post, a few miles away from Judi's lawyer's office. Sandy had expected to meet a stylish and voluble femme fatale, a Mata Hari in high heels, but Judi was wearier, heavier, and dowdier than the slender woman who had last appeared in San Jose six years earlier to confirm her affair with Bill Melcher. She wore a frumpy brown track suit, flat sandals, and no makeup. Sandy felt almost relieved to note her fresh pedicure: that, at least, was in keeping with the character she'd envisioned.

Judi said nothing as Sandy advised her of her rights, after which the cops drove her to the Genesee County Jail. At a subsequent court hearing, she was charged with death-penalty murder and conspiracy. The judge refused to grant bail.

About two weeks later, Sandy Williams was back in San Jose in time to watch Bob Singer muster his courage once again in the service of his efforts to prove he could be a reliable prosecution witness. This performance would test him even more than the set-up phone call to Judi.

When Bob incriminated Judi in her ex-husband's murder, he had to reveal his own role to prosecutors for the first time. But he hadn't yet told his family. Joan, his first wife, had remarried him shortly after he and Judi had divorced. For a full decade, she and Bob's three sons had appeared to accept his story that he'd had no part in the murder—that he was a blameless victim, as he'd said more than once, of "the system."

By then the Singer children were young adults embarking on their careers. Their eldest had just started work as a county prosecutor in Fresno; their middle son was a U.S. Air Force captain, and their youngest had followed Bob into the restaurant business. Together with their mother, they had visited Bob often in prison and attended his parole hearings. But in recent weeks Sandy and John Luft, the prosecutor, had been coaxing Bob to tell his wife and kids the truth so that they could then be questioned as to whether any of them might have evidence to support Bob's new narrative.

Bob chose September 18, which was Yom Kippur, the Jewish Day of Atonement, to summon his family to an office at the Santa Clara County Jail. He told Joan that the prosecutors had given him a special visiting privilege for the Jewish holiday, which was more or less true.

Bob was sitting at a table in his orange jumpsuit, shackled at his wrists and ankles, when Joan and the boys entered the room. Sandy Williams and John Luft leaned against a wall at a discreet distance. Bob's wife and kids kissed and hugged him before taking their seats, listening expectantly as he began to ramble. He spent several minutes making nervous small talk—long enough for Sandy to wonder whether Bob might be rethinking the advantages of life without parole.

At last she took a step toward him. "Bob, it's time," she said, adding, "I think Mr. Luft and I need to step out of the room for a few minutes, and you need to speak to your family and tell them the truth."

For the next few minutes, the investigator and the prosecutor waited in the hall. At first they heard only Bob's muffled voice, but then the room exploded in shouts, wails, and the sound of someone banging on the wall. They rushed back in to find Bob's sons crying and his wife screaming that she didn't want to hear anymore but in the next breath demanding that Bob keep talking, that he explain how he could have done this to them, and how he could have lied for so long.

Embarrassed at intruding on such an intimate moment, Sandy Williams and John Luft at first looked at the floor. But as Sandy raised her eyes, she noticed that Bob's youngest son Eric, the restaurant owner, was calm and dry-eyed. Bob's news hadn't surprised him. Sandy remembered that Eric had lived for a brief time with Bob and Judi in Michigan, when he was still a teen, and she made a mental note to speak to him alone as soon as she could.

29

As hard as it initially was for Bob Singer to tell the truth about his plot to murder Howard Witkin, he picked up steam after he atoned with his family. I was cheered by how readily he agreed to meet with me after I wrote to him in prison, and how thoroughly he answered every question I asked over two long meetings in the visiting room of Soledad Prison, where he'd been transferred in January 1992. All through his two trials, he'd struck me as taciturn, even surly. Now he was warm and effusive—actually, too much so.

"I didn't know whether to shake your hand or hug you or give you a kiss!" he said on a collect call the evening after my first visit.

It made me nervous. I hadn't consciously been flirting, although I'm not the first to have observed that there's a thin line between that and the journalist's work of trying to entice someone to tell you their secrets. Still, after all that time in therapy that I'd spent confronting my habit of manipulating men, I monitored myself so that I'd have no later regrets. I reminded Bob two or three times that he was speaking on the record, keeping my notebook in sight as I scribbled down his answers. On our second meeting, after his "hug you" comment on the phone, I wore a boxy blouse and jacket and tried to smile less and not make as much eye contact. I was haunted by Dr. P's voice in my head, warning that I might be trying to make a monkey out of Bob. It's not like that wouldn't be fair, I'd thought darkly on the two-and-a-half drive down from Hillsborough, where I was once again availing myself of my parents' hospitality. After all, he'd co-conspired in that libel suit that had nearly wrecked my career. And everything I'd heard about him during the trial made me think the worst of him. I didn't relish spending time with him. But I still needed his story.

In both of our meetings we sat across a wooden table from each other, as I struggled to hear him over the noise of other inmates and their visitors. It was clear he'd been ruminating over the case during all those ten years in his cell, as he tried to understand how after a life in which his only transgressions were a few parking tickets he'd reached the point where murder seemed like a reasonable option.

Not once in our conversations, however, did Bob express any regret about Howard Witkin's death. In Bob's new chronicle of the murder case, *he* was a victim.

He began by telling me the genuinely sad story of his childhood in New Rochelle. Bob was just sixteen when his own mother, in his account a warm affectionate woman who kept a kosher kitchen, died of a cerebral hemorrhage. The elder of two sons, he was sent to live with an aunt, which left him with a lifelong sense of having been cheated. Many years later, when he created his first Facebook profile, he would list his educational experience as the "School of Hard Knocks."

Bob told me that he'd married his first wife, Joan, when they were both twenty years old. They'd met on a blind date while he was on leave from the army. But the romance barely outlived their engagement. In her first year of marriage, Joan suffered a kind of mild nervous collapse, as Bob recalled. Inexplicably she became convinced that she would get sick and die before Bob could get her to a doctor. He ended up driving her, night after night, to the parking lot of the nearest hospital, the only place she managed to sleep.

This lasted several months, until Joan's parents found a doctor who advised them that Joan might be cured if she started a family. In those days this wasn't unheard-of advice, and Bob agreed to give it a try. The first of their three sons was born in 1956, after which Joan did seem to improve, as Bob recalled. But by the time Bob met Judi in 1977, he was desperate for a change.

"I was tired of being so responsible," he told me. "Judi made me feel like a kid again."

He was entranced from his first glimpse of her at that 1977 synagogue fundraisers' meeting. As he recalled, she appeared a few minutes late, and with all eyes in the room on her, walked jauntily over to the rabbi to give him a kiss on the cheek.

Bob already knew a lot about Judi through the grapevine: how she'd graduated (supposedly) from an elite college, married into one of Santa Clara County's richest Jewish families, and quickly risen as a leader in Hadassah. "She was Jewish high society," Bob said. "Whereas I was a nouveau riche schlep."

Still, the two of them soon hit it off. Their friendship began with frequent phone conversations about synagogue business and quickly moved on to private lunches at the Sambo's diner near the temple. Judi brought over casseroles to Bob's family and sent him affectionate greeting cards— always marked with her little smiley face—at his office. She showered him with the maternal warmth he'd missed as a teen, gazing at him during their most unexceptional conversations as if he were giving her a series of vital emergency instructions she needed to memorize in sixty seconds. Her attention was addictive, as was her air of self-assurance. Bob couldn't imagine Judi ever second-guessing herself, like he did all the time.

As they grew closer, Bob confided in Judi about his boring marriage and the stress of working with his father and brother. Judi told Bob about her troubles with Howard. He was gambling, using drugs, and dating cocktail waitresses, she said. Sometimes, she said, he even beat her. Bob had met Howard at the temple and found it difficult to imagine that smiling, roly-poly man being violent. But by then he was in no condition to doubt anything Judi said.

By early spring they were holding hands across the table. Once or twice, Judi put Bob's hand on her growing belly to feel her baby kick, telling him: "It knows your touch. It knows you love it; you care about it."

The baby's birth was traumatic. Nine weeks premature, Nathan suffered a heart murmur and respiratory distress. Judi told Bob that Howard had left her to deal with his problems all alone, refusing to even accompany her to the hospital. Bob was appropriately outraged. Just two months later, on a sticky, midsummer evening when Howard was playing racquetball, Judi drove her new red Cougar to meet Bob at a cheap motel, where Bob signed in as R. Roberts.

Bob was in such a confessional mode during my visit that from the moment he started talking he seemed anxious to spare no detail. He told me all about the motel's king-sized waterbed—he'd never slept on one before—and his brief disappointment in Judi's "matronly lingerie": an unadorned beige slip that did nothing to hide her post-partum weight.

Over the next couple of hours, however, Judi behaved in a manner he never would have dreamed possible for a Hadassah chapter president. "She did some very imaginative things with grape jelly!" Bob said, with a sly smile.

I wrinkled my nose. *What had I gotten into?* I could not imagine writing about this middle-aged pair, who even now seemed like people I might have met at my parents' synagogue, frolicking with grape jelly, and I didn't want to know more.

Luckily Bob was already talking about something else. Just before they left the hotel, he said, Judi lifted a painting from the wall over the bed and tucked it under her arm, to carry out to her car.

I raised my eyebrows.

"It wasn't any great work of art," Bob said. "It was some tacky scene of a forest. The hotel could afford it."

Besides, Bob said, Judi told him it would be her souvenir of their first tryst. Bob thought that was adorable.

He paused at this point and looked at me as if he expected me to criticize him.

Instead I moved on. "Tell me why Judi wanted Howard dead," I asked.

Bob willingly complied, telling the story he'd later repeat in court.

"It was only after we moved to Flint and bought the restaurant and I started getting into debt that her behavior started to change," he said. "This sexy blonde I'd married became frigid!"

She talked about Howard all the time. "She called him 'that asshole,'" Bob said. She couldn't stand that he still had partial custody of the children. She complained about his driving too fast and feeding the kids pizza rolls and Cheetos on their visits. But the last straw was Howard's plan to take them on a houseboat.

"She just couldn't stop thinking about it or talking about it," Bob said. "She started saying things like 'I wish he'd just drop dead.'" Then one night, he said, she became more explicit. She really did want Howard dead, Judi told him.

By then, this didn't come as much of a surprise, but Bob said he tried to laugh it off, pretending he couldn't tell that she was serious. Judi responded by pressing him harder. "She'd say 'If you really loved me, you'd help me,'" he said.

It was his responsibility as a father to help protect her children—their children—Judi told him, Bob recounted.

When he continued to balk, she refused to sleep with him. Then she threatened to leave him, taking the kids. At last he broke down and agreed to consider a plan.

One thing I've always loved about reporting in a hurry is how it forces me to clear everything else out of my head so I can meet the deadline. The dishes in the sink, the overdraft notices, the car that's overdue for maintenance: They all have to wait. Sitting with Bob, knowing our time was limited by the scheduled visiting hours, I listened closely, taking notes, while also trying to figure out my next question. Still, even then, part of my mind was wandering off course. I remembered Judi's testimony, nearly ten years earlier, that she'd left Howard because of his drug use, fearing her children were unsafe with him. Bob's story seemed to make sense. What else, other than that level of fear, would have driven her to give up her cozy perch in Los Gatos, trading one unattractive man for another? And had the same motive inspired her to nag Bob to commit murder? It didn't make it right by any means, but it was at least a little more comprehensible than her hoping to cash in on the life insurance, which had never seemed convincing to me or Jack Marshall or Bob's jurors.

Bob was still talking, as if no longer needing my questions to guide him. I tuned back in, hoping I hadn't missed anything important.

"Our first thought was that I'd do it myself," he was saying. "We talked about disguises, like a false beard and mustache—and how I could get to California and back without being missed at work."

But at last, Bob said, he told Judi that he couldn't imagine killing anyone in cold blood. He would have to find someone else to do it, which is why he eventually recruited Gary Oliver, his employee, in that almost inexplicably boneheaded move.

Once the plot was underway, Judi oversaw most of the arrangements with the same eye for detail as she'd had when she'd ordered the invitations for their wedding, Bob told me. She even thought to rip two Polaroid photos of Howard out of one of her albums so that Bob could give it to his hitman to help identify the target. Then she made her most chilling request of all.

"She told me to make sure he wouldn't be shot in the face," Bob said. "She didn't want the children to be traumatized at his funeral."

I put down my pen and sighed. I wasn't all that shocked by his portrait of Judi, after getting to know her dark side through her love letters to Bill Melcher. But after two days of listening to Bob, my emotions had morphed from sympathetic curiosity to something close to disgust. Bob was so ready to put all the blame on his ex-wife, painting her as such a villainess, without taking a shred of responsibility himself. It was time for my last question.

"Why did you wait until now to tell anyone?" I asked.

"Look," Bob said, staring into my eyes. "I still loved her, and I trusted her, before I heard about her and Melcher. And I had hopes for my appeal. And someone had to stay home and take care of the kids."

But now the children were nearly grown. Bob had reconciled with his first wife and three sons. He had grown to hate Judi with the same intensity with which he'd previously loved her. Most importantly, he now had a chance to leave prison alive. I saw his point: What reason did he have to spare Judi?

Two days after my second meeting with Bob, I flew to Phoenix to meet with Judi's daughter, Marie. On the plane I'd worried that she might change her mind and not show up, but when she answered the door of her small apartment, its walkway strewn with trash and broken glass, she told me that she'd woken up at four in the morning to prepare for our visit.

Marie was fourteen when I'd last seen her, at Bob's first trial in 1981. In 1986, I'd read her testimony confirming Judi's affair with Bill Melcher. Over the next few hours in Phoenix, as I got to know her better, it struck me that in a cast of characters all eager to portray themselves as victims, Marie had some of the best grounds to do so, even as she complained the least.

In the five years since she had run away from home, Marie had worked at a series of marginal jobs while moving from boyfriend to boyfriend. At the time of our interview, she was living with a man named Sam, the father of her two-year-old baby, although he didn't appear while I was there. She said Sam sometimes beat her, and she wore thick makeup that looked like it was covering a bruise.

The one time her face truly lit up all that day was when she remembered her trip to the Bay Area to testify, to try to help Bob Singer. The Hallinans had flown her and her then-boyfriend, Greg, to San Francisco, booking them at a high-priced hotel near City Hall, where maids turned their sheets down each night and put little chocolates on their pillows. They ate thirty-dollar breakfasts, shopped, worked out at Gold's Gym, and swam in the Hallinans' pool in Marin County. It was the best week of her life.

Marie told me she'd agreed to testify because she still loved her stepfather and was grateful for the way he'd looked after her and her brothers. This was surprising, given that she also said she'd been convinced for years that Bob had hired Gary Oliver to kill her father. She was somehow able to forgive Bob for that, but she couldn't forgive Judi. She blamed her not only for Howard's murder, but also for years of cruelty toward her.

Judi had treated her like a "maid" from the time that she and Howard had adopted her, when she was still in grade school, Marie said. She'd made her wash the dishes, clean bathrooms, and look after her younger brothers. "She said I came from the gutter, and could always go back there," she told me. "And whenever I didn't work hard enough, or did something wrong, she'd throw things at me. She threw glass jars, shoes ... once she even hit me with a golf club. Once I had to go to the ER and get five stitches on my head."

Even knowing what I knew about Judi by then, these stories surprised me. I was more than willing to believe she'd had a role in her ex-husband's murder, but still believed she was a devoted mother. I also found it hard to imagine her being that out of control, even behind closed doors. What made it all the harder was the way Marie told me her stories, always smiling her sweet smile, even as her tales became increasingly lurid. Two years after running away, she said, while living with a girlfriend in Tempe, she'd been raped repeatedly over two days by an intruder who broke into the apartment with a sawed-off shotgun.

I did all I could to check out all these stories. Over the next few days, I tracked down Marie's old boyfriend, Greg, who told me he'd seen Judi slap Marie in the face. Greg's mother, Audrey Dove, then told me that Marie had complained to her for months about Judi's mistreatment before Audrey finally decided to help her run away from home. I also found a 1988 local newspaper report confirming Marie's account of the break-in and rapes, although it didn't mention Marie's name. The story said the victim had been treated at a hospital but the intruder had escaped arrest.

In later years, I'd ask everyone who might have had some knowledge of Judi and Marie's relationship what, if anything, they'd seen. Phillip Frandler, a close family friend, said he believed that only Howard, her father, had shown her any love. Eric Singer, Bob's youngest son, who lived with Judi and Bob for a few months when he was fourteen said he'd seen Judi slap Marie's face. One of Judi's in-laws remembered going to dinners at their home in Michigan, during which Judi would make Marie wait on the guests. "We all felt sorry for that girl," she said.

I asked Marie why she hadn't said anything about Judi's mistreatment when she testified in 1986. When Jack Marshall, the prosecutor, had asked her about the relationship, she'd simply said it had been a little "shaky," adding, "You know, mother and daughter have their normal arguments." She told me she'd wanted to avoid further antagonizing Judi, but that she'd failed. Within a few weeks after the hearing, Judi's lawyer, Richard Goldstein, had written her—she showed me the letter—to say that he was cutting off her payments from Howard Witkin's trust. Around the same time, both of her brothers, whom she'd loved and cared for over several years, stopped responding to her calls. "That was the hardest," she told me, her fixed smile briefly fading. "That really hurts."

Throughout the hours I spent with Marie, I tried to keep my journalist's face on. But this got harder as the day went by. At first, as she was telling me about her partner Sam's abuse, I hesitantly suggested: "Maybe you ought to think about why you are drawn to men who hurt you." By the end of the day, I was no longer suggesting anything, much less hesitantly, but rather urging her to get out of that apartment, to see a therapist, to read books I recommended about victims of abuse. She responded to all my suggestions with the same sweet smile. By the time I finally left to catch my plane, I wanted to adopt her myself. And I was angrier at Judi than I'd ever been before. What would make someone that cruel?

30

Flint, Michigan, January 1992

Judi leaned forward, her brown eyes intent and liberally enhanced with teal, Wet n Wild eyeshadow from the Genesee County Jail inmate commissary. She wanted to give me advice about writing my book about her husband's killing—the crime for which she had been locked up in Flint for the past five months, as she fought extradition to San Jose.

"Will you start with the murder?" she asked. "That's the way I'd start."

In the same month that I interviewed Bob Singer and Marie Witkin, Judi had surprised me by immediately answering my letter requesting an interview. She agreed that I could come see her right away. In our first of what would be four visits that week, she was as chummy as she'd been more than a decade ago, just before she sued me—even to the point of offering that writing advice.

And maybe, I found myself thinking, starting with the murder *was* a good idea.

I nodded encouragingly as I wrote down Judi's suggestion while silently cursing myself for my reflexive sheepish grin. After all these years, and all the terrible things I now knew about her, she still managed to intimidate me.

She was wearing a light-green cotton jail jumpsuit and white converse tennis shoes. I was decked out in an expensive black cashmere sweater, skinny black jeans, and the new black leather boots I'd bought two days after getting my book advance. But I still felt less confident and feminine next to her, a feeling that was painfully familiar. It was just the way I'd always felt with my mother, as if the two of them knew secrets about being a woman and a mother that I'd probably never learn.

Judi and I were alone and free to talk for as long as we wanted, thanks to the extraordinary indulgence of the warden, Sheriff Joe Wilson, who let us use his office without a chaperone. Snow flurries beat against the office window, but we were warm inside, the furnace blasting.

Our privileged time together was just one of the special favors Judi had cajoled from Sheriff Wilson, who was already such a notorious softie that local reporters called him Never Say No Joe. Wilson had taken a special interest in Judi during her time in Flint, as he told me when I took him to dinner that week to thank him.

"She's by far the most articulate prisoner I've ever met," he said. She had impressed him so much in her first month in his custody that he'd even invited her to speak to his community college class, on the topic of: "An Insider's View of the Criminal Justice System."

But Wilson also wanted me to know he wasn't hoodwinked. "She's highly *goal-oriented*," he ventured, cutting into his veal.

"Is she guilty?" I asked.

"Oh, yeah, but she'll be acquitted," he said. "The crime was so long ago, and someone's already in jail for it."

I wondered if he were right. Judi had certainly seemed optimistic about her chances. Her mother had recently died and left her money, which she was using to fight extradition to California for as long as she could. She said she knew she'd have to go back eventually, but that it made tactical sense to stretch it out. "They've got a weak case, and a weak case gets weaker over time," she said. "And you can delay for *illimitable* reasons."

What Judi didn't have to explain, because it was so obvious, was that once she resigned herself to waiting in jail, doing so in Flint made a lot of sense. Compared to the crowded San Jose facilities, the Flint jail was deluxe: clean, modern, and spacious, with liberal visiting hours, generous access to phones, and opportunities for lots of extra perks. Soon after she arrived, Judi joined the housing unit, an elite cleanup cadre whose members got soft drinks and videos when their work passed inspection. She pioneered a project in which women prisoners knitted gifts to be donated to local senior citizen's homes. She'd also charmed several of the guards, who smuggled in salads for her from McDonald's and let her use the Jacuzzi when she complained of a pinched nerve.

For Christmas, she boasted, she'd even managed to set up a conference-call system whereby she could call her sons collect and have them connect her to Saks Fifth Avenue to shop by catalogue. But most importantly, in Michigan she was near her family: her father, stepfather, and sister. Between them and old friends, she routinely had more visits than any other prisoner.

I learned from Sheriff Wilson that the other, mostly younger inmates looked up to Judi and confided in her. With more disposable income than anyone else, she rewarded her best friends with coveted small gifts—little bottles of shampoo and conditioner and emery boards. Several of them called her "Mom."

What did my "goal-oriented" interviewee think she might gain by agreeing to speak with me? In recent weeks, her father, sister, and several friends had all refused to be interviewed, saying this was at Judi's wish. In San Jose, the chapter president of Hadassah hung up on me when I called. Despite my frustration, I admired Judi's command of such loyalty in her moment of disgrace. Maybe now she was merely trying to find out what I knew, to size me up and find a way to control me if she could. Or maybe she was just bored. "It's pretty great to be talking to someone who isn't a whore or a drug addict," she confided on our first visit. Either way, she seemed confident in her ability to keep her secrets.

She listened carefully to all of my questions and told me a lot about her life in jail, but every time I tried to get her to discuss why, for instance, the San Jose prosecutors thought they had enough evidence to convict her, she skittered away.

"I've always said I wanted this whole story told," she said on our first visit. "It's just that I don't trust my instincts. I have to do what my lawyer tells me." Her lawyer, she added, didn't want her to talk to me at all, but she couldn't resist.

"Well, thanks," I muttered.

"Despite everything, I've always liked you, Kathy," Judi said suddenly, flashing one of her sunniest smiles. "I think if we'd met under different circumstances, we'd have been friends."

"I could see that," I agreed. Despite everything, I really could.

Judi's social success at the jail, and for that matter with me, illustrates a widely acknowledged truth about narcissistic people, which is that they're often at least initially endearing. One study suggests that narcissists charm others with their seeming self-assuredness and their attractive, often expensive clothes. Their vanity leads them to present themselves well and seem successful, whether or not that's true. Yet after some time—another study put the average at seven weeks—these surface impressions wear off, as the narcissist's other traits, such as thin skins, self-absorption, and exploitation of others become obvious.

I saw the seeds of Judi's jail mates' disillusionment with her during my visits. Judi couldn't seem to help herself from making snarky comments about them behind their backs, as when she told me she was tired of talking to addicts and whores. At one point I watched her hug a black deputy sheriff and then brazenly ask Joe Wilson, the warden, once the deputy was out of sight: "Any way we can get a Clorox moment?" by which, as she had to explain to both of us, meant a white guard.

Already by then, at least a few other inmates had begun to envy her privileges and doubt her sincerity.

"She asks everyone about their cases but won't say a word about hers," said Tracey Oskey, a red-headed woman in her twenties awaiting trial for selling cocaine. "She knows everything about everybody and what do we know about her? Nothing."

Before the end of Judi's first year, as I'd later hear from Sheriff Wilson, several inmates had turned against her. Some suspected her of giving information to the guards to win their favor. Others decided she was cruel. During my visit, one inmate told me how Judi had reacted after another inmate's boyfriend was stabbed to death. The woman hadn't yet heard the news, and her friends were planning to break it to her gently. But before they could do so, Judi ran up and told the woman herself, in front of everyone else.

"Nobody understood why she had to be so mean," the inmate said.

Today I'm still embarrassed to recall how nice I was to Judi in Flint, how gentle my questioning was, and how before each visit I brought her little treats, like sodas or paperback books from a nearby drugstore.

None of it got me any closer to the truth. Throughout our interviews, Judi steadfastly refused to talk about Bob's phone call or any other potential evidence against her. Only a few times did she even allude to her tangled relationships with

Howard, Bob, or Bill Melcher, and then it was only in the most general terms. When, on our second to last interview, I summoned my nerve to ask what she had been thinking when she went along with Bill Melcher's plan to stage a shooting in East San Jose, she looked at me impatiently. "As a woman, you should understand," she said.

"I really don't!" I blurted out, in an exception to my otherwise ingratiating behavior.

She rolled her eyes at me, as if I were simply too thick to be worth further effort.

I stopped myself from rolling my eyes back at her in the hope of preserving whatever relationship this was. Writing a book was different than daily reporting, I told myself: I had to make longer-term investments. Which maybe was smarter than it felt at the time. When I asked if she'd be willing to write to me after I left, Judi agreed. At some point, I figured, she might want to tell someone the truth, and I wanted her to choose me. Still, I did take a risk on one question she might not have liked, but which I'd wondered about for years. She was obviously bright, and in her way ambitious, and she'd come of age when feminists were still riding high. Why hadn't she ever considered a career?

Judi insisted she wasn't that much of an anachronism.

"That was my generation," she retorted. "I wanted the two-point-three kids."

I wondered if that were really true. She was born in 1948, and technically a Boomer. Her generation was the *sixties*. But I didn't push it.

On the morning of our last interview before I planned to fly back to San Francisco, I made my usual stop at the drugstore to pick Judi up a little gift. I laughed when I caught myself reaching for a book I thought she might find interesting: Sue Grafton's *F is for Fugitive*.

Maybe not a great idea. Without thinking twice, I then picked up another paperback that had gotten even better reviews. Today I'm still impressed by how my brain once again seemed to turn off for an instant, much like it had in 1981 when I erroneously accused Judi of murder.

When I handed her the book, Judi said drily, "That's nice, Kathy."

I looked at the cover again and blushed.

"Oh, jeez, sorry!" I said. I'd told myself I was buying her a gift sure to win her goodwill. How could I have missed the implications of presenting Judi with Anne Rice's *Interview with the Vampire*?

As easy as I'd found it to be friendly with her, my subconscious still wasn't on board.

31

Flint, June 1992

Not that surprisingly, three months was nowhere near enough time to finish my book about Howard Witkin's murder—especially since, as my leave ended, Judi was still fighting extradition, and no one knew when she would go to trial. I stored my notes away and plunged back into reporting on Mexico and Central America, but on my next home leave that June, I stopped in Flint for a few more days to do a little more digging. As usually happens when you're reporting, sources lead you to more sources, and I'd gotten a few tips that seemed worth following up.

One of these tips led me to the Genesee County courthouse, where I found to my delight that Judi's parents had been as litigious as she was, providing a trove of documentary evidence of what I soon learned had been her awful childhood.

The trail began in 1950, with a personal-injury lawsuit filed by Judi's mother, Serene Morris, against her country club. Such lawsuits were rare at that time, but Serene was a pioneer. She'd been hit in the head with a golf ball, which she claimed had resulted in chronic headaches, dizziness, "traumatic neurosis," and "emotional instability," all conditions that she said interfered with her "housewifely duties," including caring for her only child, Judi, who was then just two years old. Jurors rejected the lawsuit after just fifteen minutes of deliberation, but I'm guessing Serene's various illnesses explained why she proceeded to send Judi to live with her parents, kosher immigrant grocers in Bay City, on the banks of Lake Huron in eastern Michigan. Madonna, Bay City's most famous native daughter, would later dismiss the place as "a smelly little town." Yet for Judi, it may have been a refuge from the growing turmoil of her parents' marriage.

Serene returned to the courthouse in 1953 to file for divorce from Judi's father, Bob Barnett, after a marriage of less than seven years. Friends of the couple were surprised they lasted even that long. Serene was tall, attractive, and flamboyant, with some obviously narcissistic traits, while Bob was soft-spoken, retiring, and modest. It took Judi's mother less than a year to find a more like-minded partner in a wealthy entrepreneur named Bobby Adell.

No one would have described Bobby Adell as modest. While courting Serene, he was building his future twenty-five-million-dollar fortune from his car-parts manufacturing firm and inventions that included a rubber door-edge guard that became a standard feature in U.S.–manufactured cars. He liked to hand out hundred-dollar bills as gifts, and joked about his "golden rule," namely: "He who holds the gold makes the rules." He helped elect Detroit Mayor Jerome Cavanaugh, who appointed him as Fire Commissioner, after which Adell drove around with a siren on the fender of his bright red Cadillac.

Adell befriended local celebrities including the comedian Jackie Mason and the Teamsters boss Jimmy Hoffa. Michigan cops long suspected he had ties with the local mafia, but his "personal security advisor," a former FBI agent named William Lamb, told me he was more of a wannabe. "He used to like to go to restaurants where they were," Lamb said when I spoke to him that week in his cabin overlooking the Lake of the Clouds, in Michigan's Upper Peninsula. "It's not so much that he wouldn't have wanted to join—I wouldn't put that past him," Lamb said, "but he was Jewish, so they never would have accepted him." During Prohibition, Detroit hosted a notorious Jewish mafia, known as the "Purple Gang," but in the late 1920s a rival Sicilian group began a campaign to eliminate them, and within another decade the Purple leaders had either been murdered, jailed, or run out of town.

Serene and Bobby had two children together: Larry, born in 1957, and Joan in 1962. Judi moved back in with them just before Larry was born, although Adell, who was generous and protective with his own offspring, never adopted her and always kept her at arm's length. "I raised her, but I wasn't her father," Lamb told me Adell would say. Judi nonetheless called him "Dad" and used his surname through her years in high school.

While living with Serene and Bobby, nine-year-old Judi, much like seven-year-old Marie many years later, became the family's "live-in babysitter." It must have been hard work, but when Judi and I talked about those years during our interviews in Flint, she smiled, telling me how much she adored Joan and Larry and enjoyed being their stand-in mom. "It gave me a sense of purpose; I felt useful," she told me, which must have been particularly important in that house where she never entirely belonged. In high school, she said she would rush home early to find little Joan waiting in the front yard for her to take her to Sherman's Drug Store for ice cream.

In 1963, when Judi was fifteen, the family moved into a nine-bedroom mansion on a corner lot in Birmingham, a wealthy Detroit suburb, where they were waited on by what were then called "colored" housekeepers. Serene drove her own baby-blue Cadillac and wore diamond earrings and a necklace valued together at twenty-five-thousand dollars, according to court documents. But her conflicts with Bobby were already becoming the stuff of local legend. In court papers, Serene accused Bobby of adultery, drunkenness, bugging her phone, threatening to kill her, and having her investigated for drug abuse by his friends in the police. He filed a counterclaim charging that she was addicted to barbiturates, which he said compromised her "ability to discharge her marital obligations," even as she also "lasciviously" consorted with other men.

A family friend I interviewed that week said that Serene, who had paid little attention to Judi as a child, began to focus on her after Judi started high school. She put her daughter on a diet, supervised her wardrobe, and taught her to lighten her hair. Starting around this time, as I read in the divorce papers, Serene also recruited her daughter as an ally against her husband, a dynamic familiar to me, although in this case under more dramatic circumstances. Serene brought Judi with her as she cruised the parking lots of Detroit's motels, looking for Bobby's red Cadillac. Her hope was to catch him in the act of adultery, thus winning an advantage in court. All this further alienated Bobby from his stepdaughter.

When Judi was sixteen, Serene won a restraining order against Bobby after charging he had beaten her and Judi. She supported the claim with emergency room records that noted she had arrived at night with her clothes ripped apart and contusions on her face and arms. (The records make no mention of Judi's condition.) But the injunction didn't stop the violence. Serene soon filed another affidavit describing another melee. Bobby, she reported, had shown up at the house, gulped down a fifth of whiskey, and thrown his glass on the floor. When Joan began to scream and Judi tried to comfort her, Bobby picked up a vase and struck Judi with it in the face.

Serene filed for divorce three times, dropping the suit twice before finally following through in 1964. Shortly thereafter, Bobby developed heart trouble and moved to Palm Springs. Over the next few years, the two of them each married two new spouses yet stayed in close touch. Each time Serene divorced, she would return to using Bobby's surname, and he would return to paying her bills, Lamb told me. The family also convened periodically for restaurant meals and vacationed together in Bobby's motor home.

I visited Judi in jail just once during that second trip to Flint. What I'd read in the divorce papers had made me feel as if we'd shared a similar sort of wound, and one that had become increasingly worrisome for me. Abundant research confirms how common it is for abused children to grow up to be abusive parents. Did that explain why Judi had been so terrible to Marie, and possibly why she had committed a murder? And did it mean I was doomed to be a failure if I ever decided to have children myself?

Of course, lots of traumatized people obey the law all their lives. Childhood trauma is no justification for the crimes of which Judi was accused. Still, it seemed at least part of an explanation. After learning about Judi's upbringing I felt new compassion for her and a resolve to better understand her. But I still regretted my earlier fawning, so this time I forced myself to be more direct. She'd earlier described her childhood as idyllic, I reminded her, but what was it really like to live with Bobby Adell? What about those beatings?

She looked at me blankly.

"That never happened," she said. "Bobby was a wonderful father to me. I always looked up to him."

In that moment, she looked just like my mother whenever I'd tried to get her talking about my dad's abuse of my brothers. By then I'd learned that denial, and even dissociation, is a common reaction to extreme stress. I also knew how much work it takes and how much help you need to see past your own defenses. So I just nodded, grateful for the hard evidence of Bobby's abuse in all those documents. They reminded me of the written records I'd kept as a child, when my parents pretended that nothing was wrong to the point that I doubted what I'd seen.

A few days after Judi denied that her stepfather had ever hurt her, I got further confirmation of it from one of Judi's formerly closest friends from Mills College, who'd become a lawyer in Saint Petersburg, Florida. Her name was Adrien "Dusty" Waller, and in an interview she recounted a conversation she'd had with Judi over the telephone during their freshman year winter break. Judi told her that as a punishment for something, Bobby had tied her to a hot furnace in the basement. "She was terrified. I think she was even burned," Dusty told me. Dusty also said that Judi had told her that Bobby had beaten her as a child, and that she feared for the safety of her two half-siblings who were then still living with him. But the next time I spoke to Judi, over the phone years later, she said Dusty must have been mistaken. Nothing like that had ever happened.

Judi and her friends did agree on one point, which was that even as a teenager, Judi had longed for the kind of conventional stability represented by her grandparents in Bay City. In her senior year at Seaholm High School, while Serene and Bobby were still fighting in court, Judi joined the Future Social Workers club and was secretary of the National Honor Society. "Judi was entirely different from Serene—refined, quiet, anxious to do everything well," a former neighbor told me. She studied hard and got good grades and high scores on her college entrance tests, winning admission to Mills, where she planned to major in religious studies. She enrolled in September 1966.

It was in college that Judi first showed her talent for making loyal women friends—and manipulating people. Dusty Waller and others said she was the leader of a group of girls who took regular outings together to San Francisco. On Halloween, she got them all to dress in matching skirts and sweaters as characters from Mary McCarthy's 1963 novel, *The Group*, which followed eight close friends after their years at Vassar College. The girls wore tags with the names of the characters, some of which weren't flattering— McCarthy had described a girl named "Pokey," for instance, as fat, rich, and lazy. But most of Judi's friends hadn't read the book.

"I adored Judi," one of her pals told me. "She was sweet, kind, and generous. I remember once being blue, and she surprised me with a little greeting card. I remember her telling me to smile more. I was bashful and frowny."

Yet just as she'd later do at the Flint jail, Judi eventually alienated some of her friends at Mills. Gloria Ziskind, who lived across the hall from her, described the afternoon that she lost faith. While sitting in Judi's room reading a book, she overheard her persuading two of her friends in succession to run for student body president, promising to be each girl's campaign manager, and telling neither of them about her promise to the other. Perhaps it was an innocent misunderstanding, but Gloria was sure it was evidence of Judi's manipulativeness. "I could never understand why she would do it, except as a cruel psychological experiment," she said.

It bothered her so much that Gloria told the two girls what she had witnessed. But to her surprise, neither took offense. Instead they told Judi, who complained to the housemother that Gloria was spreading rumors about her. The housemother held a meeting to try to get Judi and her accuser to resolve their conflict. Nothing was settled, but as the meeting ended and Judi was walking back to her room in her pajamas, she collapsed in the hallway from what she would later tell friends was a bladder infection. Her housemates flocked around her, and the girl who had complained understood that she was now on the outs.

In the summer before she'd enrolled in college, Judi met Howard Witkin through a family friend and the two began to date.

Phillip "Flip" Frandler, who was then Howard's best friend, had a girlfriend at Mills and remembered seeing Judi in the dining room one night that fall. He wasn't impressed. "Mink hat, mink muff, mink stole," he recalled. "It was a sad sight. Nineteen going on forty."

But Howard was smitten, Frandler said. "I never saw him so excited. He was all smiles from ear to ear."

Judi and Howard got engaged when she was still a freshman. She announced the news, according to a Mills tradition, by asking that a lit candle be passed around the dinner table, keeping everyone guessing until it arrived at her seat, where she blew out the flame. She would drop out of Mills the next year.

Judi and Howard got married on June 10, 1968, a year distinguished by the escalating war in Vietnam, riots in Chicago, and the murders of Martin Luther King, Jr., and Bobby Kennedy. In Atlantic City, women's liberation activists threw false eyelashes and mops into a "Freedom Trash Can" to protest plans for the next Miss America contest. Many of Judi's contemporaries at Mills were reading Betty Friedan's *The Feminine Mystique* and Sylvia Plath's *The Bell Jar*, while dreaming of big careers. Yet even in those years, shows like *Leave it to Beaver* were still popular, pigeonholing women as mothers, nurses, schoolteachers, and secretaries. In 1964, a *San Francisco Chronicle* critic could still get away with describing a crowd of female Beatles' fans as "shrieking with the agony of unfulfilled motherhood."

Judi told her college friends that what she wanted from marriage, most of all, were babies: lots of them, and as soon as possible. She also reveled in becoming the daughter-in-law to Howard's long-married parents. Her friend Dusty Waller remembered Judi as "hysterically happy" after spending an afternoon shopping for lingerie for her trousseau with her mother-in-law to be, Geraldyne Witkin. Howard's mother was a pillar of her synagogue and Judi was determined to follow her lead. "Her conception of her future was to be the matriarch, the person who made the business gracious, the party-giver, the strong woman behind the man," Dusty told me. "I never got the sense that she thought Howard was intelligent. But he didn't need to be, because she was."

The Witkins celebrated the engagement with a weekend of old world–style festivities, including a band and champagne, followed by a series of showers, lunches, and formal dinners leading up to the June wedding. Judi and Howard then left for a three-week honeymoon in Europe.

"Howard and the Witkins were her salvation," Dusty told me. "They loved her unconditionally. It was supposed to be her happy ending."

It didn't work out that way, however. Judi and Howard returned from their honeymoon trip a week earlier than they had planned, looking, according to friends, much less in love. Judi later told Bob Singer, who told me, that Howard was "all but impotent."

In the fall of 1968, the couple moved to Tacoma, Washington, so that Howard could finish college at the University of Puget Sound. Daniel was born the following spring, after which the family returned to California, settling into their new home in Los Gatos.

Judi adored her "Little Messiah" and couldn't wait to have more children. But she went on to have two miscarriages, after which her doctor advised her to stop trying. In tears, Judi called one of her old college friends, weeping, to say she had always counted on being a fulltime mother, "But how can you do that with just one child?"

To fill her time, Judi ramped up her volunteer work, signing up for the Diabetes Association, serving on the board at Temple Emanu-El, and in 1973 being elected president of the six-hundred-member San Jose chapter of Hadassah. "Hadassah was de rigueur for Witkin women," Judi explained to me in Flint. Both Geraldyne Witkin and Geraldyne's mother, Sylvia, had served as chapter presidents before her.

Sylvia was known as the chapter's "angel," who for as long as anyone could remember had sponsored the annual donor luncheon. But in short order, Judi surpassed both women in her fundraising talent. She helped turn the group into one of the nation's most dynamic chapters, topping that off by becoming vice president of the larger regional organization, which included all of California and parts of Nevada. Yet as she dedicated more of her time to Hadassah, Howard spent more of his at the Garden City Card Club.

To her friends, Judi seemed resigned to make whatever family life she could in Los Gatos. In 1974, she convinced Howard to adopt seven-year-old Marie Natanya, who had bad teeth but a contagious smile. But that October, Judi heard devastating news. She was hosting a Hadassah meeting at a friend's house when Serene tracked her down by phone to say that Judi's beloved half-brother, Larry, had gone missing the day before. Early that morning, Bobby Adell had gotten an anonymous call. Larry had been kidnapped, the caller said, and the ransom was four-hundred-thousand dollars in small bills.

William Lamb, Bobby's "personal security advisor," told me what happened next, some details of which I'd later confirm in newspaper reports.

Larry, sixteen, had been living with Bobby on his estate near the Palm Canyon Country Club in Palm Springs. But Bobby had failed to control his son's growing drug habit. The last thing Larry told his friends before he disappeared was that he was headed for a meeting with his marijuana dealer.

Judi was distraught when she got off the call with Serene, and her friends gathered around her. Some of the women exchanged looks of disbelief as Judi told them what she'd heard. It seemed so impossibly dramatic, one friend recalled.

As a favor to Bobby Adell, the Palm Springs police kept Larry's disappearance out of the newspapers for several weeks while he tried to bargain with the kidnappers. Those efforts failed but gave the FBI time to track down and arrest two suspects: Angelo Inciso, a former union president, and Hugh Pheaster, a convicted robber. The two were charged with extortion, but both refused to talk until Bobby assigned William Lamb, his right-hand man, to work on the case. In a creative if ethically questionable move, Lamb became Pheaster's lawyer and worked out a deal with prosecutors to give Pheaster limited immunity in exchange for the truth.

Pheaster said that Larry had willingly participated in his own kidnapping, even informing his abductors that Bobby had recently earned four-hundred-thousand dollars from selling some bonds. The plan was to split the ransom three ways. But then, as Pheaster claimed, Inciso accidently killed Larry with an overdose injection of phenobarbital.

Over the next three years, Bobby's passion to find his son alive became determination to give him a proper burial. In November 1977, Pheaster agreed to lead Lamb and the police to Larry's body. For three days the convict, in chains, wandered through the arid wilderness near Desert Hot Springs before he could locate the unmarked grave. Bobby rented heavy equipment to dig everywhere Pheaster suggested. When at last part of the skeleton was unearthed, Lamb told me he watched as Bobby clawed at the sand with his bare hands until he found the skull, which he raised in the sunlight, searching for confirmation. The jaw dropped open, revealing metal braces, and Bobby wept.

Those three years between Serene's phone call to Judi and the discovery of Larry's remains spanned the decline and end of Judi's marriage to Howard Witkin. As she testified at Bob Singer's murder trial, she first caught Howard smoking marijuana in 1974, the same year Larry disappeared. What she never said publicly but did tell Bob Singer soon after they first met, after which Bob told me, was that Howard gave Larry his first joint. Later, she also told Bob that she blamed Howard for Larry's death. Her divorce from Howard became final the same year Larry's body was found.

As I listened to Lamb tell this story, in his lakeside cabin, I felt as if I'd picked up the missing piece to Judi's puzzle: the clue to how she could hate her ex-husband—and fear his influence on her children—so much as to want him dead. I had been driven for so long by an urge to understand her, and after that long interview was prepared, to a limited extent, to empathize. Even not being a mother myself, I could imagine how easy it might be to be blinded by fear for the safety of my children. Yet after I returned to California, and Judi and I spoke on the phone, she refused to say anything about Larry's death or his relation to Howard.

After that, there seemed to be little else to say. Judi was keeping her secrets even as I kept some of my own. I didn't even consider telling her about my plan to travel next to Atlanta, where I had one more interview on my list. It was a meeting Judi surely would have tried to prevent if she had known about it. My interviewee was an FBI agent with whom Judi had lived for several months in Flint, and whose marriage she had helped destroy.

32

Atlanta, June 1992

I first learned about Judi's affair with the FBI agent from Judi's daughter, Marie, who had still been living with her at the time. The agent was listed in the phonebook in Atlanta, where his Michigan supervisors had transferred him after learning about the relationship. I didn't expect he would agree to talk with me when I first tracked him down, but he seemed oddly eager to meet. He hadn't talked to anyone about Judi besides his wife and mother, he said, and was still trying to understand it. He just asked that I not use his real name in print, so I promised to refer to him as "Stan."

We met at the Hampton Inn coffee shop near the Atlanta airport. Stan was in his early forties, tall and muscular, with a touching *what-hit-me?* expression. Our interview stretched over six hours as we transitioned from breakfast rolls and coffee to more coffee to a late lunch. I was already familiar with Judi's seduction techniques from my interviews with Bob Singer and her letters to Bill Melcher. But Stan's recollections were exceptionally clear and detailed, an advantage of his professional experience. He reconstructed his affair with Judi much as if he were investigating a crime.

Stan and his wife, a corporate executive whom I interviewed by phone a few days later and agreed to call "Sally," met Judi through a mutual friend in the summer of 1982. This was several months after Bob Singer was sentenced in San Jose, although Stan and Sally had no idea then of Judi's involvement in that crime. The three of them met for the first time over happy hour at Mr. Gibby's, a Flint fern bar hangout for local young professionals. After that, Stan started seeing Judi there regularly on muggy summer nights while Sally was working late.

Judi had rented a townhouse that year in Grand Blanc, an expensive suburb of Flint. She told all her new friends that she was a widow whose husband had died in a car accident and left her with a trust fund. She was having quite a lot of fun for someone whose first husband had only recently been murdered and whose second husband had been sentenced to life in prison.

Both Stan and Sally liked Judi right away and were delighted to find that Stan's thirteen-year-old son by his previous marriage got along so well with her three kids.

This was especially convenient for Sally, who felt frazzled that summer. She had recently been promoted to a high-level job that required her to work many more hours, sometimes even weekends, and occasionally to travel out of town. Her friendship with Judi seemed like a timely gift, since Judi seemed to have so much free time and was so happy to help out. Judi offered to pick up Stan's son at school when Sally and Stan were working and was soon also bringing sandwiches and freshly baked casseroles over to the house. Sally couldn't believe her good luck. "I've never been into all that Betty Crocker stuff," she told me. She probably would have felt guilty spending all that time at the office, she added, if it weren't for Judi filling in as earth mother.

On weekends, Judi brought her kids to the new house that Sally and Stan were busy building on Lake Fenton, about thirteen miles south of Flint. The children swam together, watched TV, and ate popcorn. The three adults kept saying how it felt like one big family, although Marie recalled one moment when it didn't—when she caught her mother ogling Stan in his black Speedo, and whispering to her: "Doesn't he have the best body?"

"I could tell she was interested in me," Stan confided at the Hampton Inn. To his surprise, that excited him. "Until then, I'd always been a play-by-rules kind of guy," he said. He'd never before cheated on a wife or even on a steady girlfriend. But he'd also never met anyone like Judi.

"She was so beautiful—so slim and blond—and also so smart," he said. Relaxing together at Mr. Gibby's on evenings when Sally was still at the office, they talked about books and politics. Stan couldn't remember the last time he and Sally had enjoyed such leisurely, thought-provoking conversations. And Judi had a way of making Stan feel cozy, even in the crowded bar; she listened so attentively, repeatedly touching his arm, and she seemed able to guess his moods, sometimes even his thoughts. He began to joke with her about it, asking, "Are you sure you're not a witch?" It was heady stuff, he said, especially for Flint.

What impressed Stan the most in those early months, he said, was Judi's extraordinary kindness. He was moved watching the way she drew people to her and treated them so well that in a short time she was able to win their affection and loyalty. Shortly after they were first introduced, Judi began sending him cheerful notes on her elegant, cream-colored stationery. Then she presented him with a small gift: a little statuette of a golfer. He was flattered to realize that she'd paid attention when he said he liked golf. Similarly, she listened closely when he told her how much he loved salads, and after quizzing him on precisely what he liked, shopped for the freshest ingredients—radishes, avocados, and feta cheese were his favorites—and invited him over for lunchtime vegetarian feasts at her apartment. "No woman other than my mother ever treated me that well," Stan told me.

In September, Stan and Sally and their son moved into their new house by the lake. Over a late dinner there, three days before their third anniversary, Sally asked Stan if he were happy. She didn't suspect he wasn't, as she told me later; she just wanted to show she cared. His response shocked and dismayed her. "No," he said. "We've made a mistake. I want this marriage to be over."

Stan wouldn't tell Sally what was wrong, and when she pressed him, he clammed up. At two in the morning he'd fallen asleep but she was still sobbing and frantic enough to risk waking the one friend she felt sure would console her, even at that hour. She was right: Judi didn't seem to mind being woken up and also seemed truly concerned. Sally wouldn't understand the depth of Judi's duplicity until the next week, when Stan left home to move in with her.

While Sally nursed her hurt and anger, Stan guiltily enjoyed himself. He and Judi were behaving like teenagers, grabbing each other in elevators and cars, he told me. "Making love with Judi always felt so easy," he said. "I never had to initiate anything."

I nodded and smiled and slid my tape recorder closer to his plate.

Between the coffee and the cheap croissants and being obliged once again to picture Judi—with all her outward similarities to my mother—in the bedroom, I was starting to feel queasy. I appreciated Stan's honesty but just as I had with Bob Singer, with his talk of grape jelly, I couldn't help but wonder why Stan was so eager to trust a stranger with a story that made him look so gullible. Had Judi recognized and exploited this naiveté in both of these men?

"I was actually starting to think that we'd get married," Stan was saying now. He'd come to feel so close to her in such a short time, but still had one nagging worry. Judi, he was sure, was lying to him. Despite her repeated denials, Stan was convinced she had an eating disorder. She was always so thin and so concerned about her weight. And whenever they went out to eat, he noticed how she gobbled down her food and then slipped off to the bathroom—to vomit it up, he assumed.

My hand started shaking as I tried to set my coffee mug back on the saucer without spilling. I hoped Stan wouldn't notice. Apparently Judi and I had one more thing in common. Stan was describing bulimia, the same disorder I'd suffered through from age fifteen to twenty-four. I knew what it was like to be repeatedly doing that violence to yourself, while feeling you have no choice but to lie to cover up such crazy behavior. I used to think I'd never be free of it, but six months into my sessions with Dr. Y, the first person I'd ever dared to reveal it to, it vanished. Today I see this as another strange gift from Judi's lawsuit, which first pushed me into therapy.

Eating disorders were much less familiar in the mid-1980s as they are today. But Stan had studied psychology as an undergraduate and believed he recognized the symptoms.

"I finally asked her about it, but she told me she had colitis," he said. "I just didn't believe that, and I felt hurt that she didn't feel she could confide in me."

Stan dropped by the local library and did a little research on bulimia. Lying and hiding, as he learned, are often part of the addiction he suspected. Judi's lies repelled him more than her self-induced vomiting, but Stan kept telling himself that she deserved his sympathy, and that he might be able to help her. He kept encouraging her to stop lying and trust him, until she relented. And then he was sorry he'd pushed her, because Judi had an even bigger secret to reveal. She wanted to talk about Howard Witkin's murder.

Like most newspaper readers in Flint at the time, Stan vaguely remembered the town's strange connection with the killing of a California businessman two years earlier. He'd had no reason to link Judi to that story until then. Judi insisted that she'd had nothing to do with the murder, but the more she talked about it, the more Stan felt that wasn't true. "I could see from our own relationship that she wasn't the kind of woman who would ever accept less than total honesty from a lover, and I just couldn't imagine Bob Singer being able to hide something like a murder from her," he told me.

He admitted his doubts to Judi, who despite her usual intuition hadn't grasped the fact that she was fraying Stan's trust with her continual talk about the murder. She told him it was such a relief to finally be able to tell her whole story, and so, Stan said, he learned all about her stepfather's cruelty, which she had denied to me, as well as Howard's drug use during their marriage and even how she'd come to see Bill Melcher as her "life preserver" during Bob Singer's murder trial.

What she didn't say, but which Stan now realized with a jolt, was that she was looking for another life preserver: him. Gradually—at first in subtle ways but soon more and more explicitly—Judi revealed her fear of being charged with Howard's murder. "She kept asking me, how did I see it? How would I behave if I were in her place?" Stan told me.

When he was honest with himself, which he acknowledged wasn't often in those days, he understood that Judi was trying to mine his law enforcement expertise, and perhaps even hoped to gain from his stature in Flint, where everyone knew him and where he served on the YMCA board. His misgivings about her grew. What if she *did* become a murder suspect? And then what if their affair became public? How would people, including his bosses, not see that as a terrible lapse of judgment on his part?

He moved out of Judi's apartment and got back in touch with Sally, who surprised him with her willingness to reconcile. By then she felt that Judi was entirely to blame for their breakup.

But Stan discovered that saying goodbye to Judi wasn't as easy as he'd hoped, and this held true even after August 1985, when the *Flint Journal* reported that Bob Singer had filed his petition detailing the affair between Judi and Bill Melcher. Even then, while living with Sally, he secretly continued to see Judi every so often, and didn't completely stop for another two years.

The last straw for him had nothing to do with the murder case. Instead, he got fed up with hearing rumors about Judi's involvement with other men. The word at Mr. Gibby's was that she'd been seeing two dentists, a gas-station owner, an optometrist, and a professional pigeon-breeder.

Stan was transferred to Atlanta in 1988, and Sally followed him, but their marriage had taken a lethal hit. They divorced in early 1992, a few months before I spoke to them.

By the time he reached this part of his story, Stan had kept his eyes on his plate for several minutes. When he looked up, that stunned look I'd noticed in his eyes when we sat down six hours earlier was still there.

"And I guess that's the story," he said, shrugging.

We both looked down to check our watches. I shut off my tape recorder and removed the last tape I'd inserted, taking a moment to write on the label: "STAN #6." I needed that pause, that necessary task. I couldn't think of anything to say. Stan walked me out to his car to drive me to the airport, but he stopped in the parking lot as he remembered one more thing he thought I should know.

"There were signs all along that I never should have trusted her, but I think the biggest warning sign was something that happened right at the beginning," he said.

About a month after they met, after a few hours of flirting at Mr. Gibby's and after Judi had given him the golf statuette, but before they first slept together, Stan came home early one afternoon and by chance found an anonymous letter in the mailbox, addressed to his wife. Recognizing the cream-colored stationery, he opened the envelope and read a letter warning Sally that her husband cared for another woman. Stan drove immediately to Judi's townhouse and confronted her, but she denied having anything to do with it, and somehow he was able to ignore his instinct not to believe her.

Stan leaned on the hood of his car, still talking. I wanted nothing more by then than to get to my flight, watch a stupid movie, maybe have a glass of wine, or two, and get the whining sound out of my head. But what he said next forced me to refocus.

"Did she ever really love me?" he asked. "What do you think she really wanted? What if I'd gone ahead and married her back then? How do you think she would have dumped me?"

I raised my eyebrows. Did he truly think I could answer these questions? What made him think I could read Judi's mind?

Then I shook my head, and Stan shook his head back, and we said nothing more until we reached my terminal and said our goodbyes.

It was only after I'd downed three glasses of wine and watched *Thelma and Louise* that I felt ready to reflect on Stan's descriptions of Judi's behavior. Despite everything I'd learned about her until then, including her treatment of Marie, this was the first time I seriously wondered if she might altogether lack a conscience, which can be true of extreme narcissists but is also a defining feature of something considerably worse: namely, a psychopath.

"Psychopathy" isn't a recognized mental disorder, but rather a term that judges, lawyers, and prison officials apply to the most incorrigible criminals. The nearest clinical cousin is "antisocial personality disorder," a diagnosis that encompasses behaviors such as law-breaking, lying, and lack of remorse. All psychopaths (and sociopaths) are narcissists, sharing that grandiosity that covers for an insecure self, but not all narcissists are psychopaths. Evidence suggests that psychopaths have a clear neurological deficit, which is probably genetic, sets them apart, and may help explain their singular cold-bloodedness. A common belief is that psychopaths can't be cured, although some researchers claim to have had success in reducing their symptoms. Again as with narcissists, the trick may be to get them into therapy—they're notoriously unwilling—and keep them there until it starts working.

Psychopaths are universally despised. The Harvard anthropologist Jane Murphy has found such traits to be familiar even among an isolated group of Inuit near the Bering Strait, who use the term *kunlangeta* to describe someone who lies, cheats, and steals, and ignores rules and punishment. When Murphy asked one of the Inuit how a *kunlangeta* would be treated, the answer was: "Somebody would have pushed him off the ice when nobody else was looking."

This was Jack Marshall's reaction to Judi. To my surprise—because Jack was otherwise usually so kind—he'd later tell me that he felt just fine about picturing her in prison for the rest of her life. Jack shared none of my mixed feelings about Judi, particularly not my flickering sympathy. Otherwise, as he explained, he wouldn't have been able to do his job without endless agonizing. For similar reasons, Jack didn't pay much attention to debates about whether pathological narcissism or even psychopathy are genuine mental disorders, stemming from childhood traumas and possible brain malfunctions, which would suggest that even serial killers deserve treatment rather than punishment. He also rejected psychologists' theories that narcissism and even psychopathy fit on a spectrum, implying we all may have a little Judi Barnett in our souls. Judi, he concluded, was simply "a born criminal: like a heifer with a defect. It just happens sometimes."

As my plane headed for San Francisco, I asked myself—again—why on earth I'd spent so much time and energy trying to understand this troubled stranger's behavior. Initially Judi had attracted me due to her similarities with my mother. Next I was drawn in by fear, as I realized the deeper ways that she and I were alike. Talking with Stan finally put my mind to rest that while Judi and my mother and I may all have fit on the same self-absorbed spectrum, my mother and I were far enough apart from Judi to make a huge difference. My own family's problems weren't insignificant, but nor were they sinister. Or inevitable.

All this felt reassuring in that summer of 1992, as I found myself giving more thought to having children of my own. My work with Dr. Y had rid me of the fear I'd had for so long that I'd make the same kinds of mistakes that Judi or my mother had, blindly repeating that cycle of damage with my own family. Now more than ever I wanted to see Judi's story through to its end. It had somehow become wrapped up with my longing to understand—and forgive—my parents. And, once and for all, to stop thinking of myself as a victim.

33

Montevideo, August 1994

My husband Jack and I had just finished a half-bottle of Malbec and two big plates of pasta at our favorite Italian restaurant in Uruguay, where we were reporting on upcoming presidential elections. I caught his eye and smiled and made a cradling motion with my arms.

He knew what I meant. "Check, please!" he said. It was our code for: *Time to change the subject!* It usually got a laugh. This time my eyes welled up.

"You're such a jerk!" I said, throwing down my napkin and pushing back my chair.

Jumping up from my chair, I hurried out of the restaurant and back to our hotel, a couple blocks away, leaving Jack to pay the bill.

My psychiatrist sister Jean, in whom, as usual, I'd been confiding, told me that couples often split their ambivalence about big decisions. And indeed, the more I talked about having a baby, the more Jack hit the brakes. Yet whenever I dropped the subject for any length of time, he found a way to pick it up. I had just turned thirty-seven. He was forty-eight. We didn't have much more time to decide, and if we were going to have kids, we'd probably have to start making some changes.

We had moved to Rio de Janeiro a year and a half earlier, after I'd finally left the *Mercury News* for a bigger paper. The *Miami Herald* had hired me as chief of their South America bureau, a job that had me traveling constantly, responsible for major breaking news in six countries. The move made sense. Jack spoke fluent Portuguese and had longed to live in Brazil again after his time in the Peace Corps, while I was excited to report on the region for a newspaper so seriously engaged with Latin America. Jack quit his teaching job to freelance again, stringing for *Time Magazine* and the Associated Press, which gave us more time to travel together. I had yet to miss a flight or make a mistake—that I knew of. I'd reported on an attempted coup in Argentina, U.S.-sponsored human rights abuses in Paraguay, deforestation in the Amazon in Brazil, and attacks by the Sendero Luminoso guerrillas in Peru. The Buenos Aires newspaper *Ultima Hora* referred to me as "*La prolifica Ellison.*" I won awards for feature writing. On weekends, Jack and I went to bossa nova concerts and headed for the beach.

It's reasonable to wonder why I was considering blowing all of that up by having a baby. But as any mother can tell you, the desire for a baby isn't a reasonable thing. Throughout my life, I'd had many solid arguments against becoming a mother, ranging from rational observations about the kind of world I'd be bringing a child into to terror over all the ways I might personally screw them up. Somehow they all got outweighed, a couple weeks before that argument in Uruguay, by two days at a hotel in Rosarita, a beach town near Tijuana, with a fellow correspondent who'd just had a baby. While my friend swam in the infinity pool, I sat in the sun inhaling the scent of her infant's head.

After that I felt as if total strangers could recognize how I'd changed. Every time I got in a cab, the driver would ask if I had kids. In Argentina, an elderly Jewish woman Jack and I interviewed for a story on Holocaust refugees peered at us as we said goodbye at her apartment door, and whispered, apropos to nothing, "Hurry up!"

"Should we do it right here?" I asked Jack on the elevator ride to the ground floor.

I kept trying, comically, to involve my rational brain, interviewing new mothers and reading books with titles like: *A Baby? ... Maybe: A Guide to Making the Most Fateful Decision of Your Life.* But my subconscious mind was made up. In a dream, a man I didn't recognize solemnly told me: "The purpose of life is to have kids, so *they* can have kids."

"Was it the Pope?" Jack asked when I told him about it over breakfast the next morning. "Was he wearing a beanie?"

"Are you scared?" I asked Jack in the hotel in Montevideo, as we lay in bed half an hour after he'd chased me to our room.

"Maybe a little," he said. There it was again: his seeming willingness to let me make so many big decisions. Yet after eleven years together, I trusted his backbone. This wouldn't have happened if he really was decided against having kids.

Six weeks after we got back from Uruguay, I caught Jack smiling as we stared at our first ultrasound view of the embryonic offspring we were calling, for the time being, Montevideo. When I got home from the gynecologist's office, I wrote a new list:

1. Find a nanny.

2. Research maternity-leave laws.

3. Ask my new-mother correspondent friend how she broke the news to her editors.

4. Figure out everything I want to do while still childless and do as much of it as possible.

One of the things I was determined to do while still childless was to finish my book about Judi. I'd been working on it off and on for the previous three years, writing in the evenings and during vacations from my beat, and a few weeks after the ultrasound I turned in a nearly finished manuscript to my publisher, with one caveat: I still had to wait for Judi's trial to conclude, as I'd promised Jack Marshall. This had been more of a problem than I'd anticipated. Judi had managed to delay her extradition for nearly three years, earning her the dubious status of the Genesee County Jail's longest-serving unconvicted criminal. But at last she had run out of arguments and was now in jail in San Jose. Her trial was set to begin in mid-September, and I scheduled some of my vacation time to cover it. I so looked forward to the closure.

I'd promised my editors at *The Miami Herald* one more feature story before my trip to California. It was a piece on Candomblé an Afro-Brazilian religion gaining a lot of young devotees, and I was focusing the story on a famous *mae-de-santo*, a Candomblé priestess, whom I'd heard was a skilled fortune teller.

I met the priestess at her home on Rio de Janeiro's northern outskirts. She must have been in her eighties, regal in her lacy white turban and long white dress adorned with long strands of red and blue beads. She ushered me into a darkened room where we talked for nearly an hour about the story, after which I told her about Montevideo. The *mae-de-santo* chuckled, like she'd finally understood why I was there, and beckoned me closer so she could tie a colored ribbon, a *fita do Bonfim*, around my wrist to keep the evil spirits away and ensure that the wish she knew I was wishing for would come true. "Green—for new life!" she said. Then, holding my wrist, she peered into my eyes and told me what I'd hoped to hear.

"You're going to be a wonderful mother," she said.

34

San Jose, California, September 1994

I lost my *fita* on September 15, 1994, while I was on another home leave and attending Yom Kippur services with my parents. All afternoon, bored and hungry while we sat and fasted, I'd been tugging on the ribbon, and during the closing service, just before the rabbi blew the shofar, I looked down at my wrist and saw that it was gone. I searched all around my seat but couldn't find it.

This wasn't good. The folklore about *fitas* says your wish will come true if the band falls off by itself, the implication being that you don't mess with nature. Did that mean I'd be punished somehow for my anxiety and restlessness, two evil spirits all that therapy still hadn't chased off?

Between the boredom and the tugging, I'd been praying: mainly for Montevideo, but also for my embryonic book. Two days after I'd arrived in California, my New York editor had called me at my parents' house and said, "You're having trouble with this."

She was right. Nothing I'd ever tried to write before had been so difficult. But what she said next stung as much as any of the memorable insults I'd previously endured, including "opportunistic groupie," "not Shakespeare!" and "doubts about your stability."

"I hate to say this," she said, "but you're a *first-class reporter.*"

It was clear what she meant. Not a writer, but a soul-less scribbler.

There were many excuses I might have offered her. The whiplash of thinking about Judi in between flying to cover events in Chile, Argentina, and Bolivia. The fact that it was only my second book, and I was still finding my way. Trying to decide whether to get pregnant. Being pregnant. But I knew what she meant. The writing was flat. The plot was suspenseless. My ear had failed me. And more than any of that, I hadn't yet understood, much less conveyed, why this particular story had held me in its grip for most of my adult life.

In the synagogue, surrounded by families meditating on the sins of the past year, I silently catastrophized. The contract would be canceled. The publisher would ask for the advance back, even though I'd already spent it and more. I would never write another book. I'd get so depressed I wouldn't be able to keep my job. Jack would divorce me. Our dog would get hit by a car.

The next morning, I borrowed my mother's BMW to drive to the Santa Clara County criminal courthouse.

As I parked in the lot, all I could think of was why on earth I'd tied myself to this train-wreck of a tale that was now, if you started with Howard's murder, well into its fourteenth year. Over that time the Cold War had ended. Three U.S. presidents had come and gone. The U.S. had invaded Iraq. Terrorists had made their first attack on the World Trade Center.

Santa Clara County's population had grown by two hundred thousand, with crime, and fear of crime, growing apace. Now there was a giant metal detector screening everyone who entered the remodeled county courthouse.

I arrived about twenty minutes early to take my seat in the back of the windowless courtroom with its blasting air conditioner as I waited for my first glimpse of Judi Barnett. If she hadn't been led in by the guards, I might not have recognized her. She was now forty-six-years old and at least fifteen pounds heavier than she was in 1992 when I last visited her in Flint. Her hair was dull brown, hanging in limp curls. She still dressed well, in a deep-blue silk jacket the judge had OK'd for her appearances in court, but her formerly proud posture was gone. She walked stiffly, like a much older woman, and sat with her shoulders hunched forward. I'm sure I wasn't alone in that courtroom in wondering what had become of the comely Jewish siren who'd driven so many men to their ruin.

Bob Singer was the first witness for the prosecution, and as he limped to the witness stand, he seemed even more worn-out than Judi. His old back injury had flared up and his eyes looked red and watery. In the three years since he'd made that desperate late-night phone call to Judi in West Bloomfield his dream of freedom had dissolved. Disregarding all his teamwork with the DA's office, the Santa Clara police opposed his appeal for early release. On a collect call to Rio earlier that year, Bob told me he'd gone back to fearing that he would die in prison. The thought, he said, made him wake in the middle of the night, night after night, his heart racing in a claustrophobic panic.

But now he felt he had one last chance to save himself, and slim as it was, he was going for it. Over the next three days, breathing heavily, Bob again recited the story he'd told me and the prosecutors: how Judi had come to fear her children were unsafe with Howard, how she had pestered him endlessly to do something about it, how she'd threatened to leave him if he didn't arrange the murder.

The jurors expressed no emotion during much of this story, until Bob got to the part where he had tried to commit suicide in 1982. "That was Judi's idea," Bob murmured. "She said it would be for the good of the children."

At this, three jurors swiveled their heads to glare at her. I wondered if this might be the moment she lost everything, when she morphed, in their minds, from a carpool-driving Jewish mother to a monster.

Still, Bob himself lost some sympathy under cross-examination by Judi's lawyer, James Blackman, who questioned Bob's claim that he acted under "extreme pressure."

"And you seem to define this extreme pressure as Judi wouldn't talk to you?"

"Correct."

"And she was cold and aloof?"

"Correct."

"And she refused you sexually?"

"Correct."

"But she was never physically violent with you?"

"No."

"Did it ever cross your mind to just leave?" Blackman demanded.

"Yes."

"But you didn't want to *break up the family*?" Blackman asked, with heavy sarcasm.

Bob's voice until then had been strong and defiant, but this answer came in a murmur.

"I didn't want to admit I made a mistake."

The San Jose prosecutors knew what a weak witness Bob would be and had done their best to try to prop him up. Judi's adopted daughter Marie had returned to California to describe how she'd seen her mother grow enraged when she first learned of Howard's plan to take the kids on a houseboat. Tom Maciolek, the convicted getaway driver, showed up to say he'd met Bob in prison back in 1982 and heard him blame Judi for the murder, saying, "that fucking bitch caused all this." But the DA's most powerful ammunition came from Eric Singer, Bob's youngest son.

Sandy Williams, the DA investigator who three years earlier had noticed Eric's odd reaction when Bob finally told the truth to his family, had cajoled him to explain. Now Eric told the court, just as he'd previously told Sandy, that while staying with Judi and Bob, when he was just fourteen years old, he had overheard Judi telling Bob that she wanted Howard dead. Eric had kept this a secret for eleven years, and as he publicly confessed it now, he broke down in tears. "I've felt bad I'd never told Howard what I'd heard so that he could protect himself," he said.

I felt my own eyes watering as I listened to this, but there was worse to come when Judi's lawyer called on her son Nathan to contest the DA's claim that she'd tried to evade arrest. In a hesitant voice, the seventeen-year-old described the last-minute journey as a normal summer vacation—"just a break from the grind, I guess." He said Judi first took him to a hotel in Saginaw for a couple of days, after which they moved to a different hotel in Clio.

On cross-examination, however, Deputy District Attorney Richard Titus grilled Nathan about a call he'd made to his girlfriend from a payphone, telling her he was scared and couldn't reveal where he was. Nathan said he couldn't remember the call. He kept his eyes fixed on his mother as he answered the questions, his expression apologetic. Judi held his gaze.

"Did you ever remember telling your friends you didn't know if you would go back to school?" the prosecutor asked.

"No, I don't remember much of this at all," Nathan said. "This was a long time ago, and a lot's happened."

When Titus asked Nathan what he had done at the hotel in Clio, the boy said he swam in the pool. But under further questioning, Nathan conceded there wasn't a pool at the hotel, and that all he and Judi had done was "hang out and order room service."

"It was upsetting," he burst out. "I didn't know what was going on. I didn't know what I'd do—if my mom got ...."

By then he and Judi were both crying. As I watched, I felt a sudden sharp pain in my belly.

At last Nathan returned to his seat, and Daniel, Judi's "Little Messiah," took his place.

Daniel was now twenty-five. He wore a dark suit, a small gold earring, a thin Fu Manchu mustache, and an air of indignation that became audible when Judi's lawyer asked him to talk about his life with Judi and Bob Singer in the months before his father's murder.

"We were a *family*. We had a *family* life," Daniel said, his gaze trained on Judi as his brother's had been. "We did *family* things together. We went out as a *family*." In California, he said, his father, Howard Witkin, hadn't been available. "He worked very hard. And it was nice to do things together. It was a family life. A family lifestyle."

None of this meant he hadn't loved Howard, Daniel added. He had loved his father very much, and he believed his mother when she said she still cared for him. "I have never heard my mother make a negative statement about my father," he said.

Judi took the stand the following morning. I'd wondered whether she'd do so but wasn't surprised that she did. She had always prided herself on being a good witness. Her testimony held no bombshells as she stayed faithful to the story she'd followed in our conversations at the Flint jail. She called Howard a "drug addict" but insisted she "felt just fine" about him, adding that they'd had no serious disputes.

"Do you have a personal habit involving the use of personal expressions?" her lawyer asked.

"Sure." Judi brightened. "I say things like I wish he'd take a long walk on a short pier. I wish he'd take a slow boat to China .... I wish he'd just drop dead."

"Do you use the word 'asshole'?"

"Yes." Now she was smiling, although none of the jurors smiled back. "I like that word."

"Why would you make that kind of statement in regard to Howard Witkin?"

"Well, we were divorced. If he did something to anger or frustrate me, I'd use that expression.... It didn't have to be a big thing. That's how I react."

"Now, when you said you could just kill somebody or that they should take a long walk off a short pier, did you mean that should happen to him?"

"No."

Judi's lawyer paused as he moved behind his desk.

"Now, as to the killing of Howard Witkin, did you assist with that in any way?"

"No, I did not."

"Did you ask Mr. Singer to have him killed?"

"No, I did not."

"Did you attend any meetings with Andy Granger or Gary Oliver?"

"No."

"Did you make any arrangements whatsoever?"

"No, I never would have drawn up a plan like that."

"Did you put any pressure on Robert Singer for the purpose of having him kill Howard Witkin?"

"No."

By then I was so used to hearing Judi lie that I felt little emotion on hearing all this. But the pain in my belly was continuing and starting to scare me. I hurried out of the courtroom as soon as the day's session ended and drove the half-hour back to my parents' home. Later that evening, I noticed I'd been bleeding.

I had to fly back to Rio the following morning without waiting for the jury's verdict. Brazil's presidential election was scheduled for October 3, and I needed to write an advance story. My mom came in to try to help me pack, but

I told her I had it under control. I may have been a little brusque as I told her I wanted to be alone. I didn't want her to see me cry, since I could already tell what was in store.

Later, in my journal, I wrote that a miscarriage feels like a car crash inside your body. This was one more thing that Judi Barnett and I would have in common—and it seemed, in my wretched state, like her parting curse. I blamed myself for rushing around, getting stressed, and drinking coffee in those key first weeks of pregnancy, but as always it was easier to blame her. Ever since the lawsuit, justifiably or not, I'd counted myself among her victims, and now the timing seemed to make it clear, at least in my mind, in that moment, that she was still out to get me.

Over the next two days, the bleeding became heavier and cramps left me curled up and weeping for most of the flight back home. At my ultrasound appointment in Rio, the technician gently told me: "*Nao tem boas noticias.*" It's not good news.

Hearing the words in melodic Portuguese took away none of the sting. The only thing that helped was sobbing on Jack's chest for an hour, listening to him tell me, over and over, that we'd try again.

35

San Jose, October 1994

Before I left San Jose, Jack Marshall promised to keep me informed about the trial's conclusion. He kept his word, calling me on the evening of October 4.

Just before noon that day, Jack got the call that the jury was ready with a verdict. He hadn't expected it that early; the jurors had spent barely two days discussing the case, a remarkably short time for a special-circumstances murder.

He decided not to go to the courtroom to hear it, he told me. He feared it wouldn't be good news, and he didn't want to risk having to watch Judi and her lawyer celebrate a win. But after hanging up the phone, he skipped his usual lunch-hour walk along the Guadalupe River in favor of pacing around his sixth-floor office. He walked over to his window to peer out at the gray clouds, turned around to stare at his phone, strolled to his open door to check the hallway, then retraced the route. His sandwich—onion, tomato, and cucumber, a small offensive in his ongoing war against cholesterol—remained untouched in his desk drawer.

In his fifty-eighth year, Jack had slowed down a lot. His kids were grown and gone and his litigating years were all but behind him. He seldom took work home anymore, as a rule, or dwelled on it. He spent most weeknights watching reruns of sitcoms after dinner and turning in early, doing his best to keep the stress levels down. Still, he'd been brooding over the Witkin case and couldn't deny how much he still cared. This was largely due to how much the Witkins still cared. For all these years, the family had been patiently waiting for Judi to pay for her crime. "We will never pardon her," one of the Witkin cousins had told Jack.

Now, for his own peace of mind, to know things could turn out right after so much time, effort, and heartache, Jack longed to see Judi convicted. But he worried that justice might not be done. Even though the prosecutors weren't seeking the death penalty, the crimes they charged entailed a life sentence, and reasonable people might disagree that Judi should spend the rest of her days locked up for what even Jack had to admit boiled down to nagging. Judi hadn't ever spoken to Gary or Andy, much less bought a gun or fired it.

What worried Jack most of all was the chance that this trial, like the one back in 1981, would end in a hung jury, which would mean he'd have to choose between a costly fourth trial or abandoning the case once and for all. He walked once again to the window, then back to the door. His wife called but he hustled her off the phone, telling her he needed to keep the line clear.

In the courtroom, Judi watched the jurors file in, and noticed, as she would later tell me, that not one of them was looking her way.

She leaned over to her attorney. "I need to go; I have to get out of here!" she whispered, in a comment that the *Mercury News* court reporter overheard.

The foreman stood to read the verdict: Guilty of first-degree murder. Guilty of conspiracy to murder. The judge would have no leeway in sentencing. The convictions meant Judi would be going to prison for life.

Judi raised her hand to her mouth and kept it there while the judge asked each juror by name if he or she agreed with the verdict. A clerk passed Judi a box of tissues and she took four, staring straight ahead. One of the women jurors wiped away a tear, and as soon as the judge said they could go, the group hurried out of the courtroom, ignoring shouted questions from reporters.

A few minutes later, Richard Titus, beaming, strode through Jack Marshall's door. Looking at him, Jack fondly remembered his own blissful exhaustion twelve years earlier after Bob Singer was convicted. This just about made them blood brothers, he thought.

Titus told Jack he was going to lunch and that he planned to take off the rest of the day.

"That's fine," Jack said.

"Come to think of it, maybe I'll take the rest of the week."

"Go ahead."

"And next week, too."

Jack returned to his desk where his phone was ringing. Howard's mother, Geraldyne Witkin, told him how grateful she was, and how she hoped, somehow, that Howard knew.

On November 3, 1994, Judi was formally sentenced to life without parole. The *Mercury News* reported that only her son Daniel showed up to offer support as she left the courtroom, bound for the maximum-security Central California Women's Facility in Chowchilla.

"I think injustice was done in all respects," Daniel told the reporter. "My father's dead and my mother's going to be in jail for the rest of my life."

One day later, Judi called me in Rio. Normally inmates can't make calls outside the country, but Daniel had figured out a way to patch me in on a three-way call.

Her upbeat tone surprised me. "They said in the newspapers that after fourteen years, this case is finally over," she said. "I don't think it's over. The case is not done. There are other things that will come up ...."

She was already planning her appeal, she told me. "I believe I have very good issues. Very good issues."

Judi wanted me to know that she felt no responsibility for Howard Witkin's murder. "I didn't ever pressure Bob," she said. "I know you all think he was whipped. But the only thing he ever allowed me to do was to pick out the color of the carpeting." She insisted that the first time she realized Bob had something to do with the crime was in his phone call to her in 1991, when he "admitted" it. "I still don't believe he did it," she said. "It just doesn't square with how I see him."

I wasn't surprised that Judi was sticking to her story. I'd long since given up believing that she might ever tell me the truth. But I was intrigued by a chance to talk to Daniel, who had never before agreed to an interview, on the basis that his mother was against it.

Now on the phone, he sounded furious and eager to say why. He blamed the legal system, saying it was unfair that strangers would judge his mother without having any clue about the kind of person she was. "I have never doubted my mother, not for a second. There's nothing to doubt," he said. "And I don't think there's anybody in the world that knows her as well as I know her—isn't that right, Mom?"

Judi agreed.

"The legal system doesn't work in this country, unless you have money," Daniel said.

"So then how do you think it happened?" I asked him as gently as I could. "If Bob Singer really did kill your dad, why did he do it?"

"I don't waste time thinking about it," Daniel said. Then he said something I'd later understand was ominous: "It doesn't matter. I'm not going to be able to live with any explanation."

Daniel told me he'd become his younger brother's legal guardian and had been working at odd jobs to help pay their expenses while Nathan finished high school. He added that he was making plans to settle in or near Fresno, the closest big city to Chowchilla.

"I'm not going to leave my mother," he said.

"My boys have been incredible," Judi said, with some of her old confidence returning to her voice. "As long as my family is with me, everything will be alright."

We said our goodbyes shortly afterward, after which I sat staring at my phone. Appalled as I continued to be by Judi's dishonesty and willingness to manipulate others, including her own kids, I felt a tug of compassion for her as I wondered once again how much choice she'd truly had about the way she was behaving.

In the fall of 2018, I would hear an eminent Stanford biologist give a nearly three-hour lecture on all the external influences on our behavior, from evolution to genes to hormones to neurotransmitters. He concluded by saying there was no such thing as free will.

I can't find my way to agreeing with him, on top of the fact that I don't want to. It would seem to imply that all the work and attention I've devoted to try to do better were never my own praiseworthy choice but preordained by the initial hand I'd been dealt. Instead I've come to believe that narcissism, self-absorption, ADHD, and every other mental and emotional obstacle to our doing the right thing are like addictions. Once an alcoholic, always an alcoholic, but the choice is still always there whether or not to take the drink, and, beyond that, to arrange your life so as to reduce temptations.

In other words, I believe in free will. The catch is that I also believe in opportunity. I'm still amazed to think that without the catastrophe of Judi's libel lawsuit, I might have missed my chance to change. After all of my flip-flops of feelings about her, I've ended up on the side of sorry for her that she didn't get the same opportunity until it was too late.

36

My mother's voice on the phone was triumphant.

"I did it!" she said. "I finally did it!"

I was sitting at my computer in my backyard shed office, staring out the window at the gray day in our garden: the dying apple tree, the unraked leaves.

"What did you do?"

"I left him! Just like you always said I should!"

She was calling from the Hillsborough mansion of her friend Phyllis, a wealthy widow of ninety-four. She'd had yet another fight with my father the night before, and had decamped there that morning with Alma, her saintly caregiver, and two boxes of diapers.

So much had changed in the twenty-three years since I'd last lived with my parents while attending Judi Barnett's murder trial. But so much remained the same.

I'd quit the *Miami Herald* in 1999, after which Jack and I had moved back from Brazil to the Bay Area with our two sons—then babies, now teenagers. We bought a fixer-upper in a small town north of San Francisco, an hour's drive from my parents. I switched to freelancing while the "Jew without a job" got hired as a newspaper editor in San Francisco.

My mother was eighty-nine and dying of ovarian cancer. She'd been diagnosed five years earlier after the abdominal pain her doctor had thought was gas turned out to be caused by a tumor the size of a baseball. By that time she'd become so outspoken about her long-simmering anger at my ninety-three-year-old father that she told me she had named the tumor "Ellis," after him.

What made my mother most furious was my father's failure, at the end, to do his part in maintaining their facade. In 2008, the spending sprees finally caught up with them, forcing them to move out of the big, over-mortgaged Hillsborough house that my mother loved and into a two-bedroom condo in neighboring San Mateo.

My father tried to redeem himself by sparing no expense on remodeling. More granite counters, another Wolf stove, another Sub-Zero refrigerator, and a self-flushing Japanese toilet with a heated seat that my kids loved to sneak in and use when my father wasn't looking. He paid for all of it and more as he had in the past, by reducing the equity in the condo, but my mother continued to mope until he exploded, drinking harder than ever, throwing chairs across their small kitchen floor, and speeding off into the night.

He was terrified. They'd been married for nearly seventy years, during which she'd cooked his every meal at home and washed his every dish, and now he was going to be left alone. As usual, his fear made him furious, and he continued his tantrums even as she endured a hysterectomy that almost killed her, followed by seven rounds of chemo and a colostomy. "I want to die!" I heard him shout as she lay in her bed, emaciated and groggy from painkillers.

After he told my sister that he'd had suicidal thoughts, she prescribed him antidepressants, which he told us he was taking. But given that he was drinking more than ever, the combination of alcohol and pills may have counteracted each other or even made his depression worse. The result was that my once-elegant, fun-loving parents were spending their last months together in a squalid hell.

"I can't help her!" he'd moan to me, which broke my heart, even as it again was making it all about him, while he refused to do the one thing that would have made it easier—get sober and stop mistreating her.

"I told him I won't come back until he stops drinking!" my mother said now.

I'd wished for those words for so long. I was stunned and encouraged, until she got to the part about what she needed from me. She asked me to drive down to their condo to pick up some clothes and her beloved Cavalier King Charles spaniel, Charlie.

I had work to do that day and it was already close to rush hour. The traffic would be awful and I dreaded seeing my father. One year earlier, I'd betrayed him, as he saw it, by calling the DMV to report his failing eyesight and increasing deafness and drinking and erratic driving. That had led to the suspension of his license, a humiliation for which he'd never forgive me.

On the way down I realized I was trembling. Five months shy of sixty, having covered rebellions, military coups, and invasions, and been arrested, tear-gassed, and shot at on three continents, I was terrified of facing my father. Would he be drinking? Would he attack me? This was my only excuse for doing the second thing for which he'd never forgive me: calling for a police escort.

Two officers met me outside the building. We took the elevator together to the second floor, where they pounded on his door. My dad, who may have been sleeping or was too deaf to hear them, didn't respond until we got a key from the building manager and let ourselves in.

I edged by him, cringing and silent, and swept up the dog and some of my mother's underwear and track suits. He glared at me groggily, speechless.

Ten minutes later, I arrived at my mother's refuge, on a hill shaded by redwood trees. I breathed in the calm of the living room, watching the two elderly friends recline on leather chairs, with matching afghans on their laps, sardonically toasting each other with Ensure.

"You gave me the strength to do this," my mother whispered to me just before I left.

It was an interesting thing to say, I thought, as I drove away. Around the same time I reported my father to the DMV—and then felt horribly guilty about it—I'd summoned the courage to finally tell my mother that I wasn't going to listen to her complain about him anymore. Not if she wasn't going to do anything about it.

More than a decade had passed since my first watershed moment, when I'd left her alone with him in the restaurant. But I'd needed this second one, which like the first was less about trying to fix my parents than fixing myself. We hadn't been well-trained in setting boundaries. Still, as soon as I'd said it, I wondered why I hadn't done so years ago. Perhaps it was part of my old lack of humility. All my life, I'd wanted so much to keep being my mother's Little Savior that I'd helped keep all three of us stuck.

"I understand," my mother had said, before hurrying off the phone. She didn't call again for several days.

I had wondered what she'd do with all that anger at my father, which she'd previously handed to me. Now I knew. By leaving him, she must have felt as if she were hauling her dirty laundry up a flagpole.

She stayed at her friend's house for the next month, despite my father's entreaties. My siblings and I held several worried conference calls. What should we do about our dad, alone in that condo? Free of my mother's weak influence, would he drink himself to death?

Instead, he proved us all wrong. He stopped drinking the day after my mother left, continued to take his antidepressants, and as far as any of us could tell, didn't take another sip of alcohol for the remaining fifteen months of his life. "I don't need it," he told us. He didn't go to AA; he didn't see a doctor; all he did, after those first two weeks, was to cajole my mother to allow him to visit her at her friend's house—she asked me to drive him there, and I did—where he leaned over her bed and promised that he'd try to be a better man. She'd finally given him the opportunity.

My mother stayed away until my California brother confirmed that my father had been sober for a month and had removed all the liquor from the condo. She returned just one week before their seventieth anniversary, which I suppose was her way of telling the world that her laundry was now clean. "I was strong to leave and I was strong to return," she told me, and I agreed. She seemed in that moment as unlike Judi Barnett as I ever could have wished.

I was with her when she died, late at night on May 5, 2017. For her last several hours, it was just me and Alma, her caregiver, and my father in the condo. When he and I locked eyes after I felt her arm grow cold, I knew I'd never make good on my earlier vow to myself that I would leave him to his karma after she was gone.

While waiting for the Neptune Society to arrive, he got up to rummage in a drawer and returned with my mother's huge diamond ring. Sitting back down on the bed, he handed it to me.

"*She* wanted you to have it, and *I* want you to have it," he said.

I slid it on my finger, looked up at him and shrugged.

I remembered how much I used to long for a big diamond ring, to show the world how much someone cared for me. And here it was. But now as I looked down at my ragged fingernails, it seemed completely wrong for the life I'd chosen, and loved.

It was the kind of ring you could never forget you were wearing, the kind that knocked into things. I couldn't see myself wearing it to type in my garden shed office or to go to my volunteer job, teaching writing to kids detained in Marin County's juvenile hall. Jack and my kids would surely make fun of it. But more than anything else, that ring was a hurtful reminder of the worst side of my parents' marriage. I couldn't bear to look at it, and put it away in a drawer.

I visited my father often over the next fifteen months and called him most days. My California brother stepped in even more, bringing him food many nights of the week. Alma stayed with him for increasingly long shifts, providing him with the same steady, cheerful, compassionate care she had given my mother.

During that time, my father kept surprising us. He was sad and bereft, but we'd seen the last of Hyde. Before his death of pancreatic cancer, in August 2018, he apologized to my psychiatrist brother for not being a better father to him. "Can you imagine if he'd been that way all our lives?" my sister asked me more than once.

Two months after my mother's death, when I had bills to pay, I sold her diamond ring, which paid for one month of one of my son's college tuition. I had other jewelry from her that made me feel happier, and, more importantly, in her last weeks she'd given me some intangible gifts of greater value.

At the end she'd behaved like the role model I'd always longed for her to be: honest, independent, and resourceful. By doing so, she finally helped my father be the better man he'd always wanted to be: self-disciplined, even-tempered, and kind. I was with him, too, on his last night. Just before he lost consciousness, he reached out his open knuckles, as he'd done so often when I was a child, beckoning for me to put my nose between them.

Of course, I did.

Epilogue

*"Droll thing life is—that mysterious arrangement
of merciless logic for a futile purpose. The most you
can hope from it is some knowledge of yourself—that
comes too late—a crop of inextinguishable regrets."*
—Joseph Conrad

I last saw **Judi Barnett** in June 2019, during her parole
hearing at the Central California Women's Facility in
Chowchilla, the largest women's prison in the United States.
The previous year, Governor Jerry Brown had commuted
Judi's sentence, along with those of more than one hundred
and fifty other inmates serving life without parole. In a press
release, Brown cited Judi's participation in several prison
self-help programs, including "Commitment to Change,"
"Personal Integrity," "Life Planning," and "Relationships."
Over the years, she had served as an inmate liaison with
prison officials, taught a memoir-writing class, mentored
younger prisoners, and helped care for aging inmates. She
had also studied Hebrew, becoming the first bat mitzvah in
the facility's history.

Brown said he'd been moved by Judi's "dedication
to nonviolence, her service to those around her, and
her commitment to self-improvement." Her parole
commissioners received forty-three letters from prison staff,
inmates, and volunteers, testifying to her good character,

although the Santa Clara County District Attorney's Office continued to oppose her release.

"This was a horrible heinous murder that sucked victims into its web for twenty years," said Deputy District Attorney Aaron West, who attended the parole hearing.

Judi arrived at the small meeting room in a wheelchair. She was seventy-one years old, and told commissioners she suffered from lupus, scoliosis, stenosis, back spasms, chronic pain, nerve damage, and hearing loss.

I was covering the hearing as a freelancer, writing for my old paper, the *Mercury News*. I felt awkward wearing my old obsession on my sleeve, all the more so since I knew Judi didn't want me there.

Until just a year earlier, we'd exchanged friendly letters and even holiday cards, and in the summer of 2014 I'd visited her at the Chowchilla prison. It was unnerving to imagine Judi there; our backgrounds were so similar that I too easily could see myself in her shoes. Ringed by concertina wire, buzzing with flies in the summer heat, the prison was designed for two thousand inmates but at that time held nearly twice that many. Judi shared a cell with seven other women. "It's never dark, it's never quiet, and you're never alone," she said.

In 2018, a year after my mother died and after I'd resumed work on this book, I sent a letter to Judi asking to see her again. This time, I wrote, I hoped she'd finally tell me the truth about her role in Howard Witkin's murder.

One month later, I received a greeting card with a picture of a big orange orchid. But Judi's tone was frosty.

"I couldn't figure out what to say to someone who straight-out called me a liar," she wrote. "Basically that makes me sad and I have to wonder why you always assume that your sources are telling the truth when they have showed [sic] themselves to be unreliable over and over again."

She concluded: "Since you feel that way, a visit makes no sense. What could you hope to accomplish? I don't know what else to say."

One year later, she apparently was still so angry at me that she tried, unsuccessfully, to prevent me from attending her hearing, as prison official let me know. That morning I also received a barrage of hostile Facebook messages from Judi's sister Joan, who was responding to a story I had written on the case a few days earlier. "This is MY family your [sic] writing about, your facts are wrong," Joan wrote, adding: "A fellow Jew, shame on you."

At the hearing, I was the only attendee other than Judi, her lawyer, the prosecutor, and the two commissioners. Judi made no eye contact with me throughout the nearly three hours we sat just a few feet away from each other in the small room.

Often breaking down in tears, she spoke at length of the transformational progress she said she'd made in prison. A decade earlier, she said, she had finally come to accept her role in Howard Witkin's death, after participating in the Lioness Tale Prison Project, a support group based on a book about a lioness that grows up in captivity but learns to embrace her inner freedom.

"There's a moment when they take the cubs from the lioness," Judi said, weeping so hard she had to pause. "The lioness says: 'I wonder if they'll remember me as a mockery of a mother.' I knew then I had to fix *me*. I decided to get real, to just get honest. I had to accept blame and come out of denial and say: 'Ok, Judi, this is what you did and this is what it cost you .... This journey has been amazing. I've come from the dark to the light. I want to assure you I have changed. I hope and pray you can see me as someone who has grown into a better person."

Everything Judi said about the Lioness Tale project made it seem as if she'd finally gotten her chance to confront her worst behavior and change. But as the hearing dragged on, she continued to tell lies—even as doing so no longer served her immediate goal. The California Supreme Court has ruled that an inmate's "insight" into his or her crime is a significant factor in deciding if that person continues to pose a danger to society. Commissioners routinely also weigh whether an inmate seems to feel remorse.

Judi did show some remorse about the way she behaved in 1980. In contrast to how she had always previously described her actions, she said she had been "panicked" by her ex-husband Howard Witkin's plan to take their three children on a houseboat vacation and had pressured Bob Singer "to a shameful degree" to "fix" the situation.

"I screamed and hollered and slammed doors," she said. "I was a true Psycho-Barbie." She acknowledged that she'd threatened to leave Bob, adding that for that reason, "I may as well have pulled the trigger" of the gun that shot her ex-husband.

Still, when the parole hearings commissioner, Pete LaBahn, asked Judi if she'd wanted Witkin dead, she said no. "I didn't want him killed. I just wanted the situation *fixed,*" she said. "I was not part of his plan to have Howard killed."

Judi furthermore insisted that she had believed Bob Singer for "many, many years" after his trial when he told her he'd had nothing to do with Howard's murder and that Howard had died in "a drug deal gone bad."

LaBahn leaned forward and stared hard at Judi as she said this. "It seems incredible that you allowed yourself to believe that," he said. Indeed, Judi's behavior when Bob called her in 1991 didn't reflect a belief that he was innocent.

"It was an insane time," she told the commissioner. "I had to believe Bob to survive."

Over and over again, the parole commissioner questioned Judi's sincerity. When she spoke of her plans, if paroled, to move in with a sixty-five-year-old Fresno woman who had visited her in prison, he grilled her about all the details, finally saying: "If it were my elderly relative, I would want to spend time with you and meet with you and then I'd want to make a number of unannounced visits just to make sure that my mom's or my uncle's or my aunt's checkbook wasn't in your purse. To put it bluntly."

LaBahn called Judi's statements about her role in the murder "inaccurate and implausible" and said he felt "awkward" about not finding them to be a bar to her parole. In the end, however, the two commissioners determined that Judi's advanced age, health issues, and exemplary record in prison won the day in determining that she no longer posed a danger to society. That meant that she could go free in a hundred and twenty days, pending a review by the full parole hearings board and by California's new governor, Gavin Newsom. LaBahn said Judi would be required to get clearance from her parole officer before making contact with any of the murder victims, including her own children.

There's no question in my mind that Judi's kids—her ostensible reason for everything she did—suffered the most from her behavior.

In 2003 **Daniel Witkin**, Judi's "Little Messiah," died one week after his thirty-fourth birthday. Phillip Frandler, Daniel's godfather, said the death was a suicide; Daniel had overdosed on his insulin. "Daniel's conflictions I am convinced led to his overdose and death," Frandler wrote in a statement opposing Judi's parole, which was read aloud at Judi's hearing. "So in my judgment Judy [sic] killed not only Daniel's father but Daniel himself." Judi hid her face in her hands and wept as she heard this. I believe her reaction was genuine. I can't imagine hearing anything more horrible.

Angela Zeoli, a Modesto school district administrator in Modesto who was married to Daniel for just one year in 1999 said he rarely worked after graduating college, making do on about a thousand dollars a month from his trust fund and other family money. "Mostly he sat at home and smoked pot," she told me.

In the years since his mother went to prison, she said, Daniel had pierced his nose, ears, nipples, and penis, and had tattoos covering his chest, arms, and feet. The word JUSTICE covered his right forearm. Images of more than a dozen staring eyes spread over his arms and chest.

Both Zeoli and Frandler said that in the year before his death, Daniel had come to believe his mother was guilty of murder. He continued to accept her weekly collect calls from prison and listen to her pleas of innocence because "he had compassion for her," Zeoli said. "He didn't think her motive was anything to do with money, but because she wanted sole custody of the kids."

Frandler, however, said that shortly before he died, Daniel had come to him distraught, asking if Frandler thought his murdered father would have forgiven him for defending his mother for so long. "I told him the truth," Frandler said. "Through all the hell Judi put everyone through her strongest defender was always Howard. Your father would certainly understand your loyalty and reasoning. He would not fault you."

In contrast to Daniel, Judi's adopted daughter, **Marie Witkin**, not only never reconciled with Judi, but through the years has done everything she could to help get her convicted and pressure officials to keep her in prison.

In 2019, Marie was living in Norcross, Georgia, working as a part-time home health aide. She had testified twice against Judi and written to state prison authorities, former Governor Jerry Brown, and the state Board of Parole Hearings, opposing Judi's release, calling her a "psychopath" and "evil woman." In one letter she wrote: "Please for everyone's safety and peace of mind keep Judith in prison until its [sic] time for her to lay in her own coffin."

Marie blamed Judi for the loss of her brothers, with Daniel dead and Nathan having stopped talking to her, she said, since she first testified against Judi in 1986. Nathan declined to be interviewed for this book. "He was my heart," Marie said. "I raised him. I taught him to walk, talk, ride a bike, color, and helped him collect hundreds of pictures of animals that he used to tape up in his fort. I bathed him, dressed him, drove him to school daily!! and cooked for him. He always looked to me for guidance and permission. It was as though I was his mother. I loved him & still do and he was the only one that mattered to me."

Bob Singer, who planned and paid for Howard Witkin's murder, was released from prison in 2009, after serving twenty-five years, his life sentence shortened in consideration of his testimony against Judi. When I messaged him on Facebook a few years ago, he proudly told me that he owned his own home in a gated community in Sacramento. In the summer of 2019, however, after Bob had stopped answering me on social media, I learned that he was seriously ill and had only a short time to live.

Eric Singer, Bob Singer's youngest son who testified that he'd heard Judi tell Bob she wanted Howard killed— thus providing the only corroboration of Bob's story—called me after he read my 2019 reporting on Judi's parole hearing, after which we met for lunch in San Francisco. It was the first time I'd talked to him. A divorced father of two grown sons, Eric told me he had smoked marijuana heavily from 1980 after Howard Witkin's murder—until 2005. One of the first things he did once he got sober was to visit Howard's grave to apologize for never having warned him that he'd overheard Judi pushing Bob to have him killed.

Just before we said goodbye, Eric told me that he'd felt betrayed by his father, and that the one thing that made sense to him ever since then was to be a better parent than Bob had been. "I think I've done a good job with that," he said. "I've been present. And I've kept them safe."

Andrew Lee Granger, the confessed triggerman, was still in prison in 2019, incarcerated at the Richard C. Donovan Correctional Facility in San Diego, California. The previous year, Governor Brown had commuted Andy's sentence of life without parole, noting that at the age of fifty-nine, Andy had served more than thirty-eight years in prison and had been "dedicated to rehabilitation." He had participated in Alcoholics Anonymous, assisted with the start-up and coordination of the electronics program and had received exceptional work ratings from his supervisors. Brown's statement also cited a letter from former prosecutor Richard Titus, saying justice had been served in Andy's case and that further incarceration would serve no purpose.

The Santa Clara District Attorney's Office opposed Andy's parole, however, noting that he'd been disciplined twice during his years in prison for processing contraband, as well as once for gambling, and once for "manipulating staff." In May 2019, the parole hearings board voted against Andy's release, citing factors including his confessed use of heroin and methamphetamines in prison until 2016, plus what the parole commissioner said was his continuing lack of insight into why he committed the murder. Andy's next chance for parole will be in 2026.

I should note that the parole commissioners questioned Andy at his hearing about whether his father had ever abused him, as Bryan Shechmeister had told me was the case back in 1981. Andy said his father was a pedophile who had abused his four brothers, but not him, although he added, "the threat was constantly there."

Gary Oliver, the convicted middleman, was released from prison for good behavior in 1984 after serving just two years of a six-year sentence for solicitation of murder. A few years later, he married and settled near Flint, working as a machinist.

Bill Melcher, Bob Singer's Beverly Hills lawyer and Judi's lover, died of cancer in 2012. He was never sanctioned for his conduct in the Singer murder trial. After the humiliating 1986 hearing, he continued practicing law for several years, mostly working for indigent clients on appeal. Both of his sons became lawyers, and at one point the three worked together as Melcher, Melcher, and Melcher.

I last heard from Bill in 1991 after I tried to interview him. He declined my request in a faxed letter that said, "Despite extremely frequent interview requests and requests for collaboration by television, radio and the printed media, both newspaper and magazine, I have vigorously sought to protect my privacy and also that of my family. I have rejected, by my silence, all requests for interviews in this case as well as others. In fact, yours is the only such request to which I have responded at all and I do so only because you are sincere ...."

The letterhead he used was new to me, but it still listed Vincent Bugliosi as "of counsel," along with Alfonso del Castillo, of Mexico City, and a Klaus Mathes of Bundesrepublik, Deutschland. The names of four other Los Angeles lawyers were listed "in association," including a Michael Shiney and a Michael Fargo. I tracked down Michael Shiney who told me that he and Michael Fargo had at one time shared the same building as Melcher but hadn't had contact with him for four years. "I don't remember if he ever asked us to use our names on his letterhead, but we've certainly asked him to take them off," he said.

Although it made no move against Bill Melcher, the California State Bar Association did adopt a new rule of conduct for lawyers in 1992, prohibiting sex with clients that could either be considered "coercive" or that would have the effect of making the lawyer professionally incompetent. It was the first bar association in the nation to opt for such regulation, following several years of efforts by a state legislature outraged by the scandals surrounding the alleged rapes by Marvin Mitchelson. Still, it wasn't until 2018 that California—this time lagging after most other states—made it a violation of legal ethics for a lawyer to have sex with a client, unless that relationship preceded their professional one.

Jack Marshall retired from the DA's office in 1999, after which he returned to his first love, rodeo-riding. But his days as a cowboy ended in 2010, when Jack was seventy-five, after a horse bucked him into a fence and nearly killed him. He was hospitalized for six days, suffering head injuries and seven broken ribs. On his recovery, he settled into a less adventurous life, watching TV and taking occasional cruises with his wife.

On what I didn't know then was our last phone conversation, in 2017, Jack he told me he still often thought about the Witkin murder case and Judi Barnett. Then he teased me, as he often had when I was interviewing him for the book, about how much he thought Judi and I were alike, although this time he graciously added that he didn't think I would murder anyone. He died shortly after that call.

Bryan Shechmeister, the passionate genius of the Santa Clara County Public Defender's office, died of his brain tumor in 1992. Ever since that year, Santa Clara University has held a summer training program: the Bryan R. Shechmeister Death Penalty College, to prepare attorneys representing defendants charged with capital crimes.

Kay Rhea, the psychic who accurately predicted that a "fat lady" would cause trouble for Bill Melcher, died in San Diego in 2011 at the age of eighty-six.

Richard Ben Cramer, the legendary journalist to whom I briefly hitched my star in 1980, died of lung cancer in 2013 at the age of 62. He left behind a wife, a daughter, an ex-wife, and half a dozen books, most notably the more than 1,000-page "What it Takes," a highly acclaimed tome about the 1988 U.S. presidential elections. One of the truest things I've read about him, in one of the magazine eulogies written after his death, quoted a friend who said, "Cramer was a man trying to eat the world." I'm grateful that I got to share some of his feast.

Dana Priest, whom I met when she was freelancing for the *Flint Journal,* and with whom I traveled on my first trip to Nicaragua, went on to become a star national security correspondent at the *Washington Post*, writing books and winning two Pulitzer prizes.

My husband, **Jack**, at this writing is still employed as an editor at the *San Francisco Chronicle*, where he has worked for the past twenty years.

As for me, since leaving my last newspaper job in 1999, I've combined motherhood with a series of mostly short-term freelancing gigs with the advantage of flexibility. Plus I do Jack's laundry (badly).

Was I the "wonderful mother" the *mae-de-santo* said I'd be? Maybe sometimes. I've worked hard to be honest with my sons—especially if you don't count the whopper about the Good Behavior Cop at Legoland. I'm also grateful I was able to give them a warm, consistent father, who calls them out when they're wrong but always loves them for who they are and who has never physically abused them. I hope I've helped teach them good values, including the value of self-awareness.

Alas, I can't say I've never made another mistake. I sometimes revert to my scatter-brained ways, especially when I'm under stress. Had it not been for generous friends and rigorous copyediting by WildBlue's Denise Iest, for instance, this book might be full of embarrassing errors. More painful to acknowledge are the times I've slipped up in my self-monitoring and been inexcusably selfish. Yet while like most people my age, I have my "crop of inextinguishable regrets," it's a lot smaller than it might have been, had I never met Judi Singer.

On June 9, 2019, my mother's birthday, my siblings and I and our partners gathered at Rancho la Puerta in Mexico to fulfill my mother's wish to scatter her ashes on Mount Kuchamaa. She had never said anything about my father's ashes, and neither had he, but we knew he'd want to be with her, so we scattered him there, too.

I think of my mother and father every day and continue to love them for all they were able to give me, including my extraordinary siblings.

Acknowledgments

Given my decades-long obsession with this story, I'm grateful to everyone I know who never got sick of me talking about it, or at least didn't tell me they did.

Simon & Schuster canceled my original contract in 1994 after I failed to deliver an acceptable manuscript. But over the past several years I've attempted to tell it in a new, more personal and I hope more meaningful way. I would have given up if it weren't for four friends who pretty much dragged me across the finish line this year.

I am most deeply indebted to my husband Jack, for everything.

And to Dr. Y, who after all that therapy in the 1980s came back into my life in 2017 to help me cope with the deaths of my parents and to help midwife this book.

And to Elizabeth Share, a beloved consigliere who read through several drafts, offered brilliant advice, and repeatedly talked me off the ledge.

And to Jonathan Krim, my former editor on the Philippines series—and the sharpest editor I've known. Jonathan knew me at the time of the core events of this book and stepped in nearly forty years later as a member of my writers' group. After reading some of the chapters in progress, he took me to lunch where he asked many important questions, beginning with: "What were you thinking?" My debt to him is huge.

I am also grateful to:

Steve Bennett, the genius founder of Authorbytes, who not only designed my website but stepped in when I was despairing (again) with encouragement and a wonderful trailer.

Amy Friedman and Paula Derrow, for helpful advice on early drafts.

Steve Jackson and Michael Cordova at WildBlue Press, for providing an innovative, supportive home for this book.

Denise Iest, for her expert, thoughtful, and patient editing on behalf of WildBlue Press, which caught a rather startling number of typos and grammatical and style mishaps. Denise, you rok!

Many thanks also to:

My siblings, Dr. James Ellison, Dr. Jean Milofsky, and Dr. David Ellison.

My two sons, Joseph and Joshua, who make me proud every day.

Drs. Craig Malkin, Leon Seltzer, and Josh Miller, for answering some of my questions on self-absorption and narcissism by email and phone.

Randy Field at Tomorrow Media, for generous and expert help with the trailer.

The wonderful Bert Robinson, Erica Goode, and Sarah Dussault at the *Mercury News*.

The North 24th Writers Group—particularly Frances Dinkelspiel, Julie Flynn Siler, Susan Freinkel, Leslie Crawford, Alison Bartlett, Lisa Okuhn, and Jill Storey, for reading early drafts, and also to Leslie Berlin, Jeanne Carstensen, and Gabrielle Selz.

My other treasured writer and non-writer friends whom I'm guessing will be relieved if I ever stop talking about this story: Nancy Boughey, Emily Goldfarb, Jill Wolfson, Linda Zipperstein, Barbara Graham, Ginny Graves, Ronnie

Cohen, Molly Giles, Susan Keller, Laura Hilgers, Katy Butler, Stefanie Marlis, Jane Hall, and Tami Miller.

I remain grateful to my former editors at the *Mercury News*, particularly John Baker, Bob Ryan, and Pat Dillon, for giving me so many amazing opportunities and for not firing me when they had the chance, and to Pete Carey, who taught me so much more than how important it is to eyeball every word.

I'm further indebted to dozens of people who helped me understand Judi's story, chiefly including Marina Witkin, Sandy Williams, William Lamb, John Luft, Detectives William Britt and Steve Derossett, and especially Jack Marshall and Bryan Shechmeister, may they rest in peace.

A logistical note: This is a true story based on interviews, court transcripts, police reports, newspaper stories, and my journals going back to 1968. Everything is factual to the best of my ability, with a few exceptions to protect the privacy of people who are still living and weren't involved in the criminal trials. I changed a few minor identifying details and gave pseudonyms to Drs. P and Y, "Sarah" in Chapter 5, the "Weinsteins" and "Mark" in Chapter 7, and "Stan" and "Sally" in Chapter 32. I also changed some of the details concerning the boyfriend I refer to as the "lawyer" in Chapter 35.

Some written sources I relied on for understanding self-absorption, narcissism, psychopathy, and playing the victim include:

Cleckley, Harvey. *The Mask of Sanity: An Attempt to Clarify Some Issues about the So-Called Psychopathic Personality,* Echo Point Books and Media, 1950.

Egloff, Boris, Back, Mitja, Schmukle, Stefan C. "Why Are Narcissists so Charming at First Sight? Decoding the Narcissism–Popularity Link at Zero Acquaintance." Journal of Personality and Social Psychology, Vol. 98, No. 1, 132–145; 2010.

Hare, Robert D. *Without Conscience: The Disturbing World of the Psychopaths Among Us*,

The Guilford Press, 1993.

Kiehl, Kent A., and Hoffman, Morris B. "The Criminal Psychopath: History, Neuroscience, Treatment, and Economics," Jurimetrics, Vol. 51, No. 4 (Summer 2011), pp. 355-397.

Malkin, Dr. Craig. *Rethinking Narcissism: The Secret to Recognizing and Coping with Narcissists,* HarperCollins Publishers, 2015.

McBride, Dr. Karyl. *Will I Ever be Good Enough? Healing the Daughters of Narcissistic Mothers.* Atria Books, 2008.

Miller, Joshua D., Lynman, Donald R. Hyatt, Courtland S., Campbell, W. Keith. "Controversies in Narcissism," The Annual Review of Clinical Psychology, 2017, 13:291–315.

Otway, Lorna J., Vignoles, Vivian L. "Narcissism and Childhood Recollections: A Quantitative Test of Psychoanalytic Predictions," January 1, 2006 Sage Publications.

Paulhus, Delroy L. "Interpersonal and Intrapsychic Adaptiveness of Trait Self-Enhancement: A Mixed Blessing?" Interpersonal Relations and Group Processes, 1998.

Seabrook, John, "Suffering Souls: The Search for the Roots of Psychopathy,"

The New Yorker, November 2, 2008.

Seltzer, Leon F. "Self-Absorption: The Root of All (Psychological) Evil?"

Psychology Today, August 24, 2016.

WildBlue Press Women True Crime Writers Rock!

Read excerpts from books by Caitlin Rother, Anne K. Howard, and Monique Faison Ross. You won't be able to stop.

 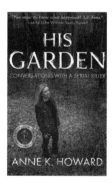 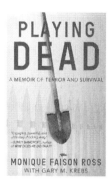

Read on for an excerpt from each!

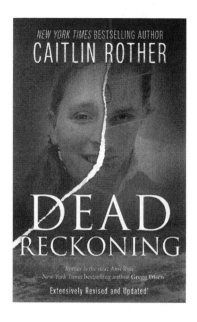

 WILDBLUE PRESS

See even more at:
http://wbp.bz/tc

More True Crime You'll Love From WildBlue Press

A MURDER IN MY HOMETOWN by Rebecca Morris
Nearly 50 years after the murder of seventeen year old Dick Kitchel, Rebecca Morris returned to her hometown to write about how the murder changed a town, a school, and the lives of his friends.

wbp.bz/hometowna

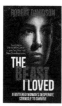

THE BEAST I LOVED by Robert Davidson
Robert Davidson again demonstrates that he is a master of psychological horror in this riveting and hypnotic story ... I was so enthralled that I finished the book in a single sitting. "—James Byron Huggins, International Bestselling Author of The Reckoning

wbp.bz/tbila

BULLIED TO DEATH by Judith A. Yates
On September 5, 2015, in a public park in LaVergne, Tennessee, fourteen-year-old Sherokee Harriman drove a kitchen knife into her stomach as other teens watched in horror. Despite attempts to save her, the girl died, and the coroner ruled it a "suicide." But was it? Or was it a crime perpetuated by other teens who had bullied her?

wbp.bz/btda

SUMMARY EXECUTION by Michael Withey
"An incredible true story that reads like an international crime thriller peopled with assassins, political activists, shady FBI informants, murdered witnesses, a tenacious attorney, and a murderous foreign dictator."—Steve Jackson, New York Times bestselling author of NO STONE UNTURNED

wbp.bz/sea

Made in the USA
San Bernardino, CA
18 January 2020